PLOWSHARES
AND SWORDS

A Schell Center Human Rights Book

General Editors:
Drew S. Days III and George Andreopoulos

PLOWSHARES AND SWORDS

The Economics of Occupation in the West Bank

**WITH A FOREWORD BY
DREW S. DAYS III**

Richard Toshiyuki Drury and Robert C. Winn
with Michael O'Connor

BEACON PRESS · BOSTON

Beacon Press
25 Beacon Street
Boston, Massachusetts 02108-2892

Beacon Press books
are published under the auspices of
the Unitarian Universalist Association of Congregations.

99 98 97 96 95 94 93 92   8 7 6 5 4 3 2 1

Text design by GDS / Jeffrey L. Ward
Map on page xii by Judith Aronson

Library of Congress Cataloging-in-Publication Data
Drury, Richard Toshiyuki.
Plowshares and swords: the economics of occupation in the West
Bank / Richard Toshiyuki Drury and Robert C. Winn with Michael
O'Connor: with a foreword by Drew S. Days III.
p.   cm.—(A Schell Center human rights book)
Includes bibliographical references (p.   ) and index.
ISBN 0-8070-6904-3 (cloth)
1. West Bank—Economic conditions.   2. West Bank—Economic policy.
3. Human rights—West Bank.   4. Intifada, 1987–   I. Winn, Robert C.
II. O'Connor, Michael.   III. Title.   IV. Series.
HC415.25.Z7W4725   1992
330.95695'—dc20   91-41457

ACKNOWLEDGMENTS

We began this project in 1989 while still law students at Yale, worlds away from Israel and Palestine. The help of numerous individuals made it possible for us to negotiate various hurdles, make it to the West Bank, and return to write this book. We would like to extend special thanks to the following people and organizations: fellow law students Maggie Zanger and Jill Hodges for being a part of the team on the West Bank; Professor Drew Days and George Andreopoulos of the Orville Schell Center for Human Rights at the Yale Law School for their financial support and editorial comments; Mona Rishmawi, Marc Stephens, Joost Hilterman, Raja Shehadeh, and the helpful staff of Al-Haq/Law in the Service of Man, in Ramallah, West Bank, the West Bank affiliate of the International Commission of Jurists, who provided us with research facilities in the West Bank, guidance, and editorial assistance on our project; Yale Law School Associate Dean Stephen Yandle, who financed much of the project when it seemed like nobody else would; Yoreh Artzi, head of the West Bank Civil Administration's Department of Agriculture, who generously agreed to be interviewed and who guided us through several Israeli agricultural facilities; numerous other officials of the Department of Agriculture who spoke candidly about agricultural practices in the West Bank; J. Murphy and Khalil Al-Aloul of Catholic Relief Services for introducing us to many Palestinian farmers and various officials who work with these farmers; the dedicated staff of Save the Children; Hagop Deldelian and staff at Al-Haq for translating the texts of the military orders found in Appendix B; Professors Ruth Wedgewood of the Yale Law School, John Quigley of Ohio State University, Burns Weston, Bessie Dutton Murray Professor of Law at the University of Iowa, and Adam Roberts, Montague Burton Professor of International Relations, Balliol College of Oxford University, for their very helpful and generous editorial comments; the helpful people at B'tselem, an Israeli human rights organization; and Lisa Daugaard, Yale Law School, '92, for her editorial comments. Thanks to all of those who became our friends, helped us in our day-to-day experience, and brought a human element to a situation which all too often is obscured by rhetoric and hyperbole; and very special thanks to our translator and friend Kawther Abu-Qutesh.

CONTENTS

FOREWORD

Four years ago, in the fall of 1987, I received a call from a friend of mine who reported that the John Merck Fund in Boston was interested in establishing a fitting memorial to Orville H. Schell, Jr., who had died the previous summer. Schell, a quintessential Wall Street lawyer, had capped an already distinguished career by devoting much of the last ten years of his life to the promotion of international human rights. He was, for example, one of the founders of Helsinki Watch, the forerunner of the human rights monitoring organization now known as Human Rights Watch.

It was not surprising, consequently, that the Merck Fund and other friends of Orville Schell envisioned a memorial that would honor his deep concern for international human rights. Yale Law School was invited to submit a proposal for such a memorial. We did so only after considering seriously what Yale, as an institution of higher learning, could contribute to the cause of international human rights. We concluded that Yale's strengths lay in scholarly research and writing, in analyzing problems and offering constructive solutions. Moreover, we thought that Yale, given its tradition of interdisciplinary scholarship, particularly at the Law School, might develop a core of scholars from throughout the university who could apply the learning of their areas of expertise to human rights issues. We believed that students—from Yale College and the graduate and professional schools—could also be encouraged to develop research projects that cut across disciplinary lines.

The Merck Fund and several other major benefactors found our vision attractive, providing us with the financial assistance necessary to launch the Orville H. Schell, Jr., Center for International Human Rights in late 1988. Since then, the Schell Center has sponsored a number of symposia on topics ranging from "Transition to Democracy in Argentina" to "One-Party Rule in Africa," all of which have been designed to contribute to research projects scheduled ultimately for publication. They will appear either as part of our Occasional Papers series or as books like this West Bank study.

The Schell Center takes special pride in the publication by Beacon Press of *Plowshares and Swords* for several reasons. Of course, the fact that it is our first major publication provides a partial explanation. But more important, the book suggests that we chose wisely in deciding to emphasize research and scholarship at the Schell Center. Operating with funds from the Schell Center and the Law School, five students (three in the regular J.D. program and two others who had completed a one-year program at the Law School for journalists) headed off to the occupied territories in the summer of 1989. Their exhaustive field work, followed by extensive documentary research and review of the literature in the field, made it possible for Richard Drury, Robert Winn, and Michael O'Connor to produce this fine study. They have proven that with proper support, intelligent, well-trained graduate and professional school students are perfectly capable of producing high quality studies like *Plowshares and Swords*.

The approach this work takes to the subject of human rights also reflects a programmatic emphasis that we hope to develop further at the Schell Center. No one can quarrel with the proposition that the international community must vigorously ferret out, publicize, and condemn torture, other physical abuses, and the denial of basic civil and political rights in violation of international human rights norms. However, adequate attention has not been given, in our estimation, to the ways in which economic, social, and cultural deprivations also deny hope and dignity to millions of people around the world. *Plowshares and Swords* argues convincingly that harsh economic practices can be, in some respects, as devastating to human aspirations and self-respect as physical harm.

Finally, everyone with any knowledge of the conflict in the Middle East is aware of the highly charged political context in which daily events occur in that part of the world and of the deeply held antagonisms between Arab and Jew that make so problematic the search for peaceful resolution. For all the political complexity and emotional dynamics of the Middle East, however, it must be kept in mind that the future of the Occupied Territories, Israel, and its Arab neighbors must turn ultimately upon whether a solution consistent with international legal principles can be devised. Through its careful exploration of the laws of belligerent occupation, *Plowshares and Swords* makes clear how adherence to those principles can contribute meaningfully to protection of human rights and to the peace process in that region.

Drew S. Days III
New Haven, Connecticut
October 1991

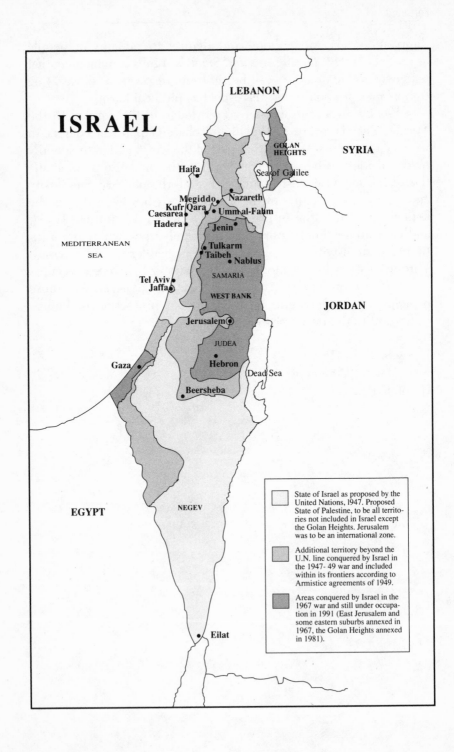

ISRAEL

LEBANON

SYRIA

GOLAN
HEIGHTS

Haifa

Sea of Galilee

Megiddo   Nazareth
Kufr Qara
Caesarea   Umm al-Fahm
Hadera

Jenin

MEDITERRANEAN
SEA

Tulkarm
Taibeh   Nablus

Tel Aviv   SAMARIA
Jaffa

WEST BANK   JORDAN

Jerusalem

JUDEA

Gaza   Hebron

Dead Sea

Beersheba

EGYPT   NEGEV

State of Israel as proposed by the
United Nations, l947. Proposed
State of Palestine, to be all territories not included in Israel except
the Golan Heights. Jerusalem
was to be an international zone.

Additional territory beyond the
U.N. line conquered by Israel in
the 1947- 49 war and included
within its frontiers according to
Armistice agreements of 1949.

Areas conquered by Israel in the
1967 war and still under occupation in 1991 (East Jerusalem and
some eastern suburbs annexed in
1967, the Golan Heights annexed
in 1981).

Eilat

INTRODUCTION

Since 1967 much attention has been focused on the often violent conflict between the Israeli military and the Palestinians in the Israeli-occupied West Bank and Gaza Strip. News reports, especially during the *intifada*—the Palestinian uprising which began in December 1987—have been filled with body counts, stories of beatings, tear gas, rubber bullets, and other forms of violent repression. Human rights groups have also, quite justifiably, concentrated their attention on the daily violence that erupts under occupation. Yet occupation is a fundamental relation between occupier and occupied that manifests itself at all levels of society. In addition to the physical violence experienced by individuals, the burden of the occupation has been evident in the West Bank economy, affecting Palestinians in quite oppressive ways and warranting serious attention as a human rights issue. This is especially the case with agriculture, which has been called the backbone of the West Bank economy.[1]

As lawyers doing research from a human rights perspective, we wanted to make connections between the individual experiences of Palestinians and the structural bases of the occupation. Two interlocking questions arose: To what extent and in what ways are the Palestinian economy and state of agriculture affected by the context of occupation? And what legal standards can be used to provide more than moral suasion in criticizing this aspect of the occupation?

In addition to thoroughly reviewing the existing literature, we found it necessary to venture into the field and piece together from primary sources a picture of the nature and consequences of Israeli control over Palestinian agriculture. For our own reasons of economy, we concentrated on the situation in the West Bank. Our stay in the West Bank started in the beginning of June 1989 and extended through the end of August. We interviewed West Bank farmers; agro-industrialists; academics from universities in Israel and the West Bank; high-ranking officers of the Civil Administration who are responsible for implementing the West Bank agricultural policy, including the top-ranked officer for agricultural affairs, Yoreh Artzi; employees from nongovernmental organizations involved in the West Bank; aid workers; diplomats from the United States and various European consulates; and members of Palestinian "popular committees" and work committees.[2] We also gathered statistics from official Israeli and Jordanian sources, when available, and observed the situation firsthand.

We found that in simple terms the "quality of life" has risen in the West Bank since 1967—the gross national product (GNP), the number of calories consumed, and the number of televisions and tractors per capita have all increased. Yet these factors do not begin to describe the economic landscape of occupation nor the way in which occupation sets the parameters for economic autonomy and development. While the rising GNP has often been advanced as evidence of the benevolence of the occupier, it could also indicate nothing more than the sudden juxtaposition of a less developed area with a capital-intensive industrialized economy. Although development has been a feature of the occupation, so have transferred inflation, retardation of the industrial base, the general shaping of the West Bank economy to complement that of Israel, and the gradual absorption of the territories into the occupying state.

Indeed, the general mood we perceived in the West Bank ranged from despair at the lack of control that Palestinians had over their lives—they felt as if their lives were not their own, despite the televisions on which they could watch Jordanian and Egyptian programs—to a sense of suppressed excitement at the self-assertion represented in the *intifada*, wherein they felt they could finally be agents of their own destiny. Farmers complained about the futility of continuing with agriculture and the impossibility of its profitability given Israeli constraints, but were also determined to persevere despite the increasing impediments.

In addition to investigating the state of agriculture, we also sought to determine appropriate guiding principles for governmental behavior in the West Bank. We found the standards by which to judge the economic aspects of the occupation in the international law of belligerent occupation expressed in the Fourth Geneva Convention of 1949 and the Hague Regulations of 1899 and 1907. These laws arose in the aftermath of turbulent periods in modern history, out of the desire of the international community to come to a consensus as to the limits of acceptable behavior in situations of international hostility.

With the aim of preventing the intentional or *de facto* exploitation of the occupied territory, the law of belligerent occupation establishes guidelines designed to keep the occupier's involvement in the occupied territory to a minimum, in order to preserve as far as possible the status quo prior to the occupation. Especially in a prolonged occupation, where "the provisional nature of the government fades away and it begins to look like a full-fledged administrative entity, but without any of the safeguards of ordinary government,"[3] there is a danger that over time minor policy preferences favoring the occupier in almost every area of daily life will culminate in an unjust situation for the people of the occupied territory. The norm of noninterference thereby strives to prevent as many major and minor policy decisions as possible from ever being made.[4]

The situation which has developed in the West Bank is precisely what this body of law was established to avoid. In the course of over twenty years, the policy choices of myriad Israeli decision makers have served to subordinate the interests of the indigenous West Bank population to those of Israel. In addition to conscious policy decisions subjugating the West Bank economy to the interests of Israel, a series of relatively minor decisions have had this same cumulative effect. Each decision has served as a playing field for special interests in a game where Palestinian concerns are denied any effective representation. Controls over agriculture—some of which are beneficial to West Bank inhabitants—become points of opportunity which are used all too often to serve Israeli domestic and political interests. The result has been the creation in the West Bank of a noncompetitive, subservient, satellite economy, which also serves as a captive market for Israeli goods and a source of cheap labor. Israeli controls over West Bank agriculture have minimized competition between Israel and the West Bank, almost always to the detriment of the latter, and have stifled West Bank Palestinian agricultural or agro-industrial enterprises which would lead the territory toward economic self-sufficiency.[5] Various Israeli agricultural practices in the West Bank have directly facilitated the transfer of West Bank land and water resources from Palestinian to Israeli hands, in violation of international law. Thus agriculture has also been an important factor in Israel's creeping annexation of the West Bank.[6] As we shall discuss in this study, the battle for possession of vast tracts of the West Bank is now being fought by Palestinian farmers using tomatoes, eggplants, and olive trees.

Given the tight cage of the occupation, almost any act of independence and self-interest is deeply threatening to the occupation and its bureaucratic structures. Especially during the *intifada*, resistance has taken many forms, from mass demonstrations to individual decisions to boycott Israeli products. Agriculture has played a prominent role. Jad Issac, a Palestinian professor of plant physiology at Bethlehem University and a resident of Beit Sahour, a middle-class community in the West Bank, described to us how he had started a small nonprofit supply store in the early months of the *intifada*, selling gardening equipment and encouraging Palestinians to grow "victory gardens" in their back yards—a symbolic gesture of Palestinian self-reliance—to decrease the need for Israeli goods in the West Bank. Though such small-scale agriculture was only a minuscule step towards Palestinian autonomy, it was quite popular and business went well. The venture, however, and the attendant media coverage, may have proved threatening to the Israeli authorities. On June 5, 1988, the shop was closed and Issac was arrested and placed in administrative detention without charge for six months. Beit Sahour was placed under curfew for twenty-one days. Despite repeated requests, the authorities would not give Issac an explanation for his imprisonment. However, it is fairly obvious that his trespass was against the occupation; the tomatoes he had promoted were, in the words of a consular official in Jerusalem, "too subversive."

The same dynamics that make tomatoes subversive make economy and agriculture human rights issues. This book attempts to explicate these particular dynamics in the context of international law, in the hope of both demonstrating the inequity of the occupation from an unusual perspective and promoting respect for the rights, in all their manifestations, of the Palestinians under occupation.

While the focus of our inquiry is upon the West Bank, the same analysis may lend itself quite readily to other occupations. Most obvious are the other Israeli occupations—of the Gaza Strip, the Golan Heights, and South Lebanon—and, as we explain below, the recently terminated South African occupation of Namibia, which displays parallels to the West Bank that make it a likely candidate for similar analysis. Other situations of international economic domination, whether or not these situations strictly qualify as occupations, are also possible areas for inquiry, including Indonesia's governance of East Timor, the governance of Tibet by the People's Republic of China, the United States' governance of Puerto Rico, Turkey's governance of Armenia, and the United States' relationship with the Native American nations. With the rise of nationalism and ethnic separatism in Eastern Europe and Eurasia, the economic human rights analysis we have used in our study may provide a useful tool for gauging the benevolence or malevolence of other relationships which arguably constitute occupations. We hope our analysis may be useful in these or other areas of the world.

PART I

ECONOMIC AND POLITICAL BACKGROUND

CHAPTER 1

Israel, Palestine, and the West Bank

In the first part of the twentieth century the confluence of Zionism, rising Arab nationalism, and the vestiges of European imperialism provided fertile ground for conflict in the Near East. Prior to World War I, the area surrounding the eastern Mediterranean had long been under the control of the Ottoman Empire; after World War I and the demise of the Ottoman Empire, the League of Nations divided these lands into various mandates administered by Britain and France. Britain, as a mandatory power, was charged with ensuring the development and eventual self-determination of the Emirate of Transjordan, to the east of the River Jordan, and of Palestine, to the west.[1]

With the rise of Zionism, mandatory Palestine saw an influx of Jewish immigrants. By 1948, there were approximately 678,000 Jews in Palestine, up from 60,000 at the end of World War I.[2] The Arab population of the area also increased, but at nowhere near the same rate, rising from over 600,000 in the early 1900s to 1,269,000 by 1946.[3] Tensions between the Arabs and the Jews increased, and hostility was also directed at the British, due to conflicting promises made to both groups. Military activities, including terrorist acts against the British, became more prevalent, and

Britain finally decided to end its problem-ridden and ineffectual tenure as mandatory ruler. In February 1947, Britain submitted the Palestine question to the newly created United Nations. A partition plan was approved by the General Assembly on November 29, 1947, which called for the creation of two states. More violence broke out between Jews and Arabs almost immediately following the passage of the partition resolution; the violence escalated to full-scale warfare when Britain withdrew from Palestine on May 15, 1948. Egypt, Syria, Iraq, and Jordan all committed military forces to the conflict.

This first Arab-Israeli war concluded in favor of the newly created State of Israel, which gained borders significantly larger than those granted to the Zionists by the UN partition; in the process, however, 700,000 Palestinians became refugees.[4] Egypt and Jordan, then Lebanon and Syria, signed separate armistice agreements with Israel. No Palestinian Arab state was formed despite the intent of the original UN partition plan. The borders set by the armistice agreements left the Gaza Strip under Egyptian control, the Golan Heights a part of Syria, and the West Bank of the Jordan River under Jordanian military control. The West Bank was soon annexed by Jordan, although this annexation was never recognized by the Arab nations or the international community. Jerusalem was divided in half, the western portion falling under Israeli control, while East Jerusalem came under the control of Jordan.

The West Bank, the focus of this book, was thus delimited by events surrounding the birth of the State of Israel. The West Bank covers one fifth of historic Palestine, an area of 5.8 million *dunams* of land, much of which is rocky and mountainous. (A dunam equals approximately one fourth of an acre.) It is possible to drive from the northern edge of the West Bank to the southern edge in less than five hours, and from side to side in less than one hour. The West Bank is bordered on the east by the Jordan River and the Dead Sea; its western border, more the result of politics than geography, is "the green line" that represents the extent of Israeli control from 1948 to 1967 and is still the official border of the state of Israel.

The West Bank has four major regions: the coastal plain and the Jenin area, the central mountainous area, the eastern foothills, and, further east, the Jordan Valley. The area around Jenin, in the north, has abundant rainfall and is part of a fertile coastal plain that extends to the Mediterranean. From Jenin south to Hebron is the mountainous region, which also has abundant rain. The foothills overlook the Jordan Valley and are very arid.[5] The Jordan Valley itself has often been called "the natural greenhouse" of the West Bank.

Under Jordanian control, from 1948 to 1967, the West Bank economy enjoyed a healthy growth rate, with its gross national product (GNP) rising an average of 8.8 percent annually between 1959 and 1966.[6] The West Bank accounted for approximately 40 percent of both the Jordanian GNP (which includes remittances from abroad) and its gross domestic product (GDP). During this period, agriculture constituted up to 38 percent of the Jordanian GDP in good harvest seasons.[7] Tourism and the service sector were also important parts of the economy; many tourists came to the holy sites within the West Bank, which include Bethlehem, the Tomb of the Patriarchs in el-Khalil/Hebron, and Al-Aqsa (the Dome of the Rock/Temple Mount) in East Jerusalem, which is one of the holiest sites in Islam, Judaism, and Christianity. (After the Israeli occupation of the West Bank in 1967, the volume of tourism, which had been largely from Arab countries, severely declined.)

On June 5, 1967, after border skirmishes between Israel and Syria and an Egyptian military buildup in the Sinai, military action once again broke out between Israel and the Arab states. Within three days the Israeli military forces conquered the Gaza Strip and nearly all of the Sinai peninsula, as well as the land held by Jordan on the west bank of the Jordan River; by the end of major hostilities on June 11, Israel had also conquered the part of Syria overlooking Lake Tiberias in the northeast (the Golan Heights).[8]

Of course, the West Bank was not unpopulated when it fell under Israeli control in 1967, although the almost entirely Arab population had decreased from 845,000 prior to the war to 596,000 just after, due to refugee flight. Approximately 1,204,000 Palestinians currently live in the West Bank, including a substantial number of refugees (and the descendants of those refugees) who fled from the coastal areas on the Mediterranean after events surrounding the creation of the State of Israel in 1948.[9] The West Bank has

been, and still is, predominantly rural, with approximately 70 percent of the population continuing to live away from major towns.[10]
After the Six-Day War, Palestinians in the West Bank suddenly
found themselves under the control of Israel.

This change in events severely reoriented the West Bank
economy from a relationship with Jordan to a relationship with Israel. Many commentators and Israelis with whom we spoke have
pointed to various economic factors as evidence of the beneficial
effects of this relationship and the benevolence of the occupation.[11]
There is no question that the gross national product of the West
Bank has increased since 1967. The Bank of Israel estimates that
the GNP of the West Bank grew by 18 percent annually between
1968 and 1973.[12] More conservative sources estimate a growth of 9
percent each year for the same period.[13] For the period 1968–1982
the annual growth rate is estimated at 10.8 percent.[14] From 1968
to 1973 real wages for West Bank residents rose by 15 percent
annually.[15] Authorities often point to a decrease in unemployment
from the postwar figure.[16] Other indicators include an increase in
house construction and in the number of vehicles and televisions.[17]

Despite the impressive picture created by these figures, taken
alone they misrepresent the economic situation in the West Bank.
As much as one half of the increase in GNP from 1968 to 1977 came
from sources outside of the territories.[18] These sources include remittances earned from work abroad, which are sent by the large
number of diaspora Palestinians to their families in the West Bank,
and a significant amount of direct aid from agencies such as the
United Nations Relief and Works Agency (UNRWA) and the
United Nations Development Project (UNDP).[19] Such income in
no way reflects the health of the West Bank economy. One third
of the GNP increase of 1968 to 1977 came from earnings from wage
labor in Israel,[20] which has had several negative effects on the West
Bank economy (discussed below).

As pointed out by Fawzi Gharaibeh, an economist who has
written about the occupied territories, the average rate of increase
in West Bank GNP is significantly inflated by very high annual
growth rates, exceeding 20 percent, immediately after the war.
Such rates are to be expected as the natural result of recovery from
the disruptions caused by war. When the postwar figures are eliminated to reflect a situation more representative of the normal

course of the economy, the average annual growth in GNP for the 1973–1982 period is a much more modest 7 percent, which is lower than the rate of almost 9 percent per annum under Jordanian rule.[21] The growth rate in the GNP from 1976 to 1986 was a mere 4 percent, including income from outside sources.[22]

In short, the economic indicators do not reflect real development of the West Bank infrastructure or the creation of a healthy, viable economy.[23] There was only a very slight growth in industry from 1968 to 1973 and an actual decline from 1973 to 1977.[24] In stark contrast, under Jordanian rule the industrial sector in the West Bank grew an average of 16.6 percent per annum.[25] The relative contribution of industry to the GDP of the West Bank dropped from 8.3 percent in 1968 to 7 percent in 1982.[26] Arab entrepreneurs could not compete with Israeli manufacturers receiving heavy subsidies from the government and benefiting from high protective tariffs. Only two factories employing over 100 workers were established in the West Bank during twelve years of occupation. Shortly after occupation, the government of Israel destroyed the West Bank banking industry, hampering economic growth.[27] Shmuel Sandler and Hillel Frisch have stated that "despite certain economic changes and rising prosperity the West Bank continued to be characterized by structural underdevelopment."[28]

Agricultural Development

Throughout the various dislocations and displacements of recent history, agriculture has remained an important part of the economy. Agriculture has consistently contributed approximately 30 percent of the West Bank economy.[29] In 1961, according to a conservative estimate, at least 40 percent of the population was employed in agriculture.[30] While the percentage of West Bank Palestinians involved in agriculture has declined since then for various reasons discussed below, over one quarter of the labor force is still employed in agriculture.[31] The vast majority of farms in the West Bank are quite small, averaging fewer than fifty dunams (around twelve acres).[32]

It is apparent that "in the early years after 1967 the rural population of the territories were the beneficiaries of an agricultural policy that vigorously attempted to develop the areas."[33] Under the

military government, new technology was introduced and import
substitutes were encouraged. There was a shift to cash crops from
the previous concentration on subsistence crops.[34] Palestinians
working within the Civil Administration and farmers alike reported
to us that they were very impressed with the quality and quantity
of assistance in the period immediately following the war of June
1967. Israeli agricultural experts reportedly advanced the interests
of Palestinian farmers vigorously, sometimes even in conflict with
the wishes of the military authorities. Agricultural extension services and a number of "inputs" such as nutrients, fertilizers, and
seeds became readily available through the Office of Agriculture.
Drip irrigation and the increased use of tractors and fertilizers are
examples of how the Department of Agriculture has helped farmers to increase production in the West Bank since 1967.[35] Farmers
were encouraged by the government to shift from high-water-con-
tent melons and legumes toward preservable beans, sesame, and
cotton. The result was a shift from West Bank exports to Arab countries to export through the Israeli agricultural exporting company,
Agrexco. The government also encouraged the growth of labor-
intensive crops, many of which could be produced more inexpen-
sively in the West Bank, where labor was cheaper than in Israel.
This had the additional advantage of creating employment.[36]

The Israeli director of the Civil Administration's Department
of Agriculture, Yoreh Artzi, gave us a tour of the Volcani Institute,
where much of the research was conducted which has benefited
Israeli and West Bank farmers. He showed us drip irrigation technology in action, as well as new olive presses and experimental
crop varieties now used in the West Bank. Artzi seemed to display
a true commitment to aiding Palestinian farmers, although the Department of Agriculture has seriously deteriorated and suffered
from under-funding in recent years. The introduction of such agricultural techniques assisted a related average rise in agricultural
production of 12 percent annually from 1966 to 1972 and 5 percent
per year from 1972 to 1977.[37]

The situation began to change following the Yom Kippur War
in 1973. Israeli public reaction against the government's perceived
lack of preparedness was harsh after the war, in which Israel came
dangerously close to extinction. There is no question today that the

Yom Kippur War was the critical event triggering the downfall of the Labor government which had ruled the country since its founding. Labor was blamed for becoming too complacent, for being overly dovish, and for letting down the nation's defenses. Partly as a result of the war, and partly for a variety of other reasons, the Israeli economy took a decided turn for the worse after 1973. By the elections of 1977, the ultranationalist, right-wing Likud party was swept into power.[38] Meron Benvenisti, former deputy mayor of Jerusalem and founder of the West Bank Data Project, has remarked that from 1967 through 1973 the occupation was viewed by many Israelis as a temporary and reasonably benevolent situation; after 1973, the occupation was seen in Israel as a permanent means for "accruing substantial benefits with negligible costs."[39] While the Labor government was reluctant to take a firm position on the status of the territories, Likud left little question that it considered the West Bank to be part of "Eretz Israel" (true or greater Israel), and therefore to be Israeli territory by right.

By the time Likud, the major right-wing party in Israel, came to power in 1977, a very different policy from that of the immediate post-occupation period was evident, reflected in the decline and eventual elimination of agricultural loans and by substantial staff attrition in the Department of Agriculture.[40] Thus, West Bank Data Project researcher David Kahan remarks, though "improvements in agricultural production and income per capita of the rural population increased markedly in the initial period up to 1975–1976 . . . in the period following 1975–1976, the rate of growth of agricultural production, value added and farm income fell."[41] The accession of Likud to power also marked an emphasis on consolidating a Jewish presence in the West Bank through increased settlement, with a corresponding increase in land being subsumed under Israeli control through expropriations and other means.[42]

Palestinian officials in the Department of Agriculture described to us a gradual metamorphosis of Israeli policy and personnel. In the early years under occupation, Palestinian farmers benefited from exposure to highly skilled and conscientious Israeli experts whose work was usually, but not always, supported by the Israeli government. After the Yom Kippur War of 1973, however, as the original extension service experts moved on to other posi-

tions, they were replaced—when the positions were refilled at
all—by individuals who were reportedly less skilled and more apt
to view all decisions through the lens of military policy. Palestinian
officials became increasingly frustrated with their Israeli counter-
parts after Likud assumed power in 1977. Any confidence and
goodwill that had been built during the early years of occupation
had dissipated by the time of our study, as was readily apparent in
our interviews.

Trade Balance

Over the course of the occupation, the economies of the West Bank
and Israel have become virtually inextricably intertwined. In 1980,
88 percent of imports to the West Bank came from Israel and 59
percent of exports went to Israel.[43] More recently, 90 percent of
West Bank imports came from Israel, and 73 percent of exports
went to Israel; in addition, the West Bank depends on Israel for as
much as 61 percent of its employment.[44] This economic relationship between the West Bank and Israel can be described in terms
of coordination and complementarity between the two economies,
as Israeli officials have asserted.[45] However, the position of relative
power is always evident in the relationship between the two enti-
ties—the West Bank complements the economy of Israel.

With the increasing of economic and political pressures in the
mid-seventies, the inequality of the relation of power became more
evident, the structural problems in the relationship between Israel
and the West Bank were exacerbated, and the West Bank was used
to stabilize the economy of Israel. For example, the encourage-
ment of cash crops was part of a policy to "orient production from
the territories toward the needs of the Israeli market. . . . The
strategy concentrated on products that had a relative advantage
and were complementary to Israel's economy."[46] Competition was
minimized through controls on inputs, crop types, and the marketing of West Bank produce. New agricultural techniques were
introduced, but almost exclusively for crops which would not compete with Israeli products.[47] This has been true at least since 1973.

The Ministry of Defense stated in 1986 its support for development, with the important qualification that there be "no conflict
with the security and economic interests of Israel."[48] Controls on

crop varieties were implemented to prevent competition with Israeli produce and the wide-reaching agricultural extension service was allowed to atrophy.[49] Likewise, as noted by David Kahan, "the selection of appropriate products tends to be dynamic and changes according to Israeli needs and requirements."[50]

In addition, the West Bank became a captive market for Israeli products, including the agricultural inputs that were necessitated by the shift in crops and agricultural methods.[51] Prior to the *intifada*, the West Bank and Gaza ranked as the number one importers of Israeli goods, accounting for fully 24 percent of Israeli exports.[52] If East Jerusalem is excluded from the calculation, the West Bank and the Gaza Strip constitute an export market for Israeli goods second only to the United States.[53]

Although West Bank produce was allowed only limited access to the Israeli market, and then only to fill in gaps in Israeli production, the West Bank has remained open to Israeli products and thus susceptible to the dumping of Israeli overproduction, which wreaks havoc on the already impaired ability to plan and stabilize the agricultural economy. "In 1980–81, of a total 87,797 tons of vegetable for sale in West Bank markets, 22,930 tons came from Israel. Of fruits, melons and pumpkins, 32,095 tons of the 62,287 total were from Israel."[54] The inequality of the competition is exacerbated by the extent to which Israeli produce is subsidized—sometimes up to 60 percent.[55] As a result of these conditions, at least until the *intifada* Israel has enjoyed an enormous trade surplus with the occupied territories. In 1987, the trade surplus in Israel's favor reached U.S. $802 million.[56]

Day Labor and Its Consequences

Another aspect of occupation has been the realization of the occupied territories as sources of cheap day laborers for Israel; this has been facilitated, during most of the occupation, by the policy of allowing free movement of persons across the green line. These day laborers work primarily at unskilled and semiskilled jobs, primarily in construction or agriculture within Israel.[57] This labor pattern is visibly manifested in "slave-markets." At designated crossroads, Palestinian men gather early in the morning to await the day's employment; Israelis in vans drive along and pick the manual laborers that they need for the day. Often people are not chosen, and if they are wages are low. Needless to say, protections for the workers, not to mention such benefits as health insurance and pensions, are close to nonexistent.[58]

The existence of jobs in Israel, combined with the decreasing profitability of farming, has drawn many farmers and their employees away from their land.[59] While the income of the day laborers has contributed to the standard of living, it has had numerous consequences for the West Bank economy. In addition to creating a permanent underclass of guest workers, it has contributed to inflation and other economic ills.[60]

By 1972, five years into the occupation, three quarters of the new jobs for Palestinians were in Israel, accounting for 30 percent of the West Bank labor force.[61] The outflow of labor resulted in a labor shortage in the West Bank and an actual decrease of 8 percent in the number of persons employed in the territory during the same period.[62] As of the mid-1980s, the portion of the West Bank labor force employed in Israel remained at 30 percent.[63] Prior to the *intifada*, between 100,000 and 130,000 workers from the West Bank and Gaza Strip worked in Israel, bringing home $600 million annually, approximately 35 percent of the GNP of the occupied territories.[64]

As agricultural workers took wage jobs in Israel, large tracts of previously cultivated land were left fallow.[65] In 1966 agriculture employed 45 percent of the working population in the West Bank.[66] By 1985 this percentage had shrunk to a little over 27 percent.[67] Farmers, induced to offer higher wages to those workers that remained, added to inflation. Due to these difficulties, marginal lands were often abandoned, leaving them open to confiscation by Israel.

Loss of Arab Markets

The steady decline of the West Bank's traditional Arab markets has also increased the extent of Israeli control over the economy. Prior to 1967, the Arab world was the natural market for West Bank produce; the West Bank also supplied much of the agricultural produce for Jordan. After 1967, despite the high cost imposed by Israeli security measures, West Bank produce continued to go to Jordan. However, since the early 1980s a dramatic increase in Jordan's agricultural production, due to improved agricultural technology, has reduced the demand for West Bank produce in Jordan as well as the possibility of marketing that produce through Jordan to the rest of the Arab world. Bureaucracy on both sides of the border substantially added to the costs and difficulties of transportation, and political difficulties, including the Iran-Iraq War, caused export markets in many Arab states to dry up.[68]

These problems were exacerbated by Jordan's "disengagement" from the West Bank in 1988, when King Hussein formally dropped all claims of Jordanian sovereignty over the West Bank. Prior to the disengagement, Jordan allowed up to 50 percent of the crops grown in the West Bank to be imported into Jordan.[69] Since the disengagement, Jordan has permitted the import of only those crops that are needed in Jordan. This factor, coupled with the prohibitive cost of shipping goods to Jordan, has greatly reduced the viability of this market.

The disappearing Arab market and the restrictions placed upon the sale of West Bank agricultural products in Israel have severely hurt Palestinian farmers in the West Bank. The other markets where buyers are interested in purchasing Palestinian produce are in Europe, and there are currently plans to direct export produce to the European Community, but progress has been slow.

CHAPTER 2

Economic Developments
since the Intifada

On December 8, 1987, an Israeli tank transport, driven by a man whose brother had been killed by Palestinians, collided with a truck carrying Palestinian laborers returning to Gaza from their jobs in Israel. Four of the Palestinians were killed instantly and seven others seriously wounded. Although this event received scant attention from the media at the time, the rumour spread through the Palestinian community that the killing had been an intentional act of revenge. The next day demonstrations erupted in Gaza, and as word spread about the event, Palestinians across the occupied territories joined in the protests. Long-simmering discontent had been ignited in the *intifada*, the "uprising" of Palestinians against the occupation.

In contrast with certain previous Palestinian activism, the *intifada* has had the support and participation of the majority of the population in the occupied territories. It is a grass-roots rebellion, arising from the experiences of living under occupation, rather than being sponsored by Palestinian organizations in the diaspora. Soon after the start of the *intifada*, the Unified National Leadership of the Uprising (UNLU) was formed. An indigenous group, the UNLU, with the cooperation of the Palestine Liberation Organization (PLO), directed the various organized activities of the *intifada* by issuing periodic leaflets calling for strike days, work stoppages, demonstrations, and other activities. The UNLU is said to include representatives from West Bank supporters of all four of the major factions of the PLO.

Self-sufficiency has been a central theme of the *intifada*. Numerous leaflets of the UNLU have called for Palestinians to boycott Israeli products and to support local enterprises. Sales of products such as olive oil soap from the West Bank town of Nablus and Royal Crown Cola (also produced in the West Bank) skyrocketed as Israeli-made Coca-Cola all but disappeared in the territories.[1] Likewise, it has been a conscious thrust of the *intifada* to plant subsistence crops and raise small animals, even to plant "victory gardens" on small pieces of property.[2] On a more organized level, various groups have attempted to sponsor development through small-scale projects. Hisham Awartani, an economics professor at An-Najah University in Nablus, described to us the work of the Economic Development Group (EDG), which is funded by the European Community. The EDG sponsors small-scale operations. Despite the tendency of the Israeli authorities to deny permits for projects, Awartani described a process of "guerilla economics," where small-scale projects are started without permission, in the hopes that they will be overlooked and will be able to continue to operate. Awartani has also been critical of the PLO, suggesting that political solutions will mean nothing without an economically viable Palestine and that the PLO should be making greater efforts toward this end.

As part of the self-sufficiency campaign, a semi-underground network of cottage industries has sprung up in the territories. New nonprofit cooperative enterprises help to replace Israeli goods and to provide an expanded market to Palestinian farmers. The cooperatives, of from two to fifteen or more women, purchase produce from local farmers and process it into pickled cucumbers and eggplants, juice concentrate, jams, tomato paste, sauces, and baked goods. Their products have been marketed through small stores throughout the occupied territories.

Although the grass-roots cooperative movement has expanded

significantly since the start of the *intifada,* the foundation for this growth was laid in the 1970s by local women's organizations loosely affiliated with the four major branches of the PLO: the Women's Committee for Social Work, which associates with Fatah; the Union of Palestinian Women's Committees, which adheres to the program of the Popular Front for the Liberation of Palestine (PFLP); the Federation of Palestinian Women's Action Committees, associated with the Democratic Front for the Liberation of Palestine (DFLP), and the Union of Palestinian Working Women's Committees, associated with the Palestine Communist Party. The women's committees have been the force behind most of the food-processing cooperatives, as well as underground schools which were established in reaction to intermittent closures of schools by Israeli authorities, small textile shops, day-care centers for working women, literacy programs, first aid courses, visits to prisoners, and a blood-grouping campaign in conjunction with the Union of Palestinian Medical Relief Committees.[3] In addition, other grass-roots committees have organized physicians and lawyers to provide professional services, extension services for farmers, construction projects and road repairs, educational seminars, and many other services.

Israeli reaction to the self-sufficiency drive has been harsh. In March of 1988, all "popular committees" (clandestine groups thought to be the organizers of the intifada) were banned and membership was made a criminal offense.[4] We interviewed leaders of two of the four major women's committees, who said that their headquarters had been raided, their files ransacked, and their membership lists, with literally thousands of names, confiscated. Numerous members of the popular committees have been arrested and placed in administrative detention without charge for months at a time. In June of 1988, the Israeli authorities, with approval of the country's High Court, deported Mubarak Awad, whose doctrines of civil disobedience were believed to have influenced the *intifada,* earning him comparisons with Gandhi.

The *intifada* has highlighted the economic underpinnings of the occupation and the extent of the interrelation between the occupied territories and Israel.[5] Economic duress has been employed both by Palestinians and Israelis as a strategic element of the *inti-fada*. On May 1, 1989, Israel imposed an indefinite ban on most imports from the West Bank. The loss of this market was particularly damaging since any agricultural development that has occurred during the last twenty-five years has been oriented toward the Israeli market. Heavy taxes have been levied and objects such as olive presses impounded when the taxes were not paid. Punitive measures have been taken which strike at economic production of small villages, measures such as the uprooting of fruit and olive trees and the destruction of farm equipment. The effects on the West Bank economy have been devastating. The West Bank GNP has dropped by 30 percent since 1987, largely because of the decrease in day laborers working in Israel.[6] According to Hisham Awartani, the income of the occupied territories has dropped as much as 40 percent during the *intifada*.[7]

But this situation of economic interdependence that Israel has created also affects Israel; the *intifada* has also harmed the Israeli economy. The Israeli construction industry, which is heavily dependent on cheap Palestinian labor, was among the sectors most seriously affected. Despite chronic unemployment in Israel, most Israelis have been unwilling to take these jobs, and when they have it has usually been after offers of higher pay. To fill the gap, Israel has imported over nine thousand foreign workers, many from Portugal.[8] Tourism also has been affected by the *intifada*, dropping by U.S. $280 million in 1988.[9] The balance of trade with the territories plummeted to U.S. $42 million by 1988.[10] As of the spring of 1989, the estimate of damage to the Israeli economy was $900 million, 2.5 percent of the GNP. By the end of the third year of the *intifada*, the head of the Israeli Defense Forces Budget Office estimated that the cost of suppressing the *intifada* was 1.5 billion New Israeli Sheckels (NIS).[11]

Economics, while contingent on political considerations, plays a very important role in the relationship between Israel and the occupied territories and will be central to the resolution of the conflict. What from one angle is a story of increasing material prosperity is also a story of deprivation and exploitation. Increases in GNP and in various other economic indicators have been inciden-

tal to occupation policies and practices which, as George Abed
comments, "have had the effect of generally directing all resource
exploitation activities to the accommodation of Israel's geopolitical
requirements."[12] Gains in material prosperity for the West Bank
have come at the price of an autonomy that is supposed to be guar-
anteed by international law.

PART II

CONTROLS ON AGRICULTURE

CHAPTER 3

The Institutions of Occupation

Israel established the framework for its control over the West Bank even before the end of the Six-Day War. Military Order No. 2 was enacted on June 7, 1967, placing "any power of government, legislat[ive], appointive, or administrative," in the hands of the West Bank commander of the Israeli Defense Forces (IDF). Since that time, the West Bank has been under the control of an Israeli military government, with the area commander as supreme legislative power.[1] Both civilian and military matters are under the ultimate authority of the Israeli minister of defense.

Legislation is in the form of military orders, and to date approximately fifteen hundred have been issued, altering the preexisting amalgam of Ottoman, British, and Jordanian law to control almost all facets of life under occupation, including agriculture.[2] In addition to general security measures, which can be used to disrupt agricultural production, more specific military orders concerning water, planting, transportation, and labeling delineate an effective system of controls over West Bank agriculture. On paper these orders are not especially egregious or reprehensible. Indeed, some of them are not even extensively enforced, and many controls have benefitted Palestinian farmers—especially those designed to prevent surplus production. Similar controls serve within Israel to regulate that economy. But because of the discretion available in implementing the orders they are often used to impede, rather than assist, Palestinian agriculture.[3]

Since March of 1981, all nonmilitary functions of the occupation have been subsumed into the "Civil Administration," created by Military Order No. 947. The Civil Administration was intended to pave the way toward the "autonomy" of the West Bank, pursuant to Israel's understanding of the 1978 Camp David Accords, by providing an autonomous governmental structure to handle the administrative and bureaucratic functions of the occupation.[4] However, it is important to note that the Civil Administration remains subordinate to the military government, and its head is appointed by and serves at the sufferance of the military commander of the West Bank. The Civil Administration was not granted power to enact primary legislation (military orders); it may only enact secondary legislation pursuant to the legislation of the military government.[5] The changes to the West Bank governmental structure were met with widespread protests. The Civil Administration was viewed by Palestinians as part of the bureaucratic institutionalization of the occupation, and hence as part of the process of annexation.

In addition, the military government tried to extend its control over the West Bank through the creation of "village leagues" composed of rural Palestinians who were willing to cooperate with the Israeli authorities. In an effort to elevate the positions of Palestinian "moderates," broad powers and privileges were extended to the village leagues, including preferential housing, the power to distribute development funds and patronage positions, the power to grant or withhold permits for travel and trade, and, eventually, even the right to form armed militias.[6] The U.S. Department of State reported that the purpose of the village leagues was to "transfer patronage and authority from elected and established Palestinian nationalist leaders whom Israel objects to as being supporters of the Palestine Liberation Organization."[7]

At the same time, PLO supporters came under direct attack. Popularly elected pro-PLO mayors and municipal council members were dismissed and replaced with Israeli officers. Eventually the most outspoken pro-PLO mayors were deported from the country, with the approval of the Israeli High Court.[8] Pro-PLO newspapers were closed and many of their journalists arrested. Students at West Bank universities protested the actions of the new Civil Administration, only to see the universities closed. Rioting in other areas of the West Bank was met with curfews and other collective punishments.[9]

By 1982, the Jordanian government had decided to treat membership in the village leagues as treason, and both the Jordanians and the PLO had threatened village league supporters with death. Despite tremendous Israeli support, or perhaps because of it, the village leagues were never able to generate a substantial Palestinian following, and their members were generally perceived as collaborators with the Israeli military. After 1983 the village leagues withered into obscurity.[10] However, through a combination of deportations of elected officials, arrests, curfews, and disruptions of the social structure, the military government and the newly created Civil Administration were able to destabilize and disempower the pro-PLO popular leadership, effectively preventing any indigenous political institutions from developing.

In contrast, Israeli political groups play an important role in setting policy in both Israel and the West Bank. Interest groups are not only influential in Israeli elections, but also exert substantial influence over the appointment of officials to bureaucratic boards. This results in a situation in which many important decisions are made informally, on the basis of private conversations between elected or appointed government officials and well-connected interest group representatives.[11]

Because of the special position of agriculture in Israeli society, agricultural interests have been extremely effective at ensuring that they are well represented in Israeli government. The early Zionist pioneers were farmers who settled new land and performed the strategically crucial task of claiming and defending that land for the State of Israel. Even today agricultural settlements play a crucial role in claiming land in the occupied territories. As a result of this history, farmers have always wielded political power in Israel that far exceeds their numerical strength. Israeli politicians, starting with Ben-Gurion, have chosen to identify themselves as farmers, even when they have not pursued that occupation for decades. Farm interests control major economic institutions such as the Citrus Marketing Board, the Bank for Agriculture, the Agrexco export company, and the Farm Center of the powerful Histradrut labor union. Through these and other less formal channels, agricultural interests have been able to influence governmental policy, especially in the Ministry of Agriculture, to an extraordinary degree.[12]

Not surprisingly, the structure of the Civil Administration is similar to Israel's own bureaucracy and furthers Israeli interests. Within the Civil Administration, there are various departments which roughly correspond to the equivalent Israeli ministries. In fact, the Civil Administration is often staffed by people from those very same ministries. The close ties between the Department of Agriculture of the Civil Administration and the Israeli Ministry of Agriculture have led to a coordination of strategies which often benefits Israel at the expense of the West Bank. These ties have been a means for Israeli domestic interests, including the strong farmers' lobbies, to protect their own interests from Palestinian competition. Consequently, West Bank Palestinians live under the control of a government selected and influenced by the population of a foreign country whose interests are often directly antagonistic to their own.

CHAPTER 4

The Permit System

The permit system established by military orders and the regulations promulgated pursuant to them compose the most extensive set of rules governing West Bank agriculture. Under the permit system, permission is required from the area commander or suitable representative in order to register a company, import or export certain goods, transfer land rights, plant trees and certain fruits and vegetables, construct water-related projects and buildings, and engage in other activities. Often conditions are attached to the grant of permission. The permit system is an opportunity for extensive control and such control has been used in Israel's interests, especially as the Israeli economy has worsened. Such controls have also served a political purpose and have occasionally led to a patronage system. Eyal Benvenisti, of the West Bank Data Project, writes, "Those who 'behave' get permits, those who are 'bad' do not."[1]

Permits and Crop Varieties

Starting in 1982, as the Israeli economy began to weaken, military orders were promulgated controlling crop varieties which could be

planted by Palestinian farmers in the West Bank. Military Order
No. 1015, effective August 27, 1982, gave the power to "relevant
authorities" to require permission for the planting or possession of
fruit trees or seedlings other than for the production of fruit for
personal consumption; the order also allowed conditions to be attached to the grant of permission. The appendix to this initial order
limited its effects to grapes and plums. Military Order No. 1039,
effective January 31, 1983, extended the list of plants to include
eggplants and tomatoes in the Jericho region. Military Order No.
1147, effective August 1, 1985, extended the coverage of 1015 to
onions and onion seeds throughout the West Bank. Section 9 of
1015 allows the military commander to amend the appendix to
bring more products under the scope of the military order. From
various interviews, we gathered that this process can be effec-
tuated through a simple telephone call from a high official in the
military government or the Civil Administration to an official in
the administration's Department of Agriculture.

The Department of Agriculture of the Civil Administration
determines the acreage that may be planted and what crops may
be grown.[2] These quotas have sometimes served to help prevent
gluts from overproduction, in much the same way that quotas are
imposed in Israel, but they have also been used to further the interests of Israeli growers. Quotas are routinely set to protect Israeli
farmers from West Bank Palestinian competition.[3] One Palestinian
official in the Department of Agriculture informed us that before
the *intifada* he routinely received phone calls from members of
Israeli marketing boards concerning the size and variety of expected crops in his jurisdiction. These inquiries were invariably
followed closely by orders from his Israeli superiors in the department detailing how many dunams of each crop would receive
planting permits; these figures would later control the marketing
permits received unless Israeli production was hampered by un-
forseen events such as frost.

After crops are harvested in the West Bank, the local agricultural officer in the Civil Administration receives inquiries from the
relevant marketing council in Israel as to the amount of produce
available. The marketing council, together with the Ministry of Agriculture, then determines the amount of produce that may be imported into Israel.[4]

These restrictions are enforced only on a few priority crops.[5] There are several reasons for this. Limitations on land and water, in addition to market forces, are a prior effective control on agriculture. Also, because of attrition there is simply not enough person power in the Department of Agriculture of the Civil Administration to effectively monitor what is being planted.[6] Because most of the office personnel are Palestinian, there has been a tendency to overlook any discrepancies. Consequently, farmers who are able to obtain seeds through the black market are generally able to plant them without much interference.[7]

Large-scale farmers who grow items that might compete with Israeli or Jewish settlement production are most affected by the restrictions. Eggplants and tomatoes grown in the Jordan Valley are heavily restricted. In the early 1980s, the soil and the water supply in the Jordan Valley became increasingly saline due to Israeli over-pumping of water.[8] Farmers then turned to eggplants and tomatoes because these were among the few crops that could grow in the deteriorating conditions. Overproduction of eggplants and tomatoes resulted, and limitations were set by the Civil Administration on the acreage that could be planted with these particular crops. In 1985, Palestinian farmers in the Jordan Valley were allowed to plant a combined total of 11,000 dunams of tomatoes and 9,000 of eggplants; in 1986, 9,000 of tomatoes and 7,000 of eggplants; in 1987, 6,000 of tomatoes and 4,000 of eggplants. The unused land is often planted with other crops in an attempt to diversify, but tradition, inertia, and lack of knowledge about other appropriate plants and technology make this difficult for farmers.[9]

In the Jordan Valley the restrictions on eggplants and tomatoes had the effect of providing controls in a situation where they were necessary. However, the same mechanisms that can be used to guide production and prevent gluts can be and have been used in a self-serving manner to prevent competition or to sanction certain populations. For instance, Palestinian farmers in the Jordan Valley have been unable to obtain improved varieties of tomatoes from the Israeli authorities because of the competition this would pose to Jewish settlements.[10] It is also important to remember that West Bank surpluses result at least partly from prior Israeli involvement in the West Bank agricultural economy, such as the unrestricted dumping of cheap Israeli subsidized produce in the West Bank,[11] or the over-pumping of water to satisfy the needs of Jewish settlements in the West Bank and agriculture within Israel.

Potatoes are also closely controlled, and West Bank farmers have not been permitted to grow quantities commensurate with local demand, with the result that Israeli imports are needed in the territory.[12] Tobacco is another crop for which few, if any, permits are granted.[13] Flowers are a very profitable cash crop grown in Israel and by Jewish settlers, but West Bank Palestinian farmers have been denied permission to begin a flower industry, pursuant to Military Order No. 818.[14]

With the above exceptions, most seasonal crops are not viewed as a threat to Israeli producers and are tolerated. However, trees—especially olive trees—have been much more of a problem because they are a more permanent sign that the land is being cultivated, making land confiscation more difficult.[15] According to Meron Benvenisti, Military Order No. 1015 has been used to require written permission for planting any fruit tree in an orchard.[16] In addition to olive trees, West Bank farmers have been unable to obtain permission to plant date palms, which could be quite profitable.[17]

Through the military orders which regulate the crops that can be grown, Israeli interests have been allowed to supercede those of the Palestinians. This has become increasingly true during the *intifada,* when a great many tree uprootings have been ordered under the authority of unrecorded military regulations issued pursuant to Military Order No. 1015.

Permits and Transportation: Access to Markets

Transportation restrictions and restrictions on the movement of goods across borders are much more stringently enforced than permits to grow various plants. One of the first military orders promulgated after the Israeli military assumed control over the West Bank was a quarantine prohibiting the transport of any plant or animal out of the West Bank. This was replaced by Military Order

No. 47, effective July 9, 1967, which prohibited the movement into or out of the West Bank of plants, animals, or products made out of them (except for canned goods) without a permit.[18]

Military Order No. 47 was replaced by Military Order No. 1252, effective September 1, 1988, which broadly regulates the shipment of all merchandise, including agricultural goods and organic products; all of the restrictions in the previous military orders regarding transportation were retained under the authority to specify in the permit any conditions of transport. Thus, variance from the permit of cargo, route, or date of transportation can be considered a violation. Potential penalties include fines and the possibility of a five-year prison sentence for noncompliance.

The bureaucratic requirements imposed by the military government on the basis of these military orders substantially increase the costs of bringing produce to market, if it is possible to do so at all.[19] Recent limitations on export to Israel and Jordan's disengagement from the West Bank have compounded the difficulties. The permit system has helped allow Israel to establish a virtual one-way valve, which prevents many goods from entering Israel from the territories while allowing heavily subsidized Israeli goods to flood the West Bank market.[20]

Permits are required to transport large quantities of produce bought at the major central markets within the West Bank. The transit permit is obtained from the local office of the Department of Agriculture, which specifies the date, the vehicle licence number, the type and amount of produce, and the destination.[21] A relief worker with Catholic Relief Services informed us that these permits used to be much easier to obtain before the *intifada*. Since the beginning of the uprising, however, such permits are nearly impossible for farmers from certain regions to obtain. With curfews, strikes, and area closures a common occurrence, the rigidity of the permit system is a problem, especially since noncompliance is often met with confiscation of goods.[22] The Jerusalem Media Communications Centre, a Palestinian press agency, cites one example in which a truck, delayed for a day because of a sudden curfew, was stopped at a checkpoint. "On discovering that the per-

mit was out of date the officials confiscated the truck, sold the produce being carried in an Israeli market (without compensation) and
only released the truck on bail pending a court case."[23]

The permit system regarding transportation of produce operates as
an effective control on what produce can be exported to Israel,
when, and how. In general, produce is only allowed into Israel if
such permission serves Israeli interests, such as filling gaps in Israeli domestic production, while imports of products which would
pose competition to Israeli producers are not permitted.[24] The influence of the Vegetable Marketing Board insures the protection
of Israeli interests.[25] In contrast, Israeli exports to the occupied
territories are subject to no restrictions or taxes.[26]

From 1983 until the *intifada*, it was possible for West Bank
Palestinians to export vegetables to Israel, except for tomatoes,
eggplants, onions, potatoes, and carrots. (There were also intermittent bans on olives, olive oil, nuts, raisins, and shoots of
fruit-bearing trees; and citrus, cucumbers, zucchini, cauliflower,
and cabbage were subject to restrictions.)[27] Before the *intifada*,
800 tons of grapes, 300–500 tons of plums, and 100 tons of figs
were exported to Israel each year. For West Bank citrus, on the
other hand, there were no exports to Israel before the *intifada*,
except for 150 tons of Jericho citrus into Jerusalem.[28] There
was a temporary lift of the ban on tomatoes in the winter of
1988–89 due to a frost; because Israel didn't want to lose its
export market for tomatoes, they imported some of the few West
Bank tomatoes that had survived the frost in order to export their
own.[29]

However, beginning in May of 1989, Israel prohibited all agricultural exports from the West Bank into Israel, apparently as a
form of collective punishment in response to the *intifada*.[30] Even
the small amount of Gaza citrus that was marketed in Israel was
banned at that time.[31] One Palestinian official in the Department
of Agriculture told us of a recent conversation with one of his Israeli superiors in the Civil Administration, during which the Palestinian sought to obtain permits to ship produce into Israel. The
Israeli official informed him that these permits would not be forthcoming, stating simply, "You throw stones, you go to Amman [Jor-
dan]."

Palestinian farmers who violate the export ban often find their produce destroyed or confiscated.[32] For example, during the summer of 1989, Palestinian women often came to sell their produce outside of the Damascus Gate leading into the Old City of Jerusalem, setting up small stands along the sides of pedestrian areas. Due to the depressed West Bank economy, their prices were extremely low. We regularly observed Israeli soldiers and police conducting sweeps of the area, during which the soldiers capsized produce carts, trampled fruits and vegetables, and occasionally beat the vendors. On one occasion we witnessed an Israeli police officer force a Palestinian boy of no more than ten years of age to throw his own produce to the ground and walk over it as the officer looked on.

In addition to the decrease in Arab markets for West Bank produce following Jordanian disengagement, another obstacle faced by Palestinians hoping to export to Jordan is Israel's heavy security restriction of cross-border transportation. The costs, of course, are borne by the shippers. Only a limited number of trucks, which have been in use since before 1967, are allowed to make the trip.[33] The trucks are entirely stripped down so as to facilitate security checks; each gas tank must have five glass panels.[34] The truck driver must return the same day or else he is forced to wait while the truck is dismantled for inspection, then reassembled; this process can take from three to five days.[35] Renting a truck costs a minimum of five hundred Jordanian dinars (JD).[36] (At the time of our research, a Jordanian dinar equaled U.S. $1.50, but the exchange rate fluctuates widely.)

The driver must negotiate a wide range of bureaucratic hurdles which have a tenuous relationship to security considerations. For instance, he needs an expensive series of permits from the Civil Administration to cross the border.[37] The driver must register his name in approximately twenty different offices of the Civil Administration, proving that he is clear with regard to income tax, value added tax (VAT), the chamber of commerce and trade, the municipality, the land custody department, the post office, the military and civil authorities, and so on. It takes up to three years to get initial approval for a driver; subsequently, the whole process can take from one day to one week.[38]

The Jordanian government adds to the bureaucratic hurdles.[39] Hopeful exporters must first clear their plans with the local Jordanian representative, working through the regional agricultural marketing cooperative, which then must receive approval from Jordan of the product and quantity. The Jordanian government requires a certificate of origin from the agricultural marketing cooperative as proof that the crop was produced in the West Bank and not Israel. Each year, the cooperatives provide the Jordanian government with a list of crops, the names of farmers, their expected yields, and the expected time of transport. Before transporting crops, the certificate of origin must be taken to Jordan for approval from the Jordanian Ministry of Agriculture.[40] Also, because Jordan refuses to let Israeli products into the country, the boxes, which West Bankers are unable to produce, must come from Jordan.[41] The purchase of these boxes increases costs substantially.

When crops are brought into Jordan, they must be taken to the wholesale central market in Amman and sold through the cooperative there. In Jordan it is customary to sell fresh produce direct from the truck, but Palestinians must unload their produce at the market in order to return their trucks across the border the same day. Buyers assume that this produce is not fresh and therefore West Bank produce cannot command the same price as locally grown produce in the Jordanian market.[42]

In the end, transportation costs are approximately $1,000 per truckload from the West Bank to Amman.[43] This cost has been estimated to be $150 per ton from Jericho to Amman, compared to $10 per ton from the Jordanian village of Shoona (just across the Jordan River from Jericho) to Amman.[44] A number of people we interviewed were discouraged from exporting to Jordan by the costs associated with Israeli and Jordanian requirements. Depending on the cargo, fees account for 5 to 10 percent of sale proceeds.[45] The shipper must bear these costs in addition to the costs of delay and possible border closures. The fact that the trucks are unrefrigerated makes the delays all the more costly, as produce may rot in the desert sun. The backlog at the Allenby Bridge, one of the main border crossings to Jordan, may cause delays of up to three days.[46] Sometimes even after all of the bureaucratic hurdles are overcome the truck is turned back. In July of 1988, dozens of trucks carrying watermelons from the West Bank to Jordan were turned back at the Allenby Bridge without any stated reason.[47] Often such produce is returned to cities on the West Bank, such as Jerusalem, for impromptu markets where the producers attempt to sell the goods from the trucks.

Again, the situation has only worsened during the *intifada*. The Israeli military has struck at the vulnerable agricultural sector by limiting and sometimes cutting off exports to Jordan's crucial market. For example, in October 1988 export to Jordan of olive oil, a major source of income in the West Bank, was blocked for punitive reasons.[48]

CHAPTER 5

Restrictions on Farmers' Organizations, Physical Planning, and Agricultural Projects

Despite the increases in agricultural productivity that have occurred during the occupation, the agricultural infrastructure in the West Bank remains uncoordinated and underdeveloped. Local attempts to bring order to the agricultural production of the West Bank, or otherwise ameliorate the effect of occupation on agriculture through structural coordination and development, have been hampered by the authorities.

Farmers' Organizations

A root cause of the agricultural dilemma is the suppression of Palestinian agricultural and economic self-help organizations. The Israeli government has not allowed the development on the West Bank of any interest groups similar to the Israeli farming lobbies.[1] As a result, West Bank Palestinians, denied the right to vote for the officials who appoint agricultural policymakers, are able neither to influence those organizations responsible for directing agricultural development in the West Bank nor to take matters into their own hands.

Most often, organizations are allowed to exist if they are perceived as nonthreatening or as serving Israeli interests. For example, there do exist eight regional agricultural marketing cooperatives in the West Bank, organized under the Union of Agricultural Marketing Cooperatives. At present, however, the cooperatives do little more than arrange for exports from the West Bank to Jordan,[2] and are generally perceived as representing Jordanian more than Palestinian interests.[3] Farmers wishing to export their products to or through Jordan must obtain the proper Jordanian permits from the cooperatives. The Israeli government has favored pro-Jordanian groups as an alternative to Palestinian nationalism; thus, the existence of the marketing cooperatives furthers Israeli political interests more than it assists the development of Palestinian agriculture.

When Palestinians have attempted to create more effective local organizations to assist in the planning and development of West Bank agriculture, such attempts have been aggressively discouraged by the Israeli government. Even small-scale self-help projects, such as the "victory garden" campaigns of Jad Issac and Mubarak Awad, have encountered severe governmental resistance, namely deportation or imprisonment of their organizers. An interview with a leading West Bank agricultural development worker revealed that an attempt by the Agricultural Engineers' Union to start a "Board of Farmers" was almost immediately suppressed. The agricultural engineers had hoped that the new board could help to develop and implement some form of coordinated West Bank agricultural policy, similar to the way Israeli farmers organize themselves. The board was forced to close by Israeli officials in August 1988, after it called for a planning session to map out agricultural development in the West Bank. One of the board's Palestinian organizers told us that the Israeli government authorities closed the operation and sealed the building.[4] At the time of our research, the agricultural engineers had been promised permission to reopen the board on August 16, 1989.

We also interviewed at length members of the Palestine Agricultural Relief Committee (PARC). PARC is an example of a grass-roots effort to develop the agricultural sector independent of Israeli institutions. The organization was established by Palestinian

agricultural workers to provide support services such as nurseries
for seedlings, clinical services such as vaccination for livestock, and
advice on small-scale food processing methods. PARC's services
are especially valuable because of the dwindling support services
of the Department of Agriculture. Since before the *intifada*,
PARC's strategy has included the promotion of production for local
consumption, crop diversification, regional marketing strategies,
and the rational use of agricultural inputs. They provide an information and advisory service to West Bank farmers through pamphlets, sixteen full-time agricultural engineers, and a network of
agricultural specialists. The engineers try to organize agriculture
committees in the villages and towns to encourage cooperation in
planning and marketing produce. PARC worked with fifty-five
such committees in 1988. PARC is also involved in research and
development, organizing "popular marketing" to deliver produce
directly from the farmer to the consumer, and providing supplies
of seedlings through a separate agricultural company which it organized.[5]

PARC has met with several obstacles. For instance, it has
been unable to obtain a permit as a charitable society, despite the
nature of its work, and instead must operate as a for-profit agricultural services center, which means in practical terms that PARC
must pay high Israeli taxes. PARC employees have been subject to
frequent harassment. At the time of our visit, twelve of PARC's
field-workers had been arrested and placed in administrative detention for at least six months, and some had their detentions doubled to twelve months. When arrested they were accused of membership in a "popular committee," the term used to refer to the
banned underground groups that have been accused of coordinating the *intifada*.

This harrassment by Israeli authorities has forced these agriculturalists to become very secretive and suspicious of outsiders.
When we attempted to meet with PARC members, our intermediary had to first contact them several times to assure them that
our purpose was merely to conduct interviews for an academic
study. Only after our contact was able to vouch for our credibility
were we able to meet and conduct our interviews. A PARC director
told us that despite the continual harassment, PARC would not be
intimidated. "They cannot stop us from helping farmers. We will

continue quietly to do our work, and be careful to stay out of the newspapers."[6]

Buildings and the High Planning Committee

Physical planning is also tightly controlled under the occupation. The West Bank contains twenty political subdivisions classified as municipalities, within which there is still a limited degree of Arab control of development.[7] Arab officials grant or withhold construction licenses and are generally sympathetic to the Palestinian applicants.[8] However, most of the area of the West Bank lies outside of the municipalities, including most of the rural lands where structures such as animal sheds would most likely be built,[9] and within the municipalities many elected municipal officials have been replaced by Israeli officers.

Due to Israeli amendment of the Jordanian Planning Law No. 79 of 1966, almost all authority over areas outside of the municipalities was transferred from local and regional planning committees to the High Planning Committee (HPC), which is now part of the "Infrastructure Branch" of the Civil Administration—the same branch responsible for land expropriation.[10] The HPC has total control over granting or withholding construction licenses outside of the municipalities and also has absolute veto power over licenses granted by the Arab municipalities.[11] The HPC is staffed entirely by Israeli government representatives and was headed by a Gush Emunim settler from the Adumim settlement at the time of our research.[12] (Gush Emunim is a religiously motivated group that promotes Jewish settlement in the West Bank and opposes Israeli withdrawal from the occupied territories.) According to Meron Benvenisti, "The physical planning process reflects Israeli interests exclusively while the needs and interests of the Palestinian population are viewed as constraints to be overcome."[13]

Especially since the start of the *intifada*, it has been almost impossible to obtain construction permits outside of the municipalities. Animal sheds built without permits in the West Bank are routinely destroyed.[14] Even permits to make repairs or to move such sheds and similar structures are routinely denied.[15] We learned of numerous such cases in our fieldwork, including denial of a permit for a farmer to move a greenhouse in Rasculca, near

Ramallah, and denial of permits for construction of animal sheds near Bethlehem.[16]

Relief workers with Save the Children described numerous incidents where building permits had been denied since the start of the *intifada*. The Israeli authorities have even been requiring permits for pens in which to keep animals. These have been routinely denied. In 1985, Save the Children built five rain-catching devices on the tops of buildings in various villages. Since the *intifada*, they have tried to build numerous others; each time permission was refused and permits denied. Save the Children workers reported that many other projects were frustrated in similar fashion.

Agricultural Projects

Food processing is one possible solution to the difficulties caused by instabilities in the markets for West Bank produce.[17] Canning, for example, would help alleviate excessive surpluses during the short harvest season, especially of tomatoes, eggplants, and grapes in the West Bank and oranges in the Gaza strip. The higher added value of processed food would tend to offset the high costs of production. However, in contrast to the cottage industries which have sprung up during the *intifada*, large-scale processing ventures have not been very successful.[18]

To some extent, this can be attributed to a lack of eager capital given the uncertain investment climate. Another factor is disorganization on the part of Palestinian entrepreneurs. But perhaps the greatest obstacle to development of Palestinian industry generally is the intense competition from Israeli industry, which receives heavy subsidies and "massive protection" from the government.[19] In addition, the military government places numerous obstacles in the path of such ventures.

Business ventures are required to obtain permits from the Civil Administration in order to operate. The permit requirement has been an almost impermeable barrier to many potentially viable agro-industrial projects. As a general matter, licenses are not granted to industries which would compete with Israeli businesses.[20] Since 1967 literally hundreds of licenses to start new factories have been denied.[21] Yitzak Rabin, when he was in charge of the occupied territories as minister of defense, stated that "there will be no development in the territories initiated by the Israeli government, and no permits given for expanding agriculture or industry which may compete with the State of Israel."[22]

Permits for agro-industrial and animal husbandry projects and nurseries are rarely denied outright. Rather, there are a series of unclear and sometimes contradictory signals over a long period of time which amount to neither approval nor denial. The project may be approved in principle, but made subject to certain conditions. If the conditions are satisfied, the entrepreneur often finds that the Civil Administration imposes further conditions which again delay the permit. The consequence of these delays, which sometimes last for several years, is that entrepreneurs often lose interest in the projects.[23]

Since the Gulf War there appears to be a noticeable shift in Israeli policy. With deteriorating economic conditions in the West Bank, Israel has issued a flurry of new licenses for various industries in an attempt to avert violence triggered by mass joblessness and economic stress. While many of the licenses granted have been for industries which were already up and running without permits, some were also very important to the West Bank economy, such as a license for a Palestinian bank. However, Palestinians note that even if the newly liberalized permit policy continues, the conditions of occupation are inappropriate for any real economic growth and the policy is not likely to contribute to the development of the infrastructure.[24] Some examples follow of various Palestinian projects which have met with obstacles from the authorities.

In Gaza, Palestinian business concerns have been trying for years to establish a citrus-processing facility. The project would create great benefits to the area in terms of employment and income. Gaza citrus is difficult to market, especially for export, because Israeli over-pumping of water has resulted in increased salinity in Palestinian wells, which has in turn caused the fruit to be smaller and of lower quality.[25] Processing would make the fruit much more marketable.[26]

In 1987, the former Gaza City mayor, Haj Attashawa, arranged for a feasibility study to be conducted, financed by Gaza

Bank, which showed a likelihood of success for a citrus plant in the
Gaza Strip. At Attashawa's request, the foreign minister of Italy,
Andreotti, agreed to help finance the project through the UNDP.
Despite a great deal of advance preparation for the $12 million
plant, the project faced extreme difficulties in obtaining a license.
The Israeli Ministries of Defense and Labor wanted to ensure that
the venture would not compete with Israeli concerns and made the
operating permit contingent on completed sales contracts showing
exactly where the products would be sold. Of course it was impossible to produce completed contracts for the sale of goods which
might not be produced for years, if at all.[27] Israeli authorities also
demanded that the Gaza plant purchase much of its machinery at
second hand from a kibbutz.[28] It was only after extraordinary intervention by the Italian government and the United Nations Economic and Social Council that the permit was finally granted for
the plant, over one and a half years after the official request was
made.[29]

Hebron is well-known for its grapes, but production is so high (approximately sixty thousand tons per year) that grapes cannot be
sold profitably at harvest time.[30] For years Hebron entrepreneurs
were planning a factory to convert some of the grape harvest into
juice. A variety of factors held up the project for over five years.[31]
     Some of the delay was due to disorganization among compet-
ing Palestinian business concerns, but the Civil Administration
added to the difficulties. Despite a promise of U.S. $500,000 for
the project from ANERA (American Near East Refugee Aid),[32] the
factory was not able to obtain a license to process grapes until after
obtaining a written promise from Jordan that Jordan would import
all of the factory's production. (Now that the entrepreneurs have
the written promise from Jordan, they have been able to obtain a
building permit and an operating license, and the project is scheduled for implementation in the near future.)[33]

The Arab Development and Credit Company (ADCC) of East Jerusalem had planned a poultry slaughterhouse for the West Bank
which would allow farmers to slaughter and freeze their chickens
and then save them for sale during periods of high demand, leaving
farmers less vulnerable to the irregularities of the West Bank mar-

ket. But after learning from their attorney of the difficulties which agro-industrial projects have encountered in obtaining permits, ADCC decided not even to apply.[34] Numerous business people have been similarly discouraged from even attempting to go through the permit process.[35]

Before 1967 there was a thriving poultry hatchery industry in the West Bank, with four hatcheries operating,[36] but all four failed after the occupation, largely due to competition from subsidized Israeli poultry farms. (Of the total number of poultry cooperatives, including hatcheries, 50 percent have failed since 1983 alone.)[37] Today, West Bank farmers import chicks from Israel which they raise and use for meat.[38] These chicks are quite expensive and are often diseased or defective. Their high price makes it difficult for West Bank farmers to make a profit on poultry products.[39]

In recent years there have been attempts to establish new poultry hatcheries in the West Bank, but they have not been successful.[40] One hatchery in Bethlehem was granted a permit from the Civil Administration on the condition that the eggs to be hatched be purchased from Israeli suppliers. The original plan was to sell the chicks to Jordan. When the hatchery later began to sell chicks in the West Bank, its Israeli sources raised the price of the eggs until the venture was forced out of business.[41] In 1983 and 1984, there was a hatchery in Hebron that was also allowed to operate only on the condition that it purchase eggs from Israeli sources; this one failed due to the poor quality of the eggs that it obtained.[42]

For four years the Ramallah Poultry Cooperative has been trying to obtain a permit for a hatchery in Ramallah.[43] The cooperative has financial support from ANERA and the Arab Development and Credit Company, and the UNDP has provided logistical support and conducted a feasibility study showing a likelihood of success.[44] But the cooperative has been unable to obtain a permit because the managers insist on having their own mother hens so they will not have to risk meeting the same fate as the other West Bank hatcheries. (ANERA has had approval for the venture for over five years, but this approval has been contingent upon an agreement not to have mother hens.)[45] The cooperative is holding out for permission to establish a self-sufficient hatchery capable of producing its own eggs. According to people in the development community who have worked with Israeli officials on this project, the hatchery is being denied a permit due to opposition from Israeli farmers.[46] As of January 1991, the hatchery had not received a permit.[47]

Samir Hillele of the Economic Development Group planned to start a West Bank fish farm, since fish are a staple in the Palestinian diet. Despite the fact that Hillele had the proper expertise and facilities to raise fish, and sufficient financial backing, the Department of Agriculture denied him a permit. Hillele reported that the department representative who denied the permit told him that the Israeli Agriculture Council, which represents the Israeli fish industry, pressured the Department of Agriculture; the representative told Hillele that the council would never allow him to raise fish.[48]

After the occupation, Israeli dairy farms, which receive large subsidies from the government, put most of the West Bank dairy operations out of business. Before 1967 there were five thousand milk cows in the West Bank; as of 1988 there were only two thousand.[49] West Bank milk production has fallen by over 34 percent since 1974, and the size of the entire cattle herd in the territories has decreased from thirty thousand in 1967 to just over ten thousand in 1985.[50] Now the West Bank is almost entirely dependent on the Israeli dairy company, T'nuva, for its milk products and is only 10–15 percent self-sufficient in dairy goods.[51] The sole source of pasteurized dairy products from the West Bank, and the only major dairy producer, is the Arab Development Society (ADS) in Jericho, which was founded in 1948 to provide vocational training to orphaned boys. ADS is able to satisfy only 7 percent of the West Bank's dairy needs.[52]

Despite the pressing need for greater dairy production in the West Bank, proposed dairy projects have been denied permits or have been shut down when they have operated without them.[53] It took one dairy farmer three years to obtain a permit for his farm outside of Jerusalem. A dairy cooperative in the West Bank village of A-Sawahedeh has been unable to get a permit despite financial backing from ANERA.[54] Save the Children has also been denied a permit to operate a dairy processing plant in the West Bank.[55]

An example from Beit Sahour shows what can happen when farmers undertake a project without a permit. In 1988, twenty residents of Beit Sahour pooled their money to start an eighteen-cow dairy cooperative to provide milk and milk products to the village. Within days, Civil Administration officials ordered the project closed because it had no permit. The cooperative operated for another five months under continuous harassment. All of the organizers were interrogated and asked if they were members of the banned "popular committees," and the project was raided almost daily. At one point its water was shut off. Finally, the Civil Administration ordered the cooperative closed within twenty-four hours. The organizers were forced to sell the cows to a local butcher to be slaughtered. When authorities discovered that the butcher was keeping the cows in a cave and slaughtering them only one by one, the butcher was arrested and imprisoned for four days on the basis of nonpayment of taxes.[56]

Plant nurseries are regulated by military order and are also subject to construction licenses from the High Planning Committee. There are currently ninety nurseries in the occupied territories. Fifty are licensed and forty operate illegally. Only licensed nurseries are allowed to export to Jordan or Israel, and even then, only when other restrictions are not in place.[57] Nurseries operating without permit risk being closed at any time.[58]

In 1984 the Palestine Agricultural Relief Committee applied for a permit to build a nursery in the Jericho area. They reported that the Department of Agriculture first denied the permit on grounds that the nursery needed certain materials and equipment, which PARC then purchased. It took six months for the Department of Agriculture officers to return to inspect the site again. This time the permit was denied on grounds that the site needed to be cleaned. PARC cleaned the site, but the officers did not return for one year. This time the permit was denied on grounds that the Jericho area was not suitable for a nursery. At the time of our research, the Department of Agriculture would not grant permits for tree or vine nurseries in the Jericho area.[59]

CHAPTER 6

Collective Punishment

One of the most repressive tools of the occupation has been collective punishment. Collective punishment refers to any punitive measure imposed upon a group of people in retaliation for the actions of a few. Such punishments can be exceptionally debilitating and divisive to a community when individuals are made to suffer for acts in which they had no part and which they may even have tried to prevent. Although collective punishment is contrary to international law (as discussed below), the Israeli military has imposed sanctions on families or entire villages, often when the instigating disturbances have been caused by only a few individuals, either known or unknown.

Because of the significance of the agricultural base of the West Bank economy, sanctions affecting agriculture are a particularly burdensome form of collective punishment. Such sanctions have been a part of the occupation since 1967; however, since the beginning of the *intifada* there has been a distinct increase in punitive measures taken against Palestinian agriculture.[1] Egregious actions include the destruction of farm equipment, curfews during harvesting seasons, the impoundment of olive presses, and the uprooting of fruit-bearing trees and vines. Military orders and bureaucratic requirements are often applied selectively to areas where disturbances have occurred and so constitute a form of collective punishment. Noncompliance with requirements imposed by various regulations can serve as justification for punishment for entirely unrelated events. For instance, farmers may learn of certain taxes that they are required to pay only after there have been disturbances in their area.

Uprootings

The uprooting of trees and vines of various kinds is a common occurrence in the West Bank.[2] Without any form of judicial review before the action is taken, the army often uproots trees that belong to a village, even trees that provide the livelihood of the village, on the pretext that they have been used as hiding places for stone throwers. Estimates of the number of trees uprooted in the first year of the intifada alone range from 23,400 to 100,000.[3] Most of these have been olive or other fruit-bearing trees. One particularly egregious example is related to the widely publicized incident of April 10, 1988, in Beita, where an Israeli settler killed two Palestinians and an Israeli girl. In the immediate aftermath of the shootings, the army uprooted olive trees on thirty dunams of land belonging to the village; it was later found that the villagers were in no way responsible for the deaths.[4]

Numerous other instances of tree uprootings have been well documented.[5] During one such instance, trucks belonging to the Society for the Preservation of Nature in Israel, an Israeli environmental group, were reportedly used to haul the uprooted olive trees to their new destination in Israel, where they were replanted.[6] Grapevine uprootings are also well documented.[7] In the first year of the intifada, the financial damage suffered by Palestinian farmers as a result of the tree uprootings alone has been estimated at U.S. $3.8 million.[8]

Bans on Marketing and Exports

As a form of collective punishment, military authorities have prohibited certain villages from marketing and exporting their produce. This can have a devastating effect because the economy of a village often revolves around the successful marketing of a single crop at harvest time.

A dramatic example occurred in the small village of Tel, which relies heavily on the sale of yogurt and figs within the West Bank. Beginning in August of 1988, at the time of the fig harvest, military authorities forbade any exports from the village for forty-eight days, as punishment for a stone-throwing incident. When villagers attempted to carry figs and yogurt out of the village clandestinely by donkey, military authorities seized the goods and destroyed them by driving over the produce with jeeps.[9]

Similarly, at the time of the grape harvest in September of 1988, authorities blocked all marketing of grapes from the town of Halhoul, as well as from the villages of Sa'ir and Shujoukh in the Hebron area, all of which rely heavily on grape sales. According to the *Jerusalem Post*, community leaders in Halhoul "were summoned to military government headquarters and told that the ban would be lifted if they maintained quiet."[10] Farmers in Yamoun were prevented from exporting their crops to Jordan for an extended period during the uprising.[11] During early 1988, Jericho was also forbidden to export produce to Jordan.[12]

Because of the centrality of olive oil to the West Bank economy, perhaps the most damaging ban was the October 1988 general prohibition on marketing olive oil to Jordan.[13] Finally, as noted earlier, at the beginning of the *intifada* a general prohibition of indefinite duration was imposed on exports to Israel.

Curfews at Harvest Time

Curfews have also been extensively used in the West Bank as a form of collective punishment. The nature of these curfews ranges from forced confinement of people to their homes for twenty-four hours a day to prohibitions against leaving the village. During the first year of the *intifada* there were at least sixteen hundred curfews, at least four hundred of which were prolonged, from three to forty days.[14] Often the curfews are imposed at strategically important times such as the harvest. During such curfews, soldiers forcibly prevent villagers from spraying, irrigating, or harvesting their crops, sometimes with the result that large quantities of the produce rots in the fields.[15] To cite an extreme example, the village of Kabatiya was placed under curfew for a month and a half in 1988; no persons or things were allowed to enter or leave the village. This curfew was imposed after a suspected IDF (Israeli Defense Forces) informant was killed.[16] In such a situation, families are forced to rely on whatever stores of food, water, and medicine they might have on hand. If a person attempts to leave the house or the village in order to obtain needed supplies, she or he can be arrested, as happens often, for violating the curfew.

On September 22, 1988, Israeli military sources were quoted by the *Jerusalem Post* as stating that "the authorities are planning to use the forthcoming olive-picking season in the West Bank to hit back at villages that are centers of unrest, by banning their export of olives and olive oil."[17] Amram Mitzna, the central area commander of the West Bank, said in the same month, "We will not accept a situation in which villages or areas riot . . . and then be able to act as though nothing had happened. This was the policy during the plum harvest and during the grape harvest. It will be in effect during the olive harvest."[18]

The following weeks of the olive harvest were marked by numerous curfews throughout the West Bank, during which soldiers forcibly prevented villagers from picking the crop, and several olive oil presses were shut down by military authorities for nonpayment of back taxes, other reasons, or sometimes for no stated reason at all.[19] A twenty-five-day curfew in the village of Qalquliya, during which no field work was possible, resulted in several farmers losing all of their crops in early 1988.[20]

The effects of such curfews often extend beyond the severe costs associated with the loss of crops. One young Palestinian relief worker whom we interviewed in Gaza nearly lost his life as a result of a punitive curfew. His village had been under a twenty-four-hour-a-day curfew for several days when he left his home seeking medicine for his father, who was ill. As he walked away from his home, an Israeli army patrol turned the corner onto his street. The young man was shot six times in the chest with an automatic rifle. The *shebab*—Palestinian youths involved in the *intifada*—carried him to an area hospital shortly after the incident, narrowly saving his life.[21]

CHAPTER 7

Land and Water

Land and the Tools of Annexation

Since 1967 the Israeli government has employed numerous means to gain control of West Bank land, much of which has been earmarked for "unlimited Jewish settlement."[1] Using preexisting means where available, or creating new tools where necessary, Israel had managed, according to Meron Benvenisti, to gain control over 52 percent of the area of the West Bank by 1986.[2] The following methods have been used:

- After the Six-Day War, 430,000 dunams owned by West Bank residents who left the area before or during 1967 were declared abandoned property. The majority of this land is leased to relatives of the absentees and so is not considered under Israeli possession.[3] However, substantial areas of abandoned property have been transferred to Jewish settlements through forty-nine-year leases.[4]
- Israel, as the successor state, took 700,000 dunams which were arguably registered in the name of the Jordanian government.[5]

- Approximately 50,000 dunams have been expropriated for non-negotiable payment for arguably public purposes, often for roads, and 100,000 additional dunams are designated for expropriation under this provision.[6]
- One million dunams have been declared "closed areas," including 80,000 dunams within areas populated by Palestinians. Most "closed areas" were declared combat zones. Arab landowners in such areas receive no compensation for their lands.[7]
- About 50,000 dunams were requisitioned for "military purposes" for non-negotiable payment. The establishment of Jewish settlements is recognized as a military purpose by the Israeli High Court of Justice.[8]
- By 1984, Israel had seized over 800,000 dunams by declaring it to be state land (see discussion below), and an additional 700,000 dunams have been located or mapped for possible acquisition in this fashion.[9] In the early months of 1991, the Israeli government seized at least 30,000 dunams of formerly Arab land by state land declaration and had begun preparations to seize another 40,000 dunams.[10]

Declaring land to be state land is perhaps the most controversial method of seizing property.[11] The tactic is based on a 1980 Israeli interpretation of a law dating to 1858, when the region was a part of the Ottoman Empire. Under the Israeli interpretation of this law, unregistered lands which have not been cultivated for a period of from three to ten years can be declared state land without compensation to the alleged owner;[12] the only ways to prove title are by actual registration or proof of continuous cultivation.[13] (It is important to note that the Israeli definition of state land was not used by either the British mandatory or the Jordanian governments.)[14] The Israeli High Court has approved this practice.[15]

When Israel occupied the West Bank in 1967, two thirds of the land in the territory was not officially registered. There had been no need to register the land because it was customary for families to establish title through use under Ottoman, British, and Jordanian rule.[16] In December of 1968, less than a year after the occupation began, the Israeli military government enacted Military Order No. 291, forbidding any further registration of land.[17]

This left two thirds of the area of the West Bank unregistered and unregisterable.[18]

Thus, after the 1980 interpretation of the Ottoman law, the ultimate test of possession for vast tracts of West Bank land was cultivation.[19] Palestinians who have seen their neighbors lose land which had been in their families for generations recognize the significance of continued cultivation as well as the Israeli authorities do. Despite the unfavorable market forces which have been created and constraints and restrictions imposed by Israeli authorities, which tend to make agriculture increasingly difficult, Palestinian farmers continue to plant even when it is not profitable. Some landowners can afford to till the fields solely for the purpose of maintaining a claim to the land, without hope of having a productive crop, but there is general agreement that the area of land under cultivation on the West Bank has declined by approximately 20 percent since the beginning of the occupation.[20]

Save the Children provides agricultural extension services to Palestinians in the West Bank and Gaza Strip. In interviews with their extension service workers, we were informed of an attempt by the Israeli government to seize five hundred dunams of farmland outside a small village in the West Bank. Save the Children was attempting to thwart the seizure by maintaining a tractor in the village for the use of local farmers; the villagers' ability to hold onto their farmland depended largely upon their ability to sustain "greenlands" or cultivation. The Save the Children workers would photograph the cultivated land at various times in order to maintain a pictorial record of this cultivation.

Palestinians have also attempted to secure land against Israeli acquisition by planting trees[21]—in particular, olive trees, which have a long life expectancy and require little attention. It is estimated that 44 percent of all cultivated land in the West Bank is planted with olives.[22] The olive tree, which has long been associated with the area, has recently gained a renewed significance in the context of the *intifada* as a symbol of attachment to the land (one of the jewelry trends that has come out of the *intifada* is olive-tree pendants).[23]

We interviewed a group of students from Bir Zeit University (a leading Palestinian university) who made it their project to plant olive trees on Palestinian property in the West Bank, especially when the land appeared to be in danger of confiscation.[24] We also met an elderly Palestinian gentleman who had lost his ancestral home when the Israeli Defense Forces destroyed his entire village following the 1967 war. The village was razed to the ground and its inhabitants forced to flee. This particular man seems almost obsessed with olive trees, planting them in every open space around his new house in the West Bank, in an effort to ensure that he does not lose this home as well.[25]

Even when the land is cultivated, however, there are no guarantees against confiscation if the land is desired greatly enough. The difficulty lies not only in the extensive legal mechanisms available for confiscation, but also in the review and appeal mechanisms that exist within the military government and the Civil Administration of the West Bank. The declaration of a parcel as state land and its seizure may be effected without a showing of cause and is appealable only to a committee composed entirely of Israeli officers.[26] No further appeal is available. Such a committee is not subject to rules of evidence or procedure and may hold its proceedings *in camera*, meaning that the grounds for decisions are often not divulged to the appellant. The burden of proof is on the Palestinian appellant and is usually very high. The decision of the committee rarely favors the Palestinian party, and even when it does it is merely advisory and need not be accepted by the military commander.[27] Thus, although a legal process exists for review of confiscations, it is heavily weighted against Palestinians.

At the time of our research a case was pending involving the attempted confiscation of 1,746 dunams in the Dura-Hebron area. A group of twenty families from the Dura region have owned this land for hundreds of years and have documentation proving continuous title since Ottoman times, including documents from the Ottoman Empire, the British mandatory authorities, the Hashemite Kingdom of Transjordan, and the government of Israel. In fighting the attempted expropriation of their lands these families have gone to great expense in procuring an attorney, conducting a survey, compiling tax receipts and photographs to show cultivation, and even making a trip to Turkey to obtain Ottoman tax documents.[28] When this attempt at confiscation was begun in 1983, 90 percent of the disputed land was cultivated. The Israeli authorities have prevented the owners from continuing to cultivate, causing these families additional economic harm while strengthening the government's position in court. The farmers continue to plant surreptitiously and document this cultivation with photographic evidence.[29] The villagers pleaded with us, as Americans, to intervene on their behalf. When we inquired of Palestinian lawyers what might be done to help these farmers, their frustration was evident, and we were told that there was very little that could be done.[30]

Furthermore, Palestinian farmers will often plant crops without seeking the necessary permits because title to their land must be shown before permits will be issued. Even when farmers possess proper title, they often will not show these papers to the Israeli authorities for fear that their land will be singled out for confiscation: some Palestinians we talked to said that they have so often heard of people's land being seized even when title was held that they are afraid that a "defect" in the title could be found and used to confiscate the land. Palestinian officials in the Department of Agriculture confirmed for us that these fears of land confiscation are well founded; they often advise farmers to plant without the proper permits. In fact, some officials instruct farmers in their region to plant only olive trees, even where not economically profitable, to maintain a continuously cultivated farm, thereby frustrating confiscation.

Land on the outskirts of settlements is especially vulnerable to confiscation and various forms of harassment. We visited one family farm between Jerusalem and Ramallah, near an Israeli settlement. The night before we arrived, settlers had taken a bulldozer and destroyed a large portion of the stone wall surrounding the family's grapevines. An Israeli military checkpoint was within fifty yards of the destroyed wall, guarding the road leading to and from the settlement, but apparently had not taken any action.

Control over Water Resources

Israel has a great need for water, due to its heavily capital- and water-intensive agricultural base; about 80 percent of Israeli water consumption goes to agriculture. However, water is a scarce resource, and because most of the usable water in the area is in underground aquifers that extend beneath both Israel and the West

Bank, water usage in one area can affect availability in the entire region.[31] Thus, after the Six-Day War, Israel moved to consolidate its control over West Bank water resources.

Again, as with land and controls over agriculture, military orders provided the structure for control of water resources. Military Order No. 92 of 1967 allowed the military commander to delegate the power to regulate any matter "which deals in any way whatsoever with water subjects."[32] Military Order No. 158 specifically provided for control of irrigation schemes by the area commander.[33] Finally, the management of the water system in the West Bank was given to the Israeli water company, Mekerot, in 1982.[34]

It is clear that Israel's water policy during the occupation has reflected Israel's own needs, much to the detriment of West Bank Palestinians and Palestinian agriculture. Although Civil Administration officials often pride themselves on the introduction of new water-saving technologies like drip irrigation to the West Bank[35]— with very real benefits—Palestinian farmers have also suffered as a result of various Israeli government controls over water. Restrictions on water used by Palestinians lead directly to greater availability of water for Israel and for Jewish settlements in the West Bank.

This is particularly important because Israel exploits nearly all of its own renewable water supplies and therefore must rely heavily on water from the West Bank.[36] Currently, 25 percent of the water used annually in Israel has its source within the West Bank.[37] Between 75 and 80 percent of the West Bank water supply is diverted for use either behind the green line in Israel, or by Jewish settlements in the West Bank.[38] Israel and the Jewish settlers account for over 95 percent of the water use in the region encompassing Israel, the West Bank, and Gaza.[39]

Less benevolent means than drip irrigation technology have also been used to maintain the disparity in the allocation of, and access to, water. Following the Six-Day War, Israeli forces destroyed many West Bank water sources, including numerous wells in Jiftlik and Jericho, and scores of Jordan River water pumps in Tubas. The owners have not been given permission to rebuild these wells and pumps.[40] During the first sixteen years of occupation, only five permits were given to Palestinian residents to dig new wells.[41]

Meters are now required on existing Palestinian wells to control water use.[42] Water use is regulated according to crop variety and soil conditions. Stiff fines are imposed on Palestinians who exceed the limit. Relief workers with Save the Children in Gaza informed us that every cubic meter taken over the allotted amount is billed at quadruple the already inflated price (see discussion of prices, below).

West Bank Palestinians who owned irrigation facilities prior to 1967 must obtain permits for continued operation of their facilities or for repairs, as must Palestinians who wish to drill new wells.[43] Since the early years of the occupation, the Israeli government has adopted a policy against granting permits to Palestinians to drill new agricultural wells.[44] Permission may be denied without showing cause, and licenses may later be amended or made subject to conditions.[45]

Palestinian agricultural water use has been frozen at 90 to 100 million cubic meters per year, a level 20 percent higher than that of 1967,[46] while the Palestinian land area under irrigation is frozen at 100,000 dunams.[47] A 1978 report of the British Consulate in Israel found that "water available to Arab agriculture [had] remained at or below the amount available in 1967."[48] Official Israeli development plans do not allow for an increase even by the year 2010.[49] Save the Children reports that as of July 1989, five hundred wells, either dug or in the process of being dug without permits, had been filled in by the Israeli military since the start of the *intifada*.[50]

Irrigation remains at little more than the 1966 level of between 6 percent of cultivated Palestinian land in the West Bank (the remainder relies on rainfall),[51] compared to 69 percent for the Jewish settlements.[52] Behind the green line, within Israel, 43.5 percent of the agricultural land is irrigated.[53] Lack of access to water is exacerbated by its high cost. West Bank water prices are about twice as high as those on the east bank of the Jordan River.[54]

In stark contrast to the water restrictions on Palestinians, Israeli Jewish settlements in the West Bank have enjoyed abundant water supplies.[55] Water use on the settlements increased by an estimated 100 percent in the 1980s.[56] It is estimated that 60 million cubic meters of water each year is now available for the thirty Israeli agricultural settlements, compared to the 100 million cubic meters allotted annually to four hundred Palestinian villages.[57] The combined personal and agricultural water allocation for the West Bank's over 1 million Arab inhabitants is 137 million cubic meters each year, while the Jewish population of 100,000 receives 100 million cubic meters annually.[58] With a high subsidy from the government, Jewish settlers pay one fourth as much as Palestinians for water.[59] On a per capita basis, Palestinians use 107–156 cubic meters annually, compared to the settlers' use of 640–1,480 cubic meters per capita each year. (Within the green line, Israelis use 375 cubic meters of water per person per year.)[60]

Water for the settlers often comes at the expense of Palestinians. Israeli settlers have bored between seventeen and twenty-five new deep wells (three to five hundred meters) during the occupation. Deep wells deliver much more water than the preexisting Palestinian wells, which are generally not more than one hundred meters deep. The deep wells have caused nearby Palestinian wells to dry up or salinate, rendering Palestinian land either useless for agriculture or cultivable only for saline-resistant crops. Palestinians have been unable to obtain permits to deepen their wells to compensate for the problem.[61]

We discussed the problems of salinization and decreased water availability with the director of the Arab Development Society, the largest Palestinian dairy farm. Before 1967, the ADS farm in Jericho irrigated 50 percent of its land. In 1989 this figure had sunk to 15 percent. Most of ADS's wells were destroyed in the Six-Day War and they have not been able to obtain permission to replace them. Because of the increasing salinity and decreasing flow of the remaining wells, ADS had to uproot much of its citrus crop.[62] During our interviews in the West Bank and Gaza, the salinity of the water was readily apparent in tea and coffee that was offered to us.

The West Bank villages of Al-Auja and Bardala have lost all of their water because new Israeli wells were drilled near existing Palestinian ones. Wells have also dried up or had decreased flow in Tal-al-Baida, Jenin, Bayt Dibs, and Toubas. In Jericho and Ayn-Sultan, Israeli over-pumping has resulted in increased salinity in Palestinian wells. In Sulfit, residents requested permission from 1967 onwards to complete a well begun before the occupation. The requests were denied until 1979, when the occupation authorities completed the well and pumped the water for use by the Jewish settlement of Alqana.[63]

In the small village of Ein El-Bida, the area spring went dry after a deep well was drilled nearby by the Israelis. Civil Administration authorities have now granted the farmers permission to purchase water from Mekerot, the Israeli water company, but will only allot them half of the volume the spring generated, and the farmers will have to pay between thirty and sixty agorats per cubic meter.[64] (At the time of our research, there were approximately two hundred agorats to one U.S. dollar.) The farmers in this village informed us that only a fraction of the land capable of being cultivated was actually planted due to the lack of fresh water from the aquifer they traditionally used and the cost of buying water from Mekorot. Due to fears of land confiscation, their prime fields were replanted year after year in spite of the damage caused to the soil by salination and the depletion of essential nutrients.

Even water projects which would have no effect on the Israeli supply have encountered great difficulties with permits. In Wadi Fara'a, ANERA proposed a major pipeline project to replace a canal leading from an area spring. (The canal lost almost 50 percent of its water volume to evaporation and seepage in the soil.) It took ten years for the project to receive requisite permits. As a condition for the permits, the project developers had to agree in writing that they would not grow more crops than they had before the water project, or that if they did they would not compete with Israeli farmers.[65]

Controls on water are an effective control on crop varieties. As noted above, increased salinity from Israeli water use has forced many farmers to turn to growing saline-resistant crops such as tomatoes and eggplants, which are already overproduced. Also, because of the shortage of water, West Bank farmers are often unable to grow in sufficient quantities water-intensive crops which would be profitable, such as citrus, avocadoes, kiwis, bananas, and cotton.[66]

Israeli control of West Bank land and water is a central feature of the occupation and is intimately intertwined with the issue of agriculture. Controls over land and water very obviously set the basic parameters within which more direct controls on agriculture are implemented. Controls on agriculture, in turn, have an impact on the situation regarding land and water. The discouragement of agriculture has facilitated the process of creeping annexation and has also conserved precious water resources for use within Israel. In contrast, for the Palestinians agriculture has become a way of laying claim to the land that is steadily falling under Israeli control.[67]

PART III

INTERNATIONAL HUMAN RIGHTS LAW AND THE OCCUPATION

INTRODUCTION

There are three main bodies of law at work in the West Bank. First is the body of law which existed in the territory prior to the 1967 Israeli occupation. This is itself a complex amalgam of Ottoman, British mandatory, and Jordanian law. The second body of law comprises military legislation, "security enactments" which have been promulgated by Israel since the occupation.[1] Security enactments may be declared by the commander of the Israeli Defense Forces in the region, other military commanders, or the head of the Civil Administration, and supersede any preexisting law. Enactments may take various forms, the most familiar being the military order. To these one must add what Eyal Benvenisti refers to as "the innumerable, and unnumbered, regulations, announcements, licenses, and other enactments, many of them signed by the area commander and having the same force as the orders themselves."[2] Most of the controls discussed in the preceding sections were put in place in whole or in part through security enactments.

The third applicable body of law is the international law of belligerent occupation, which is primarily expressed in the Fourth

Geneva Convention (1949) and the Fourth Hague Convention Concerning the Laws and Customs of War on Land (1899 and 1907) and related regulations (Hague Regulations).[3] In the words of the noted international law scholar Georg Schwarzenberger, this body of law seeks to "ensure a measure of real protection for the occupied territory and its inhabitants."[4]

The law of belligerent occupation was designed to maintain a reasonably humane existence in occupied territory, given a situation of control of the territory by a nonrepresentative military regime whose ultimate accountability is to a foreign nation. The primary means by which the law seeks to keep the occupier's interests from subordinating those of the inhabitants of an occupied territory is by keeping the occupier's involvement to a minimum. Lassa Oppenheim's classic text on international law states that under international law, since an occupier "is not the sovereign of the territory, he has no right to make changes in the laws, or in the administration, other than those which are temporarily necessitated by his interest in the maintenance and safety of his army and the realisation [sic] of the purpose of war. On the contrary, he has a duty of administering the country according to the existing laws and the existing rules of administration."[5]

It is clear that Israel has interfered quite extensively with both the law and the administration of the West Bank, with results that have been deleterious to the local Palestinian population. By ignoring the requirements of international law, Israel has treated the West Bank as an exploitable source of labor, water, and land, and has used its power over such matters as agriculture to reorient the West Bank to serve Israel's needs. The law of belligerent occupation provides the measure of the extent to which the occupation has failed to respect the rights of the Palestinians as an occupied population. Israel declares many of its actions in the West Bank to have been prompted by military requirements and that many others are justified as being in the interests of the inhabitants. Certainly both claims are valid to a degree. But most of the actions discussed in this book were far from military necessities, nor can they realistically be deemed to have been in the interest of the West Bank's inhabitants. Rather than providing a humane existence, Israeli stewardship of the West Bank has been an exercise in exploitation and demoralizaton, and property has been taken in the process. Palestinians and Palestinian agriculture have suffered under an occupation that has not kept within the limits set by international law.

CHAPTER 8

Applicability of the Hague Regulations and the Fourth Geneva Convention to the West Bank

The Israeli Government Position

Israel has accepted the applicability of the Hague Regulations to its rule of the occupied territories.[1] The Israeli High Court of Justice has affirmed the applicability of the Hague Regulations as part of the body of customary international law in several cases.[2]

However, there has been a long debate over the applicability of the Fourth Geneva Convention to the West Bank, despite the fact that Israel is a signatory to all of the Geneva Conventions,[3] and despite the fact that the conventions arguably constitute customary international law, binding against all nations.[4]

At first glance it seems obvious that the Fourth Geneva Convention should apply to the Israeli occupation of the West Bank. Both Israel and Jordan are now, and were at the time of the 1967 war, signatories to the convention, which states its applicability to "all cases of partial or total occupation of the territory of a High Contracting Party."[5] The situation seems clearly to satisfy the official International Committee of the Red Cross (ICRC) definition of an occupation: "During the course of an armed conflict, of whatever nature it may be and however it is called, where a territory under the authority of one of the parties passes under the authority of an opposing party, there is 'occupation' within the meaning of Article Two of the Geneva Conventions."[6]

Immediately after the Six-Day War this seems to have been the official Israeli government position. One of Israel's first actions following the war was to pass Military Order No. 3, which declared Israel's intention to apply the Fourth Geneva Convention to the West Bank. But only four months later, in October of 1967, this portion of the military order was deleted by Military Order No. 114, and the entire proclamation was superseded in 1970 by Military Order No. 378, which made no reference to the Fourth Geneva Convention.[7]

Since that time Israel and Israeli legal scholars have advanced several arguments against the application of the Fourth Geneva Convention to the occupied territories. At least since 1971 the Israeli government position has been that Israel has no legal obligation to abide by the Fourth Geneva Convention in the West Bank, but that it would "act *de facto* in accordance with the humanitarian provisions of the Convention."[8]

Some scholars have argued that Israel's *de facto* adherence to the Fourth Geneva Convention should provide sufficient protection for the inhabitants of the occupied territories.[9] In fact, the Israeli High Court, with government approval, has applied the Fourth Geneva Convention to the military government's actions in the territories.[10] Nevertheless, Israel's *de facto* adherence approach presents several serious difficulties which leave the occupied population without some of the most crucial protections of the convention.

First, there has never been a clear articulation of what is meant by "the humanitarian provisions" of the Fourth Geneva Convention. It would seem that all of the provisions of the Geneva Conventions are humanitarian in nature since the conventions, along with the Hague Regulations, comprise one of the two main pillars of humanitarian law.[11] This is apparently not Israel's view, however, since the government has refused to apply certain provisions of the convention, such as those forbidding house demolition and collective punishment, to the occupied territories.[12] The problem of leaving to the occupying power the determination of which of the Fourth Geneva Convention's provisions are applicable is obvious.

Perhaps the greatest difficulty with the Israeli *de facto* approach is the absence of an adequate mechanism to ensure respect for international law. The Fourth Geneva Convention requires the appointment of a protecting power[13]—a neutral state selected by both belligerents to look after the interests of a belligerent or its nationals in enemy or enemy-occupied territory.[14] One of the most important functions of the protecting power is the interpretation of international law in the case of disputes.[15] Israel has failed to appoint a protecting power and has refused to allow the International Committee of the Red Cross to fill that role,[16] leaving the enforcement of international law primarily to Israeli bodies. The probability of inadequate enforcement of international law is manifest in a situation where review of the actions of the occupying government is left to bodies of that same government. It is therefore an exercise of more than mere intellectual interest to determine whether the Fourth Geneva Convention does in fact apply to the Israeli occupation of the West Bank.

Perhaps the best known argument against application of the Fourth Geneva Convention to the West Bank was first articulated by Professor Yehuda Blum[17] in his article "The Missing Reversioner: Reflection on the Status of Judea and Samaria."[18] Professor Blum concluded from both the language and purpose of the Fourth Geneva Convention that it did not apply unless a legitimate sovereign had been displaced by the occupant. Blum contended that Jordan had no legitimate title to the West Bank since it had gained control of the area by conquest following the 1948 war. The primary purpose of the Fourth Geneva Convention, according to Blum, is to protect the reversionary interest of the displaced sovereign. Blum argued that the Fourth Geneva Convention greatly constrains the power of the occupier to make changes in the fundamental arrangements of the occupied society, such as the legal system, so that the ousted power would not have to take on the potentially difficult task of undoing those alterations after the signing of a peace treaty reverting the territory to the former possessor; but since Jordan had no legitimate claim to the territory, it also had no reversionary interest, and there was therefore no reason to apply the Fourth Geneva Convention to protect that interest.

Jordanian title to the West Bank was indeed quite cloudy. From the beginning of Jordan's occupation, the Arab League held that the Jordanian presence in the West Bank should be only "temporary and devoid of any character of the occupation or partition of Palestine, and that after the completion of its liberation, that country would be handed over to its owners to rule in the way they like."[19] When, on April 24, 1950, Jordan officially annexed the West Bank, the action was recognized by no states other than the United Kingdom and Pakistan.[20]

What Blum overlooks is that the Fourth Geneva Convention is at least as concerned with protecting the population of the occupied territory from the excesses of the occupying power as it is with protecting the reversionary interest of the ousted sovereign. As the Israeli legal scholar Esther Cohen has written, "The Fourth Geneva Convention was meant to be people-oriented, not territory-oriented . . . the applicability of the Convention stems from the fact of enemy nationals having passed into the hands of the occupying power, and not from the definition of the status of the occupied territory."[21]

Cohen points out that the emphasis on the rights of protected persons, rather than on territorial sovereignty, is expressed in Article 47 of the Fourth Geneva Convention, which states, "Protected persons who are in occupied territory shall not be deprived, in any case, or in any manner whatsoever, of the benefits of the present Convention by any change introduced, as a result of occupation of territory, into the institutions or the government of the said territory."[22] Thus the population under occupation maintains the same rights under the Fourth Geneva Convention regardless of the ultimate disposition of the sovereignty over the territory.[23]

A leading expert on the law of occupation, Gerhard von Glahn, has stated that the primary purpose of the law of belligerent occupation is to protect the inhabitants of the territory and that protection of the ousted government is secondary.[24] Von Glahn writes that, of the interests protected by the law of belligerent occupation, the reversionary interests of the ousted government are only the third in importance, behind the military necessity for security and the protection of the inhabitants of the territory.[25]

Professor Blum's analysis also overlooks the question, If Jordan was not the legitimate sovereign of the West Bank before 1967, then who was? Before its occupation by Jordan in 1948, Britain had control over the West Bank; earlier, the territory was a part of the Ottoman Empire from 1516 until the First World War. If a country other than Jordan was sovereign, then the Fourth Geneva Convention would still apply due to the displacement of that government. Thus the idea that there was a "sovereignty vacuum" following the end of the mandate seems quite untenable. Such a theory would imply that the West Bank was *terra nullius* after the failure of the 1948 United Nations partition plan—land owned by no one and open to any claim of title.[26]

Blum argues that since Jordan had no legitimate title to the West Bank, Israel is free to occupy the territory without regard to the law of belligerent occupation as represented in the Fourth Geneva Convention. To argue, as Professor Blum does, that the almost universal rejection of Jordan's occupation of the West Bank somehow not only legitimates the territory's occupation by Israel but also actually permits Israel to occupy the West Bank free from the constraints of international law is to turn logic on its head.

Blum makes a related argument based on the language of Article 2, paragraph 2 of the Fourth Geneva Convention, which states, "The Convention shall also apply to all cases of partial or total occupation of the territory of a High Contracting Power, even if the said occupation meets with no armed resistance." Blum contends that if Israel were to apply the Fourth Geneva Convention, it would thereby recognize that the West Bank was the legitimate "territory of a High Contracting Power," namely Jordan, which controlled the West Bank from 1949 to 1967. Such a recognition, apparently, would also imply a recognition of a reversionary right in Jordan, even though Israel, the international community, and even the Arab League, viewed Jordan to be an occupant, not a sovereign, over the West Bank.[27] In 1971, Nathaniel Lorch, former Israeli representative to the United Nations echoed this concern, stating that application of the Geneva Conventions would require Israel "retroactively to recognize as international boundaries armistice lines which have not been recognized as international boundaries by anyone."[28] Moshe Dayan, when foreign minister of Israel, stated the formal government position that the Fourth Geneva Convention did not apply because the West Bank had been illegally annexed by Jordan.[29]

The most compelling criticism of this "missing reversioner" argument is that it is premised on the wrong paragraph of Article 2 of the Fourth Geneva Convention.[30] Article 2(2), on which Blum relies, addresses an occupation which "meets with no armed resistance." But the West Bank was occupied during the Six-Day War, and so by the terms of Article 2(1) the Fourth Geneva Convention applies without any reference to Article 2(2): "The present convention shall apply to all cases of declared war or of any other armed conflict which may arise between two or more of the High Contracting Powers, even if the state of war is not recognized by one of them."

The Six-Day War clearly qualifies as an armed conflict within the meaning of Article 2(1) and the Fourth Geneva Convention therefore applies independently of Article 2(2). Article 2(1) makes no reference to the "territory of a High Contracting Power" (as does Article 2(2)), so application of the Fourth Geneva Convention by the terms of Article 2(1) can in no way be construed as a recognition of the legitimacy of Jordan's alleged onetime sovereignty over the West Bank.[31]

Jean Pictet's authoritative commentary on the Geneva Conventions is in accordance with the above reading of Articles 2(1) and 2(2):

In case of war being declared or of armed conflict, the Convention enters into force; the fact that the territory of one or other of the belligerents is later occupied in the course of hostilities does not in any way affect this; the inhabitants of the occupied territory simply become protected persons as they fall into the hands of the Occupying Power.

[Article 2(2)] does not refer to cases in which territory is occupied during hostilities; in such cases the Convention will have been in force since the outbreak of hostilities or since the time war was declared. The paragraph [2] only refers to cases where the occupation has taken

place without a declaration of war and without hostilities. . . . [Article 2(2)] was intended to fill the gap left by
paragraph one.[32]

Therefore, application of the Fourth Geneva Convention via Article 2(1), unlike its application by Article 2(2), can in no way be
construed as lending legitimacy to any claim which Jordan may
have to the West Bank. Since the West Bank was occupied by Israel during an armed conflict, the Fourth Geneva Convention is
in force in the territory by the terms of Article 2(1), independent
of Article 2(2).

In 1971, Israeli Attorney General Meir Shamgar proposed another
argument against the applicability of the Fourth Geneva Convention to the West Bank. He stated in the *Israel Yearbook on Human
Rights* that the Fourth Geneva Convention does not apply because
of the unique—*sui generis*—nature of the occupation.[33]

Raja Shehadeh, a Palestinian human rights lawyer, points out
that to accept the *sui generis* argument would be to allow various
occupiers to carve out exceptions to the universal application of the
Fourth Geneva Convention on the basis of special circumstances
which the occupier itself deems to be sufficiently extenuating. In
this way virtually any occupier could deny inhabitants of occupied
territory the protections of the Fourth Geneva Convention, since
every occupation will be in some respects unique.[34] Furthermore,
the fact that the humanitarian law of belligerent occupation was
held to govern South Africa's occupation of Namibia, which extended for a much longer period than Israel's occupation of the
West Bank, undercuts the contention that the Fourth Geneva Convention does not apply because of the long duration of the occupation.

In 1972, Brigadier Shlomo Gazit, then "coordinator of government activities" in the occupied territories, confirmed Shehadeh's
concerns that to allow an occupier to declare its occupation exempt
from the Fourth Geneva Convention on *sui generis* grounds would
all but nullify the usefulness of the convention. Gazit stated, "The
Convention was promulgated during the post-World War Two period. Israel feels that the major conflicts which broke out after 1945
are dissimilar in essence to World War Two, and that accordingly,

the Convention is out-of-date, and inapplicable."[35] In Gazit's opinion, all modern occupations are *sui generis* for purposes of the Geneva Conventions. Clearly, if the convention is to have any force, the decision of whether an occupation is *sui generis* and therefore exempt from the Fourth Geneva Convention cannot be left to the occupier.

The International Consensus on the Fourth Geneva Convention

The vast majority of international legal authorities agree that the Fourth Geneva Convention applies to the Israeli occupation of the West Bank. Perhaps most important is the opinion of the International Committee of the Red Cross, which is the neutral body charged with supervision and implementation of the Geneva Conventions. The ICRC has unequivocally held that the Fourth Geneva Convention applies to the Israeli occupation of the West Bank. On May 24, 1968, in a communication to the government of Israel, the ICRC said that "conditions were appropriate for the application of the Geneva Conventions and of the Fourth Convention, in particular, in the occupied territories."[36] In 1985 the ICRC reaffirmed its position that the Fourth Geneva Convention applies to the West Bank.[37]

The overwhelming consensus in the international community, as represented through the United Nations, is that the Fourth Geneva Convention applies to the West Bank.[38] General Assembly Resolution 35/122A of December 11, 1980, held the Fourth Geneva Convention to apply, with 141 nations voting for application, one abstention (Guatemala), and Israel as the only country voting against. As recently as 1988, the United Nations Security Council unanimously held that the Council "reaffirms once again that the Geneva Convention relative to the protection of civilian persons in time of war, of 12 August 1949, is applicable to Palestinian and other Arab territories, occupied by Israel since 1967, including Jerusalem."[39]

Even the United States, Israel's closest ally, has remained committed to the Fourth Geneva Convention's application. The U.S. State Department's 1987 *Country Reports on Human Rights Practices* states that the United States "recognizes Israel as an occupying power" and therefore considers its administration "to be subject to the Hague Regulations of 1907 and the 1949 Fourth Geneva Convention concerning the protection of civilian populations under military occupation."[40]

In addition, Esther Cohen argues that Israel is inconsistent in holding that the Hague Regulation apply to the West Bank, but not the Geneva Conventions. She argues that if the situation qualifies as a belligerent occupation for one body of law, it must also so qualify for the other.[41] Professor Meron has argued similarly that since Israel agrees that the Hague Regulations apply to the West Bank, it must also apply the Geneva Conventions to that area.[42] Article 42 of the Hague Regulations states, "Territory is considered to be occupied when it is actually placed under the authority of the hostile army," and Article 43 conditions its appliction on "[t]he authority of the legitimate power having actually passed into the hands of the occupant." Therefore, by accepting Hague's application, even under Professor Blum's analysis, Israel implicitly accepts all that is required to make the Fourth Geneva Conventions applicable: that the West Bank is occupied territory, that it is under the control of a hostile army, and that there was a legitimate power which no longer has control of the territory.

The Fourth Geneva Convention and Prolonged Occupations

Article 6(3) of the Fourth Geneva Convention states that several articles of the convention apply for only one year following the "close of military operatons" (the remainder apply for the "duration of the occupation"). Professor Adam Roberts, Montague Burton Professor of International Relations at Oxford University, points out that Article 6 has fallen into disuse and that "Israeli authorities have never invoked it as a means of reducing their obligations."[43] Protocol I (1977) to the Geneva Conventions abrogates the one year provision and establishes that the Fourth Geneva Convention will apply until the "termination of the occupation."[44] While Israel neither signed nor ratified the protocol, the consensus in the international legal community is that the Fourth Geneva Convention continues to apply to the West Bank even after over twenty years of occupation. Professor Roberts also points out that even if Article 6 were invoked, twenty-three of the thirty-two articles of the part of the convention which deals most specifically with occupied territories would remain in force.[45] Professor Theodore Meron contends that the Fourth Geneva Convention, like the Hague Regulations, applies for the duration of the occupation. He states, "The criterion for the application of the Convention is thus the exercise of functions of government in the occupied territory by the occupying power."[46] Israel still acts as the government of the West Bank through its Civil Administration. The Geneva Convention therefore still applies to the territory.

The Namibia Case

Francis Boyle, an international legal scholar, explains the striking parallels between the histories of Namibia and Palestine and suggests that the former can provide guidance in determining the legal regime applicable to the latter case.[47] Following the First World War, a system was established to ensure the eventual self-determination of the colonial possessions of the vanquished powers.[48] Under this system, former colonies were to be governed as mandates by more developed countries, with the supervision of the League of Nations and under the principle that "the well-being and development of such peoples form a sacred trust of civilization."[49]

The mandate for Palestine was given by the League of Nations to Great Britain in 1922 as a "Class A Mandate," meaning that Palestine had "reached a state of development where [its] existence as [an] independent nation[] can be provisionally recognized."[50] Namibia, then known as South-West Africa, being much less developed than Palestine, was deemed a "Class C Mandate," which "can be best administered under the laws of the Mandatory as [an] integral portion . . . of its territory."[51] The South-West Africa mandate was also assigned to Great Britain, who designated South Africa to administer it.

Following the demise of the League of Nations and the creation of the United Nations, the League's mandate system was replaced with the United Nations trusteeship system, and mandatory powers were invited in Article 77(1)(a) of the UN Charter to place the mandates into the new system. The Namibia and Palestine mandates were the only ones not placed in the UN system. The South African government refused to do so, while the British government turned the question of the Palestine mandate over to the United Nations General Assembly. The General Assembly attempted to terminate the mandate with the Partition Resolution of 1947, but this resolution was never implemented.[52]

The legal status of the West Bank and that of Namibia are therefore quite similar. In each case, the populations never achieved self-government as envisioned by the League mandate agreement—Namibia being occupied by South Africa and the West Bank by Britain, Jordan, and Israel successively.[53] Boyle argues that by virtue of this fact and the fact that the two mandates were never turned over to the UN trusteeship system, both mandates are still in force, and so, therefore, are the safeguards written into those agreements.[54]

The International Court of Justice, also known as the World Court, is the principal judicial body of the UN, established in 1945 to resolve legal disputes between nations. While there have been no World Court opinions on the legal status of the West Bank, the numerous decisions regarding Namibia provide substantial guidance. In a 1950 decision the International Court of Justice held that with the demise of the League of Nations the UN General Assembly was the appropriate body to supersede the League in supervising the administration of Namibia under the mandate, which was held to be still in force. The Court held that the mandate involved an international commitment to the people of Namibia which could not simply vanish with the fall of the League.[55] A subsequent opinion held that a two-thirds General Assembly vote was sufficient in the exercise of the supervisory power.[56] In 1966 the General Assembly exercised its power to terminate the mandate and declared that South Africa had no right to administer the territory[57] and that its occupation of Namibia was illegal.[58]

In its advisory opinion of 1971, the World Court reaffirmed the General Assembly's legal qualification to supervise Namibia, confirmed that South Africa's presence in the territory was now illegal, and ordered South Africa to withdraw immediately.[59] Boyle notes that the Court's opinion recognizes the legally binding nature of the General Assembly resolutions concerning formerly mandated territories which have not yet achieved independence.[60] Significantly for our purposes, the Court held multilateral conventions "such as those of a humanitarian character" to be binding on South Africa's occupation of Namibia, despite the illegality of the government's presence.[61] There was little question that the International Court of Justice was referring, at a minimum, to the two pillars of humanitarian law, the Hague Regulations and the Geneva Conventions, but to remove any doubt, later that year the UN General Assembly specifically urged South Africa to comply with the Geneva Conventions in its rule of Namibia.[62] Eventually, under international pressure based largely on international legal principles, South Africa respected the requirements of international law, withdrawing from Namibia and allowing the free and fair election of an indigenous government.

Boyle argues that, based on the Namibia precedent, the General Assembly is equally qualified to supervise the occupation of the West Bank and that its resolutions are as legally binding on Israel as they were on South Africa.[63] As discussed below, both the UN General Assembly and the Security Council have consistently and overwhelmingly urged the application of the Geneva Conventions to Israel's rule of the West Bank.[64] If Namibia is precedent, then the General Assembly resolutions should remove any question that the Fourth Geneva Convention applies to the West Bank.

CHAPTER 9

International Law
and Agricultural Controls
in the West Bank

The two direct methods by which Israel controls the West Bank Palestinian agricultural economy are closely related, and so they will be addressed together. The first method of control is executed through an elaborate system of security enactments. The military orders which govern water resources, crop planting, and the licensing of agro-industrial projects fall into this category. The security enactments supersede any preexisting law.[1] Every one of the security enactments, including over fifteen hundred military orders, is an amendment to the law of the West Bank as it existed at the time of occupation. The enactments which are the focus of this study all affect the West Bank Palestinian agricultural economy.

Each security enactment is subject to the constraints imposed by at least four international legal principles of belligerent occupation: (1) Israel is required to respect the preexisting law of the occupied territory unless absolutely prevented by reasons of military necessity, or unless the alteration is made in the interests of the indigenous inhabitants of the West Bank; (2) Israel is forbidden to interfere with the agricultural economy of the West Bank except as required for military necessity or for the interests of the inhabitants of the territory; (3) any controls which are exercised as forms of collective punishment violate both the Fourth Geneva Convention and the Hague Regulations; and (4) any controls which further the policy of Jewish settlement in the West Bank violate both the Fourth Geneva Convention and the Hague Regulations.

The second major category of controls studied herein are Israeli actions affecting the West Bank agricultural economy which are accomplished without security enactments, like the dumping of excess Israeli produce onto the West Bank market. Although these actions do not amend preexisting law, they are only within the bounds of international law if they are required for reasons of military necessity or if they are exercised to advance the interests of the indigenous population of the West Bank. Also, such controls violate international law if they have as a goal the furtherance of the illegal policy of Jewish settlement of the West Bank or if they are exercised as a means of collective punishment.

Requirement of Respect for Preexisting Laws

It is universally accepted that the cardinal principle of the law of belligerent occupation as expressed in the Hague Regulations and the Geneva Conventions is that the occupying power does not acquire sovereignty over the occupied territory, as this would be an act of annexation. Israel, thus far, has stopped short of outright annexation of the occupied territories (with the exception of the Golan Heights and East Jerusalem), deterred in part by the issue of how Israel would then treat the West Bank Palestinians.[2]

The corollary of the non-annexation principle is that the "belligerent occupant must respect, unless absolutely prevented, the laws in force in the country [prior to occupation]."[3] This amounts to a policy which favors, as far as possible, the maintenance of the "*status quo ante bellum.*"[4] This policy is expressed in both the Hague Regulations and the Geneva Conventions. Hague Article 43 states, "[The occupant] shall take all the measures in his power to restore and ensure, as far as possible, public order and safety, while respecting, unless absolutely prevented, the laws in force in the country." To similar effect, Article 47 of the Fourth Geneva Convention states,

> Protected persons who are in occupied territory shall not be deprived, in any case or in any manner whatsoever, of the benefits of the present Convention by any change introduced, as the result of the occupation of a territory, into the institutions or government of the said territory, nor by any agreement concluded between the authorities of the occupied territories and the Occupying Power, nor by any annexation by the latter of the whole or part of the occupied territory.

Article 64 of the Fourth Geneva Convention basically extends Article 47 to the criminal law, requiring, subject to certain exceptions, that the penal laws of the occupied territory are to remain in force.

There is general agreement that these provisions of the Hague Regulations and the Fourth Geneva Convention protect preexisting laws governing such matters as family life, property, contracts, and commercial activities, and that, as a corollary principle, the occupier "may not change the internal administration of the occupied enemy territory—he may not introduce a new indigenous governmental structure."[5]

Schwarzenberger states that the "*ratio legis*," or reason behind the law, of the rule requiring respect for the law which existed in the occupied territory prior to occupation "is to forestall temptations on the part of the Occupying Power to abuse its discretionary and legislative powers. . . . The Occupying Power may not interfere with the *status quo ante bellum*. . . . It prevents wartime emergency powers from being abused for purposes alien to a wartime occupation."[6]

With regard to agriculture, Israel has imposed a plethora of amendments to the preexisting law of the West Bank, ranging from amendments to land and water law to laws governing transportation, construction, agro-industry, and crop planting—laws which affect almost every facet of the agricultural economy. All of these amendments trigger the aforementioned legal norm.

Limits on Economic Interference

International law forbids the occupier from interfering with the agricultural economy of the occupied territory except as required by military necessity[7] or when the intervention is in the interests of the inhabitants of the territory.[8] Due to the nearly overwhelming incentives for an occupier to take advantage of its position to exploit the territory occupied, the law of belligerent occupation establishes norms with the aim of keeping the occupier's involvement in the economy to a minimum and sets guidelines to govern what involvement does occur.

Articles 52, 53, 55, (and 48 and 56)[9] of the Hague Regulations, taken together, establish a rule against "plunder and economic exploitation" of the occupied territory.[10] Both von Glahn's and Oppenheim's authoritative treatises note that the International Military Tribunal at Nuremberg held that Germany had violated this rule in its administration of occupied territories during the Second World War. Finding a violation of the above Hague provisions, the tribunal stated that "[the] territories occupied by Germany were exploited for the German war effort in the most ruthless way without consideration of the local economy and in consequence of a deliberate design and policy," and that "the economy of an occupied territory can only be required to bear the expense of the occupation in a measure not greater than it can reasonably be expected to bear."[11]

The Israeli High Court has recognized the need to keep the occupier from turning the occupied territory into an "open field for economic or other exploitation."[12] The United States Department of State expressed similar concerns in 1977, arguing that international law forbade Israel from exploiting oil fields in the Sinai and Gulf of Suez. A State Department memorandum of that year explains in detail the limitations which international law places on the occupier's property rights and economic involvement in the occupied territory. Based primarily on Hague Article 55 and the United Nations Charter, the memorandum states, "A rule holding out the prospect of acquiring unrestricted access to the use of resources and raw materials would constitute an incentive to territorial occupation by a country needing raw materials, and a disincentive to withdrawal."[13]

Following the First World War, many of the economic practices of the French administration of the occupied German Rhineland were sharply criticized by international legal authorities.[14]
Some of these controversial practices were strikingly similar to
those used by Israel in its administration of the West Bank.

French economic control of the occupied region was exercised
largely through administrative agencies known as *sections economiques*. The primary mechanisms of control were the granting and
withholding of operating licenses to German businesses and the
control of imports and exports to and from the occupied Rhineland.
Much criticism was directed at the undue influence which French
businesspeople exerted on the *sections economiques*. These *sections economiques* premised business licensing decisions largely on
French economic interests; they also regulated trade to prevent
Germans from exporting their goods to France, while at the same
time flooding the German economy with French products.

In contrast, in the zone of occupied Germany administered by
the United States, business licensing decisions were delegated to
local chambers of commerce. U.S. Army General Henry Allen criticized the French activities as being "scarcely . . . germane to a
holding force." Under Allied pressure, the worst excesses of the
sections economiques were eventually curbed, first through Article
5 of the Rhineland Agreement Peace Treaty of January 10, 1920,
and later through an agreement to establish a joint French-German
economic administration of the territory.[15]

The international legal norm forbidding economic exploitation
applies to all of the controls studied in our research, not only to
the controls executed through security enactments. This norm has
a purpose similar to that of the requirement of respect for preexisting law—both seek to minimize the occupier's involvement in
the territory and favor the *status quo ante bellum*. The norm discussed here, however, has broader application since it applies also
to those actions or controls which have no legal basis. As mentioned earlier, this category includes activities such as the flooding
of the West Bank market with heavily subsidized Israeli produce
and the informal communication between Israeli farmers' lobbies
and the Department of Agriculture, which often serve to benefit
Israeli interests at the expense of the West Bank Palestinians.

Derogations

It is generally accepted that international law allows the occupier to amend preexisting law or to become involved in the economy of the occupied territory if it is absolutely necessary for military reasons or for the maintenance of public order,[16] or, in the modern view, if the change is made in the interests of the inhabitants of the territory.[17] Relying on Hague Article 43, the Israeli law professor Yoram Dinstein states:

> [T]he occupant may abolish, suspend or amend existing law—or enact new ones—only in exceptional circumstances when the continuation of the preexisting legal position is absolutely prevented. . . . [A]bsolute prevention means necessity. The necessity . . . may be derived either from the legitimate interests of the occupant or from concern for the civilian population."[18]

The "legitimate interests of the occupant" are defined fairly narrowly and are limited to matters falling within the scope of "military necessity"[19] or "public order,"[20] such as laws dealing with sabotage, possession of arms, contacts with the enemy, and so on.[21]

The *Ville d'Anvers v. Germany* case points out how closely circumscribed is the occupier's discretionary power to declare an amendment to existing law "absolutely" necessary for reasons of military necessity or public order.[22] Following the German invasion of Belgium in 1914, there were scattered outbreaks of mob violence against German nationals. The German military commander amended existing Belgian law to give jurisdiction over such cases of mob violence to German, rather than Belgian, tribunals. Following the war, the Belgo-German Mixed Arbitral Tribunal of 1925 held that the creation of the new German tribunals had been unjustified and had violated Hague Article 43. It concluded that "neither necessities of war nor the maintenance of public order called for so far-reaching an interference with Belgian law. Thus, the Occupying Power could not claim that it was 'absolutely prevented' from showing due respect for the local law."[23] Germany was fined one million Belgian francs for its actions.[24] A similar standard was applied by the arbitrator in the *Chevreau* case, which arose between France and Great Britain in 1931 over a dispute concerning a deportation during occupation which was held to be justified neither by military necessity nor by the need to restore public order.[25]

Von Glahn points out the importance of determining both whether a claim of military necessity is valid and whether the action "exceeded the demands of a necessity."[26] In a 1962 official pamphlet, the United States Department of the Army argued that claims of military necessity must be closely scrutinized and pointed out that the "doctrine [of military necessity] when advanced in the various war crimes trials following the Second World War was universally condemned."[27] It is clear from these cases and authorities that claims of military necessity must be extremely compelling in order to justify an amendment to existing law as "absolutely necessary" within the meaning of the Hague Regulations.

Israeli claims of military necessity should be all the more suspect because of the duration of the occupation, now well over twenty years. Esther Cohen divides occupations into two phases: (1) the "wake of battle, when some armed, organized resistance remains, but control of the area is in the hands of the occupant; and (2) resistance is quelled entirely and administration predominates over battle."[28] In the latter situation of prolonged occupation, there is a much lower level of military necessity and therefore the "highest standards of humanitarian conduct apply." Cohen argues that the more than twenty-year-old Israeli occupation of the West Bank certainly qualifies as prolonged and that therefore claims of military necessity must be even more closely scrutinized than if similar claims were made shortly after the close of combat.[29]

Under these internationally accepted standards, the overwhelming majority of the controls studied in this report would not qualify as military necessities. Controls on crop plantings, business registration, and marketing simply may not be maintained as militarily necessary under international law. Harvest-time curfews, tree uprootings, and punitive marketing bans are no more justified by military necessity than were the military tribunals established in response to mob violence and later successfully challenged in *Ville d'Anvers v. Germany.* The transfer of numerous legal matters, including most land disputes, to Israeli military tribunals is so similar to the situation addressed in *Ville d'Anvers* as to require no comment. The sole control studied which clearly qualifies as a military necessity is the inspection of vehicles entering Israel from Jordan.

Modern interpretations of the law of belligerent occupation allow amendment to the preexisting law of the occupied territory or economic interventions not only for reasons of military necessity but also if the alterations are made to benefit the inhabitants of the territory.[30] The modern view is based on the original French text of Hague Article 43, which has traditionally been translated as follows: "[The occupant] shall take all the measures in his power to restore and ensure, as far as possible, public order and safety, while respecting, unless absolutely prevented, the laws in force in the country."[31] The traditional reading would allow amendment of the preexisting law of the territory only for reasons of "law and order" or "legitimate military needs."[32] However, scholars have argued that the word *safety* is an inadequate translation of the original French, "vie publique."[33] Esther Cohen argues that the sense of the phrase is actually closer to "civil life."[34] Alan Gerson, a legal scholar who has written extensively about the legal status of the occupied West Bank, argues that the phrase refers to "allowing the life of the occupied country to find continued fulfillment even under the changed conditions resulting from occupation."[35]

Cohen argues that this reading is supported in Jean Pictet's authoritative commentary on Article 47 of the Fourth Geneva Convention:

[Article 47] does not expressly prohibit the occupying power from modifying the institutions of government of the occupied territory. Certain changes might conceivably be necessary and even an improvement. Besides, the text in question is of an essentially humanitarian character; its object is to safeguard human beings, not to protect the political institutions and governmental machinery of the State as such. The main point according to the convention is that changes made in the internal organization of the State must not lead to protected persons being deprived of the rights and safeguards provided for them.[36]

Thus the occupier would be allowed to make changes in the preexisting law of the teritory in order to benefit the local population.

The obvious difficulty with the modern approach is that the occupier's professed motivation may be less than sincere. Gerson points out that humanitarian motives for the occupier's amendments to existing law are "suspect," and that such motivations "could serve as a ruse for creation of *faits accomplis* to the occupant's advantage." He points out that "claims by occupants that such change as they initiated was humanitarian, dictated by 'the imperative needs of the population,' would, during the course of occupation, be exceedingly difficult to disprove."[37]

Concerns for the interests of the occupied population are especially acute in prolonged occupations like that of the West Bank. In a changing world, freezing the laws and economic arrangements of the occupied territory at the beginning of occupation presents obvious problems which become exacerbated with the passage of time. The Israeli High Court stated in the early 1970s that in a prolonged occupation the needs of the inhabitants of the territory become more "valid and tangible,"[38] which seems to be an argument for allowing wide discretion to the military authorities to make changes in the occupied territories during a prolonged occupation. However, the Court's analysis ignores countervailing considerations.

The noted international law expert Antonio Cassese explains that "in prolonged occupation, the provisional nature of the government fades away and it begins to look like a full-fledged administrative entity, but without any of the safeguards of ordinary government." He points out the danger that in a prolonged occupation the powers of the occupier may "crystallize and consolidate, much to the detriment of the population."[39] Indeed, the Israeli Civil Administration in the West Bank after twenty-four years does look like a "full-fledged administrative entity." Cassese suggests that in prolonged occupations changes in the legal system of occupied territories must be treated as suspect even when they are justified by the occupier as being in the interests of the occupied population.

One way to ensure that economic intervention in the occupied territory is in the interests of the inhabitants is to allow the intervening party to consider *only* those interests, and not the interests of the occupying state. The Israeli High Court stated in *Cooperative Society v. Commander of the I.D.F.* in 1982:

> The Military Commander is not allowed to consider any national, economic or social interests of his own State; not even national security interest, but only his own military needs and those of the local population . . . therefore, for example, it is forbidden for a military administration to impose taxes on the inhabitants of the occupied territory in order to fill the coffers of the occupying state.[40]

The *Cooperative Society* case arose from a proposed project to build a road through parts of the West Bank. The project was challenged by certain West Bank residents who owned property which would have been affected by the project and who claimed that the road was unnecessary. The Israeli High Court held that only the interests of the inhabitants of the West Bank could be considered in the decision of whether to build the road, not the interests of the Israeli population.[41] As a further control on the occupier, the High Court said that authority over the territory is vested solely in the military commander and not in the government of Israel.[42] This ruling attempted to place authority in the hands of an official directly responsible for the territory, rather than in a party, such as an elected Israeli government official, who is necessarily accountable first to Israeli society and Israeli interest groups and at best only secondarily concerned with the territory.

Under this analysis, the agricultural policies studied in this project cannot be justified as being in the interest of the occupied population and must be deemed to violate international law. First, it is clear that elected Israeli government officials and special interest groups are directly participating in economic interventions in the occupied territories. Departments within the Civil Administration are staffed by people from the relevant Israeli ministries, facilitating communication links and coordination. Second, that involvement has had the expected result of subordinating West Bank interests to those of Israel, in violation of international law.

Almost all of the controls studied in this project either cumulatively or immediately advance Israeli interests at the expense of the West Bank Palestinian population. While certain controls (like the control of surplus production of certain crops) may have had a beneficial effect for West Bank farmers, in light of the overall effect of the controls studied, it cannot be maintained that they are justified under international law as being for the benefit of the occupied population. We have documented how Palestinian agricultural and agro-industrial projects have been thwarted to protect Israeli economic interests. We have also explained how the rising gross national product is not an accurate indicator of the economic health of the West Bank and that, in fact, the West Bank suffers from severe structural underdevelopment as a result of the occupation.

The controls studied clearly violate the standards of the Hague Regulations as articulated by von Glahn, since the West Bank economy has been "manipulated in such a way as to create a maximum benefit for the occupying state instead of for the local population."[43] In violation of the law of belligerent occupation, Israel has in fact turned the West Bank into "an open field for economic and other exploitation."[44]

International Law and Collective Punishment

Both the Fourth Geneva Convention and the Hague Regulations contain absolute prohibitions against collective punishment. Article 33 of the Fourth Geneva Convention explicitly forbids collective punishment and states that no resident of an occupied territory "may be punished for an offence he or she has not personally committed." Article 50 of the Hague Regulations, states, "No general penalty, pecuniary of otherwise, shall be inflicted upon the population on account of the acts of individuals for which they cannot be regarded as jointly and severally responsible."

Many of the actions we have described above qualify as collective punishments according to the above definitions. Collective punishments we have witnessed and/or documented include tree uprootings, crop destruction, punitive bans on export and marketing, curfews, and other measures. All of these actions clearly violate the prohibition against collective punishment.

CHAPTER 10

International Law and West Bank Land and Water Resource Control

Water

The occupation has been an opportunity for Israel to extend to the West Bank its control over scarce water resources in the region. Numerous new laws and security enactments have been put into place in order to facilitate the management of water resources. However, in practice these laws have been used to benefit Israel to the detriment of the West Bank, in clear violation of the law of belligerent occupation. Numerous preexisting laws have been altered to facilitate the Israeli exploitation of water resources. In addition, as noted by Jeffrey D. Dillman (of the Legal Counseling Project of the Washington, D.C., office of the United Nations High Commissioner for Refugees) in 1989, Israel's water resource management violates legal norms forbidding the confiscation of private property.[1]

The applicable law is found in both the Fourth Geneva Convention and the Hague Regulations. Article 46 of the Hague Regulations provides that "private property . . . must be respected . . . [and] cannot be confiscated." Any unauthorized interference with such property amounts to illegal confiscation. Similarly, Article 53 of the Fourth Geneva convention prohibits "any destruction by the occupying power of real or personal property belonging individually or collectively to private persons, or to the State, or to other public authorities, or to social or cooperative organizations . . . except where such destruction is rendered absolutely necessary by military operations." Article 46 of the Fourth Geneva Convention states that "[r]estrictive measures affecting property [of protected persons] shall be cancelled . . . as soon as possible after the close of hostilities." Pictet's definitive commentary defines the "close of hostilities" as "the actual end of the fighting and not the official termination of a state of belligerency."

Also, the law of belligerent occupation requires the occupier to respect "unless absolutely prevented, the laws in force in the country [prior to occupation]." In this case, the state of affairs under Jordanian rule provides the proper baseline for international legal analysis, since the Geneva and Hague prohibitions against confiscations of private property would be meaningless if the occupier could circumvent the law simply by redefining private property as public. In addition, if Israel were able to disregard Jordanian law on the basis that Jordan's title to the West Bank was contested, then the legal norm would be all but without force, since occupiers commonly question or deny the legitimacy of the ousted regime. Clearly, the baseline must be provided by the immediate previous regime if this legal norm is to have meaning. Under Jordanian law, unlike in the Israeli system, water was considered private property and landowners could claim ownership of waters on or under their land.[2]

However, Israeli Military Order No. 291 of 1968 redefined surface and underground water in the West Bank as public property, and Israel has used its control over West Bank water to integrate those resources into the Israeli national water system. As explained in the above section on water controls, permission is now required for any water projects. Permits for new wells and irrigation schemes are almost never granted to Palestinians. While Jordanian Law No. 31 of 1953 required permission from the Department of Irrigation and Water for irrigation projects, according to Dillman, "such authorization was routinely granted unless the project posed a threat to any land, road or other property."[3]

Thus, Israeli water regulations deprive West Bank Palestinians of water rights which they enjoyed under Jordanian rule. Palestinians who previously had a property right in the water lying on or under their land are now denied access to that water and so have lost a form of property which is very valuable in the region. Also, there is not adequate water potential to support new Palestinian wells in most West Bank aquifers since Israel is pumping these sources to their full potential for use by Jewish settlers in the West Bank and by Israelis inside the green line. In effect, Palestinian subsurface property is being siphoned away for Israeli use. The alteration of the existing law can hardly be characterized as being in the interests of the Palestinians.

Palestinians with wells drilled before 1967 have also suffered both property confiscation and destruction within the meaning of the law of occupation. The destruction of West Bank pumps and wells following the Six-Day War is an obvious example. Metering of Palestinian wells to limit water use clearly amounts to confiscation of private property under the Hague Regulations, which state that "[a]ny unauthorized interference with [private] property amounts to a confiscation."[4] The Israeli practice of digging deep wells to provide water for Israeli use, which results in the salinization or drying up of Palestinian wells, violates the Fourth Geneva Convention prohibition on destruction of private property. The practice also violates preexisting law in the West Bank, which prohibited the drilling of new wells which would interfere with the flow of existing wells. Under Jordanian law, a permit was automatically granted for a new well if an existing well ran dry, while under current Israeli legislation, such permits are almost never granted.[5] Therefore, the property destruction is irreparable and uncompensated under the current legal regime.

The above actions clearly constitute confiscations of property within the meaning of the Hague and Geneva provisions cited above. They are most certainly "restrictive measures affecting property,"[6] and "interference[s] with [private] property,"[7] amounting to confiscation within the meaning of the applicable legal provisions.

The use of West Bank water by Israelis inside the green line and in settlements also violates international law, including Hague Article 52, which allows requisition of private property only for "use by the occupying army" and then only when "paid for by the occupying power."[8] Though preexisting Jordanian law prohibited the transfer of water from one drainage basin to another, under Israeli management West Bank water is regularly transported from one drainage basin to another for use by Israelis in areas as distant as the Negev desert.[9] According to international legal scholar Julius Stone, the occupier may only "utilize the resources of the [occupied] country within the limits of what is required for the army of occupation and the needs of the local population."[10] In a parallel situation, the *Singapore Oil Stocks* case held that Japanese exploitation of oil fields in occupied Sumatra during the Second World War violated "the laws and customs of war" because the oil was used not only in "meeting the requirements of the army of occupation but for supplying . . . civilian needs of Japan."[11]

The only exceptions to the above legal provisions would be if the property confiscations were required to maintain order or security, were for the benefit of the West Bank population, or were in accordance with preexisting law. Israel has never claimed its management of West Bank water resources were required for order or military security;[12] the property deprivations obviously do not benefit the West Bank population; and finally, the confiscations are not in accordance with preexisting law, but, in fact, are executed through military orders which alter and violate preexisting law.

The concerns expressed in 1977 by the United States Department of State in arguing that international law forbade Israel from exploiting oil fields in the Sinai and Gulf of Suez seem particularly appropriate to the case of Israeli use of West Bank water. Israel's control over, and need for, West Bank water has indeed been, in the words of the above-mentioned State Department memorandum of law, "an incentive to territorial occupation by a country needing raw materials, and a disincentive to withdrawal."[13] Israeli water policy on the West Bank poses a formidable obstacle to any possible disengagement from the West Bank and is in clear violation of international law.

Land

The creeping annexation of West Bank land is also contrary to international law. However, different legal rules apply depending on the manner of confiscation of the land. Israeli alienations of land fall into three general categories: (1) alienations of private property; (2) alienations of land formerly claimed by the state of Jordan; and (3) alienations of property declared to be state property. Under international law, higher standards govern the confiscation of private property than govern state property confiscations.

Private Property Alienations

Until 1980, the primary method used to seize private land for settlements was to requisition it for "military purposes,"[14] one of the exceptions to the general prohibition on the confiscation of private property contained in Article 46 of the Hague Regulations.[15] However, under Israeli interpretation this was a wide exception indeed. The Israeli High Court in the *Beit-El* case determined that "all Israeli settlements in the administered territories are an integral part of the Territorial Defense System of the IDF" and that use of private land requisitioned for military purposes for settlements in the West Bank was permitted since it fulfilled "urgent military needs."[16] The court found persuasive the affidavits of the government that "all settlements in the territories occupied by the IDF constitute part of the IDF's regional defence system. . . . In times of calm these settlements mainly serve the purpose of presence and control of vital areas, maintaining observation and the like. . . . [I]n time of war . . . said settlements constitute the principal component of presence and security control in the areas in which they are located."[17] (The court has also stipulated, however, that these settlements must be temporary in nature, pending international negotiations.)[18]

Despite the fact that Israel offers payment for the use of such privately owned lands, the Israeli justification is legally problematic. Article 46 of the Fourth Geneva Convention states that "[r]estrictive measures affecting [private] property shall be cancelled . . . as soon as possible after the close of hostilities," and Pictet's definitive commentary defines the close of hostilities as "the actual end of the fighting and not the official termination of a state of belligerency." The settlements are obviously restrictive measures on the requisitioned property since the former owners can no longer use the land. The government's statement to the

High Court that the settlements serve a function "in times of calm" is a virtual admission that the restrictive measures are continuing beyond "the actual end of the fighting" and therefore violate the Fourth Geneva Convention.

In a rare successful legal challenge, Mustafa Dwikat and other West Bank residents whose land was requisitioned for the alleged "military purpose" of establishing a Gush Emunim[19] settlement brought the *Elon Moreh* case to the Israeli High Court. The government's claim of military necessity was undermined in the case by the settlers themselves, who testified that they claimed a right to settle on ideological and religious grounds. The court rejected the land acquisition on grounds that it was motivated less by reasons of security than "by reasons stemming from the Zionist world view of the settlement of the whole land of Israel."[20] The court also ruled against the settlement because the Likud government had decided to make Elon Moreh a permanent settlement intended to exist beyond any possible termination of the occupation. The court stated:

> [T]he decision to establish a permanent settlement destined from the outset to remain in its place indefinitely— even beyond the duration of the military government established in Judea and Samaria—comes up against an insurmountable legal obstacle, because no military government can create in its area facts for its military needs, which are designed *ab initio* to persist even after the end of the military rule in the area, when the fate of that area after the termination of military rule is still not known.[21]

The 1979 decision of the High Court in this case temporarily complicated the requisition method of private land acquisition by requiring a legitimate security justification for confiscation and forbidding permanent settlements.

Another major category of West Bank land under Israeli control is land seized for reasons of security. Approximately 1.11 to 1.15 million dunams, one half of all the land seized by Israel in the West Bank since 1967, have been declared closed areas for security reasons pursuant to Military Order No. 3 of 1967.[22] Certain of the purported security concerns are suspect. For example, areas have been closed under this provision in order to prevent journalists from visiting demonstrations.[23] Also, some 5,000 dunams seized in this method have later been turned over for use by Jewish settlements. However, most of the land seized in this method is at least arguably seized for security reasons such as use for military training grounds and firing ranges.[24] Even in such cases, the alienation of land under this provision raises international legal concerns because private landowners whose land lies in closed areas receive no compensation.[25] This practice violates accepted international standards requiring compensation to private landowners whose property is alienated even for legitimate reasons.[26]

Fifty thousand dunams of West Bank land have been expropriated for arguably public purposes, such as roads, and 100,000 additional dunams are scheduled to be expropriated in this fashion.[27] While owners of these properties receive non-negotiable payment, the manner in which the lands are seized raises two legal difficulties.

First, Israel ostensibly bases the expropriations on a Jordanian law.[28] However, the law has been extensively amended by Israeli military orders,[29] in the words of Meron Benvenisti, "to facilitate wholesale expropriations with minimal checks and balances."[30] The original Jordanian law provided the property owner extensive procedural safeguards. These included requirements that the intention to expropriate the land be published on two occasions in the *Official Gazette*, an official publication of the Jordanian government; that the authority seeking the confiscation receive approval from both the Council of Ministers and the king of Jordan; and that the authorities inform the Registrar of Lands of the names of all of the owners in question. Appeal of an expropriation was to the Court of First Instance in the area under Jordanian law. But, as amended by the Israeli military government, appeal has been transferred from the local courts to "objections committees," bodies composed entirely of military personnel, and all of the checks and balances mentioned have been eliminated to facilitate confiscation by the military commander.[31] The High Court of Israel has authorized this elimination of the procedural safeguards of the Jordanian law.[32]

The current procedure of expropriation of land for public purposes is therefore in clear violation of the international legal requirement of the Hague Regulations that the occupier respect the preexisting law of the territory. The Jordanian law relied upon has been so extensively amended as to be unrecognizable. Further, the Israeli amendments to the law cannot be justified as being required by military necessity, since the procedural safeguards of the original law could not be viewed as in any way compromising state security. Nor can the amendments be justified as being for the benefit of the occupied population, since it is the procedures which safeguarded their rights which have been curtailed.

There is also a question as to which public's interest can justify an expropriation for "public purposes." Land acquired under the provision has been used for settlements, access roads for settlements, and roads which connect settlements, bypassing Palestinian villages as if they did not exist.[33] It appears that the public being served by such expropriations is the Israeli settlers, not the indigenous Palestinian population.[34] Eyal Benvenisti notes:

> As early as 1972, the [Israeli High] Court included the Jewish settlers as part of the local community, whose interests, therefore, the military authorities also had to take into consideration in their decisions. . . . [W]hen it considered whether the administrative act in question benefitted the indigenous population, it was satisfied if the act had been intended to benefit *also* the local community. The fact that the act served primarily Israeli interest was not seen as relevant.[35]

Justifying expropriations of Palestinian property based upon benefits which will accrue to the settler population clearly conflicts with international law, especially since the Fourth Geneva Convention prohibits settlement outright. Such a justification would allow almost any transfer of Palestinian property to settler hands, since such an expropriation would clearly benefit the settler population.

State Property Alienations

International legal standards governing the alienation of state property are substantially more relaxed than those governing private property expropriation. Lassa Oppenheim states:

> During mere military occupation of enemy territory, a belligerent may not sell, or otherwise alienate public enemy land and buildings, but may only appropriate their produce. Article 55 of the Hague Regulations expressly enacts that a belligerent occupying enemy territory shall be regarded as administrator and usufructuary of the public buildings, real property, forests and agricultural works belonging to the hostile State and situated in the occupied territory; and that he must protect the stock and plant and administer them according to the rules of usufruct.[36]

In short, the occupier is permitted to use and administer the properties of the ousted sovereign for the duration of the occupation without compensation but subject to the law of usufruct, under which "the occupant is bound to preserve the substance of the property in question but is entitled to seize as his own the product or proceeds arising out of the property."[37]

Israel has employed two major methods to gain control of land alleged to have been the property of the state of Jordan. First, by virtue of Military Order No. 59 of 1967, Israel took possession of approximately 750,000 dunams of land which had been registered in the name of the Jordanian government. This procedure is not highly controversial and is authorized by Hague Article 55. The Hague text charges the occupier with the duty to "protect the stock and plant [of the ousted sovereign] and administer them according to the law of usufruct."[38]

The second method of taking possession of state land involves the dubious characterization of land held without explicit title under preexisting Jordanian and Ottoman law to be state land, thus rendering it susceptible to expropriation as mentioned above. This is by far the most controversial method of land acquisition employed in the West Bank and has become more prevalent after the 1979 Israeli High Court decision in the *Elon Moreh* case. This judgement impeded the requisitioning of land for military purposes, which had been up to that time the most common method of alienating private land for use by Jewish settlers;[39] however, the effective outcome of the decision by no means stemmed Israeli settlement in the West Bank, but rather persuaded the Israeli authorities to abandon the cumbersome requirements of private property alienation and instead to acquire property by declaring it to be state land. Despite the 1979 decision, the Elon Moreh settlement was established later, a short distance from the original site, on land claimed through the new state land method.[40] In fact, the Likud block was yet to embark on the most aggressive phase of the settlement drive.

After 1980, instead of relying on the now cumbersome private property requisitions, the Israeli government began to declare properties to be state land, thereby avoiding the restrictions imposed by *Elon Moreh*,[41] which had two major shortcomings. These have been described by Raja Shehadeh: "(1) Only seizures of privately owned land could be prevented or reversed by recourse to the High Court; (2) [t]he High Court was not prepared to intervene in any disputes over ownership status of land."[42] Israeli authorities, relying on military orders which had already been enacted, took advantage of the *Elon Moreh* exceptions. Military Order No. 364 "render[ed] a mere declaration by the authorities that land is state land sufficient proof that the land is to be considered as such 'until the opposite is proven,'" thereby placing the burden of proof on the party asserting private ownership.[43] As noted above, Military Order No. 172 had created a military objections committee to hear appeals of such decisions.

In 1980 Israeli authorities began to declare as state land areas which West Bank residents claimed to be privately owned. Because of the shift in the burden of proof, the assumption was that the land was in fact state property and thus the claimants could no longer appeal to the High Court, but only to a military objections committee.[44]

Israeli authorities based their claims of state ownership on an Ottoman land code promulgated in 1858 which remained in effect through both British and Jordanian rule.[45] The land code divided all land in the West Bank into two categories, which can be further subdivided into a total of five types. In the first category are: (1) *waqf* land, which was land dedicated to pious purposes and whose ultimate owner was designated to be the Almighty; (2) *mulk* land, which was land in municipal areas given out by the Ottoman conqueror to residents of the area under title deeds. The second category consists of land whose ultimate ownership was claimed by the sultan by virtue of conquest, but to which various land tenures could be claimed by private users: (3) *miri* land, to which holders could claim possession by cultivation (a holder could theoretically lose his or her rights if the land lay fallow for three years); (4) *matrouk* land, open to public use such as commons, pastures, roads, and cemeteries, (5) *mawat* land, which lay further from a village "than the human voice could be heard" and was open for cultivation by "anyone who is in need."[46]

This basic system remained in force with only minor revision through British and Jordanian rule. Jordanian Law No. 49 of 1953 removed all restrictions on the uses to which *miri* land could be put, thereby eliminating any effective differences between *miri* and *mulk* land. The 1922 British Order-in-Council created the category of state land and initiated a process for settlement of land claims.[47]

In 1980 Israel began to rely on this land code to declare unregistered, uncultivated lands of the *miri, matrouk*, and *mawat* types to be "state property," based upon the sultan's ultimate right of ownership. A 1968 military order had forbidden further land registration at a time when only 30 percent of the area of the West Bank was registered, making cultivation the sole means of establishing private ownership of vast tracts of the territory. According to Meron Benvenisti, "The new definition enabled the Israeli authorities to claim self-righteously that no Arab land had been taken and that the military government was acting in accordance with both local and international law."[48] The claim was that Hague Article 55 was not violated since no private land was confiscated. The land taken, it was argued, was already classified as state property (property of the sultan) under preexisting law, and so remained open for use by the state. Brigadier General Dov Shefi, as military advocate general of the Israel Defense Forces, stated in 1982 that

"Israel has consistently refrained from expropriating private property,"[49] thereby avoiding the most difficult international legal issues involved in the expropriations. However, through the practice of state land declaration, lands held by Palestinian families for generations are being alienated by the State of Israel.

The Israeli interpretation fundamentally misconstrues the nature of the Ottoman land code. Ottoman land law is similar to many other systems of land ownership, such as that existing in England. The land ownership systems of both Palestine and England were established by invasion. When Palestine became part of the Ottoman Empire, and when England was invaded by the Normans, all land came into ownership by the Crown. In England, the Crown distributed land for various uses on the basis of a complex system of land tenures, while always retaining a right of ultimate ownership—hence the maxim, No land is without a lord. However, the Crown's ultimate right of ownership was little more than theoretical, and in practice actual ownership and possession of the lands were in their owners and users. The only lands in actual possession of the Crown were those classified as Crownhold.[50] In fact, in most English and U.S. jurisdictions, a continuous and open claim of ownership for a period of ten years would convey full possessory rights by the law of adverse possession.[51]

Even after the British creation of an official category of state land in Palestine, this category was never construed as coextensive with the categories of land whose ultimate right of ownership was defined as being in the sultan. Instead, only lands which were not claimed as private property by West Bank inhabitants were registered as British state property, and then only after a lengthy registration procedure which provided the territory's inhabitants ample opportunity to assert their claims. In the words of Meron Benvenisti,

> Neither the British nor the Jordanians claimed, declared, or registered *miri*, *matrouk*, or *mawat* land as state land by virtue of a hypothetical sultan's ultimate right of ownership; but if as a result of a process of settlement of land claims there remained tracts not claimed by anyone, these tracts were registered as state land.[52]

In fact, the British considered *miri* lands to be outside the category of state lands altogether. It is interesting to note that inside Israel, where the same Ottoman land code was in force until 1969, lands of the *miri* category are classified as full private ownership properties as of 1969 by Israeli land law.[53]

Therefore, the presumption that all *miri*, *matrouk*, and *mawat* lands are state property unless registered or in actual continuous cultivation is unfounded. Hague Article 55 does not authorize Israeli government use of lands it declared state property, since they were not in fact the property of the state under preexisting law. Instead, the lands whose ownership is claimed and recognized by West Bank inhabitants, and which may have been in Palestinian families for generations, are private property under international law. It is clear that most of the confiscations at issue would not pass the stiff international legal requirements governing private property confiscation.

While international law permits the occupier "to make use . . . of the expropriation legislation in force in the occupied enemy territory prior to the occupation,"[54] it is clear that Israel is not satisfying this criterion with its invocation of the Ottoman land code. The code was the opposite of expropriation legislation; it was a system designed to distribute unused and unclaimed property to "[a]nyone who is in need,"[55] not to take it away. The code was never interpreted to confer such broad possessory rights upon the state. While Israel may rely on the words of the Ottoman code, the meaning construed from those words is so radically different from that understood during any previous regime that it must be concluded that Israel is not, in fact, relying on preexisting law, but on the Likud government's reinterpretation, which has been tolerated by the courts.

However, not only does Israel claim that the confiscations are permissible under international law, it goes further to claim that they serve to safeguard the property rights of the ousted sovereign.[56] Indeed, the language of Hague Article 55 implies that the occupier should protect the property of the displaced government, but Israel's argument is problematic since neither Britain nor Jordan claimed the property as their own, as emphasized by Jordan's 1988 disengagement from the West Bank and disavowal of any claims to the territory. Furthermore, Israel has gone to great lengths to avoid recognizing any government as the legitimate sovereign of the West Bank, even to the extent of refusing to apply the Geneva Conventions. Finally, Israel's gradual integration of the confiscated lands into the Israeli sphere through settlements indicates a poor record at "safeguarding" any property rights other than Israel's own. In short, the method of land confiscation by declaration as state land is in direct violation of international legal safeguards.

CHAPTER 11

Settlements

The legality of land alienation methods cannot be discussed in a vacuum, separate from the use to which the land is eventually put. Even if the act of expropriation is conducted in a manner consistent with international law, such as expropriation for public purposes with compensation, if the land is then used for purposes prohibited by international law the land alienation must be viewed as illegal. Such is the case with Jewish settlements on the West Bank, to which much of the land under Israeli control has gone.

From 1967 to the end of 1976, 3,176 Israeli settlers were established in the West Bank. After that period the number rose exponentially, increasing by 1987 to 80,000 settlers in annexed East Jerusalem and 65,000 elsewhere in the West Bank, in well over a hundred individual settlements.[1] At the end of the decade the settlement drive continued unabated, with 105,000 settlers in the West Bank and another 125,000 in East Jerusalem. By 1992, the number of Israeli settlers in the West Bank is expected to rise by at least an additional 50,000.[2] Settlements have been built on land confiscated in all of the manners discussed above. In some cases multiple methods have been employed to secure land for a single settlement. For example, the settlement of Shiloh is built on 740 dunams of land requisitioned for military purposes, 850 dunams declared state land, and 41 dunams expropriated for public purposes.[3]

Settlements and the Fourth Geneva Convention

The clearest prohibition on settlements in the law of belligerent occupation is found in Article 49 of the Fourth Geneva Convention, which states, "The Occupying Power shall not deport or transfer parts of its own civilian population into the territory it occupies." The passage clearly forbids the occupying power to bring in its own citizens to populate the territory. This provision has been the basis for most of the numerous United Nations General Assembly and Security Council resolutions condemning West Bank settlement.[4]

Brigadier General Dov Shefi, then military advocate general of the Israel Defense Forces, argued in a 1982 book edited by Israeli High Court Justice (and former attorney general of Israel) Meir Shamgar, that the Geneva provision is inapposite since the Fourth Geneva Convention does not apply in the West Bank. Shefi continued that even if the Fourth Geneva Convention applies, it was meant to prohibit only settlement which would result in the deportation or displacement of the local population. This, he argued, has not happened in the West Bank.[5] However, U.S. Department of State legal adviser Herbert J. Hansell pointed out (in 1978) that "displacement of protected persons is dealt with separately in the Convention and paragraph six would be redundant if limited to cases of displacement." Hansell therefore contended that Geneva Article 49 prohibited West Bank settlements.[6] The United States government remains opposed to the Israeli settlement program in the West Bank.[7] However, despite the official opposition from the Bush administration, the U.S. Congress has continued to supply financial support for these settlements.[8]

Other Israeli commentators have argued that the government of Israel has not "transferred" its own population into the West Bank in violation of Article 49, but that the settlers have voluntarily established the settlements themselves.[9] This argument is not convincing, since, as noted by the Oxford professor Adam Roberts, "the ambitious settlements program of the 1980s . . . was planned, encouraged, and financed at the governmental level" and the IDF was heavily involved in establishing and protecting many of the settlements.[10] Furthermore, the Israeli government offers substantial monetary incentives to Israeli settlers. For instance, the per capita funding for West Bank settlements is 143 percent higher than the funding for similar Israeli towns, and West Bank regional councils receive budgets 61 percent higher than those of similar Israeli towns.[11]

Settlements and the Hague Regulations

A common justification of Jewish settlement in the West Bank is that it is necessary for Israel's security. Israeli High Court Justice Landau correctly stated that according to Hague Regulations Article 43, "the main function assigned to the army in the occupied territory is 'to safeguard public order and security'" and that therefore "the temporary use of land or buildings [is permissible] for all kinds of purposes demanded by the necessities of war."[12] However, serious questions have been raised as to whether the West Bank settlements are, in fact, motivated by security interests, whether they further those interests at all, or, if they do, whether the necessity is so pressing as to allow derogation of the general prohibitions against such land use.

Adam Roberts states that "it is doubtful whether the settlements program was primarily intended to contribute to the occupying power's security and whether, in the event, it has contributed to that end; by causing friction with the Palestinian inhabitants of the territories, the program may even have added to the work of the Israel Defense Forces (IDF)."[13] In the *Elon Moreh* case, Lieutenant General (Reserves) Haim Bar-Lev (later the minister of police) "expressed his professional assessment that Elon Moreh makes no contribution to Israel's security . . . in time of war, Israeli troops will be tied down in guarding the civilian settlement rather than in engaging in the war against the enemy's army"; in the same case, General (Reserves) Matityahu Peled submitted an affidavit questioning the military capabilities of a civilian settlement in time of war, citing the Yom Kippur war, when all settlements in the Golan Heights were evacuated, unnecessarily burdening the security forces.[14] Even if the settlements can be seen as advancing Israeli security interests to some degree (which is not at all obvious), the military necessity cannot be viewed as rising to the level required by international law to allow their presence in the West Bank.

The permanent nature of the settlements also violates provisions of the Hague Regulations. Israel's property rights are at their peak in the West Bank in areas legitimately classified as state lands. But even there Hague Regulations Article 55 requires the occupier to conform to the law of usufruct, which confers only a limited right to use the fruits of the property for the duration of the occupation, but not a broader right of ownership.[15]

The Israeli High Court, in the *Beit-El* case, recognized that "civilian settlement can only exist in that place as long as the IDF occupy the area."[16] Despite the court's holding allowing the *Beit-El* settlement because of its "temporary" nature, the Israeli government has made it quite clear that the settlements are intended to be permanent additions to the West Bank landscape, especially since the start of the massive Likud settlement drive. The International Commission of Jurists, a highly respected organization of international lawyers, with chapters around the world, has cited the "permanent character" of many settlements and the "pronouncements of Israeli leaders to the effect that they are permanent."[17] Matityahu Drobles, when head of the settlement division of the World Zionist Organization (WZO), an organization instrumental in the implement of the government's settlement policy,[18] stated, "There is to be not a shadow of doubt regarding our intention to remain in Judea and Samaria."[19] Similarly, former foreign minister Moshe Dayan stated in 1980:

> Why are the settlements necessary? Because I do not wish to see the actual boundaries of Israel on the Green Line. And the meaning of boundaries not on the Green Line is the possibility of maintaining an army in these areas, of establishing settlements in these areas up to the Jordan [River]. . . . I do not think that Israel can create a map like this if there will not be settlement in blocs, and settlement which can really stand on its legs.[20]

Because of the limited, and somewhat murky, security justifications for the Jewish settlements, as well as their permanent nature, Israel's settlement policy is directly contrary to the Hague Regulations as well as the Fourth Geneva Convention. West Bank land which has been used for settlements has been illegally alienated. In addition, because of the illegality of settlement, policies designed to advance or facilitate settlement, such as water and agricultural policies which advantage settlers, are in violation of international law.

CHAPTER 12

Enforcement of International Law

Legal standards are only meaningful given an effective enforcement mechanism. In the international law of belligerent occupation, a "protecting power" is charged with the role of neutral adjudicator of disputes as to applicable international legal standards in occupied territory.[1] Given Israel's refusal to appoint a protecting power for the West Bank, we will explore three potential alternative mechanisms for enforcing international law in the territory: (1) international supervisory bodies; (2) the Israeli High Court of Justice; and (3) military courts and special military tribunals.[2]

The Protecting Power

The Fourth Geneva Convention stipulates that in a situation of belligerent occupation, a neutral body should be jointly selected by the belligerents and charged with scrutinizing the behavior of the occupier, safeguarding the interests of the inhabitants of the territory, and ensuring that international law is respected.[3] This protecting power is also to interpret international law in the case of disputes. The parties to the conflict are bound to assist the protecting power in the execution of its duties.[4]

The introduction of the mandatory protecting power has been deemed the "most significant advance" of the Geneva Conventions over the Hague Regulations.[5] While the protecting power is a historically well established institution of the law of belligerent occupation, the protecting power concept was considerably enlarged in the Geneva Conventions of 1949.[6] The rationale underlying the protecting power requirement is that the occupier cannot reasonably be expected to scrutinize adequately the actions of its own occupation authorities or to determine whether its own officials and military personnel are respecting applicable law.

If the belligerents are unable to agree upon a neutral state to serve as protecting power, the Fourth Geneva Convention requires the appointment of a substitute in the form of "an international organization which offers all guarantees of impartiality and efficacy."[7] When even this is not possible, the convention requires the occupying power to accept and cooperate with "the offer of the services of a humanitarian organization, such as the International Committee of the Red Cross, to assume the humanitarian functions performed by Protecting Powers under the present Convention."[8]

Oppenheim states, "Protecting powers shall lend their good offices whenever they deem it desirable in the interest of the protected persons."[9] One of the most important functions of the protecting power is to resolve "cases of disagreement between parties to a conflict on the interpretation or application of the Convention."[10] The convention requires the belligerents to accept consultation with the protecting power in such instances of disagreement.[11] If the parties fail to reach an agreement during consultation, they "'should' agree on the choice of an umpire who 'will' decide upon the procedure to be followed."[12]

Despite the clear mandate of the Fourth Geneva Convention, no protecting power has been appointed in the West Bank. Furthermore, Israel has refused to cooperate with a potential protecting power substitute, the United Nations Special Committee to Investigate Israeli Practices Affecting the Human Rights of the Population of the Occupied Territories (UNSCOP),[13] and has also

refused the offer of the International Committee of the Red Cross
to act as official substitute for the protecting power.[14] In fact, although the presence of the Red Cross has been tolerated in the
West Bank, that body has been hampered by Israel in its operations there.[15] In the absence of a protecting power, it is necessary
to explore alternate mechanisms for enforcing international law.

International Supervisory Bodies

International legal scholar Francis Boyle has suggested that the
International Court of Justice opinions concerning the South African occupation of Namibia serve as legal precedent to allow the
United Nations General Assembly to take on a direct supervisory
role over the Israeli-occupied territories.[16] Boyle and other commentators have also suggested that, as was done in the case of Namibia, the United Nations should exercise its authority to request
an advisory opinion from the International Court of Justice on the
legality of actions taken by the occupation authorities in the West
Bank and of the occupation itself.[17] Recent proposals have been
made in the United Nations for the secretary general or a United
Nations body to play a direct role in protecting the interests of the
Palestinian inhabitants of the West Bank.[18] To date, no such international supervisory body has gained the approval of the Israeli
government to serve as protecting power, nor has the World Court
issued an advisory opinion.

Israeli High Court Review

The role of the High Court in enforcing international legal norms
in the West Bank has been much heralded by Israeli commentators
since the court asserted jurisdiction over the territory in 1967.[19]
Israel has incorporated customary international law as part of the
municipal law of the State of Israel.[20] Thus, to the extent that the
Israeli courts recognize customary international law, claims can be
brought under such law before the Israeli courts. The Hague Regulations have been accepted as part of customary international
law.[21] However, while Israel has signed and ratified the Fourth
Geneva Convention, it has not recognized it as customary international law.[22] Nor has Israel passed incorporating legislation which

would make the convention part of Israeli internal law.[23] Because of this, the Fourth Geneva Convention is enforceable by neither Palestinian nor Israeli individuals, except insofar as it represents customary international law.[24]

Understandably, the general effectiveness of the High Court in guarding humanitarian norms is the subject of great debate, with some commentators describing it as "a fortress defending the rights of the individual against unlawful and improper interference on the part of the executive,"[25] while others claim that "the outcome [of High Court decisions] has not been encouraging [for West Bank Palestinians]."[26]

We have found that jurisdiction over many or most of the controls studied in this study is in bodies other than the High Court. As for those controls which do fall under the High Court's purview, the court has not adequately enforced international law. "The reason for this," states Raja Shehadeh, "lies primarily in a series of self-imposed restrictions which the court placed on its proclaimed role which permitted it to avoid dealing with many of the thornier issues raised by the occupation."[27]

Perhaps the most significant limitation on the High Court's review is its refusal to apply the Geneva Conventions to the West Bank. Even when the government has submitted to review under the terms of the Fourth Geneva Convention, recent High Court practice has been to refuse to apply the document. In both *Beit-El*[28] and *Elon Moreh*,[29] although the government invited the High Court to apply the Fourth Geneva Convention, the court refused to do so on the grounds that the convention was not part of Israeli law. Instead, it merely discussed the acts in question in terms of the convention in nonbinding commentary, while deciding the cases based on customary law—which, according to the High Court, does not include the Fourth Geneva Convention.[30]

High Court review is limited even further when the government justifies its actions with a claim of security or military necessity. Eyal Benvenisti writes: "One of the court's clearest policies has been deference to the discretion of the military authorities whenever it [*sic*] invoked security considerations. . . . Whenever these concerns are invoked, the court's scrutiny is confined to an examination whether the act was not *ultra vires* [beyond authority to do an act] and whether the reasons cited were not simply a cloak that hid irrelevant or illegal factors, or motives that were relevant but not dominant."[31] The narrowness of this scope of review is displayed in a line of cases in which West Bank residents went before the High Court to challenge actions of the military government which had been justified on security grounds.

In the *Hilu* case, a group of bedouin farmers living in the Sinai brought a petition challenging an order that restricted the hours during which they could have access to their farmlands. The military commander claimed that the area needed to be closed for security reasons in order to prevent terrorist activity.[32] Invoking the narrow scope of review over security matters, the High Court dismissed the farmers' petition. Justice Landau stated that "[t]he extent of the interference of the Court with the action of military authorities relating to matters of security must needs be very limited."[33] Justice Vitkon, in the same case, relying in part on the United States Supreme Court precedent of *Korematsu v. United States*[34] (which authorized the internment of United States citizens of Japanese ancestry during the Second World War), held that "matters of army and security, like matters of foreign policy, are not capable of judicial determination and that therefore the petition in question was *ex facie* non-justiciable."[35]

A similarly narrow review was applied in *Beit-El*, where the High Court allowed a seizure of privately owned land for the alleged military purpose of establishing a civilian Jewish settlement in the West Bank. The High Court stated that it would assume that the military commander's claims of military necessity were valid absent "very convincing evidence to the contrary."[36] In the *Matityahu* case, the military commander, claiming military necessity, seized five hundred dunams of cultivated and uncultivated privately owned land near Ramallah for a Jewish settlement.[37] Both the military government and the Palestinian landowners presented the court with affidavits by Israeli generals. General Matt claimed for the government that the settlement was required for military necessity, while General (Reserves) Peled stated that the land acquisition did not advance security interests.[38] The court upheld the land seizure, holding that given conflicting expert testimony on security issues, "the Court will presume that the considerations of the persons speaking on behalf of the authorities in charge of security in Israel and in the Administration of the territories are genuine, and very strong evidence would be required to rebut this presumption."[39]

In *Taha v. Minister of the Interior*, the High Court refused to invalidate a decision based on security concerns which denied travel permits to certain West Bank residents seeking to travel to Mecca for a religious pilgrimage.[40] In *Al-Sayad v. Commander of Judea and Samaria*, the court would not strike down a security-based decision to deny travel permits to Palestinian newspaper editors who wished to travel from their residences in the West Bank to their places of business in Jerusalem.[41]

According to Eyal Benvenisti, of all of the cases brought before the High Court in which a claim of security was advanced, in only two did the court invalidate the actions of the government authorities—*Elon Moreh* and the *Jerusalem Electric Co.* case.[42] (The dispute in *Jerusalem Electric* was over the government confiscation of a West Bank power-generating company.) In both cases, the court learned from the authorities themselves that security was not the true motivation for the actions at issue.[43] Such cases will obviously be rare.

The High Court's presumption of the validity of the area commander's claims of military necessity undermines the basic purpose of the law of belligerent occupation and encourages specious claims of necessity. In order to adequately safeguard the interests of the inhabitants of the West Bank it is necessary to reverse the presumption of the High Court and to scrutinize closely all Israeli claims of military necessity. As the international law scholar Ernst Feilchenfeld wrote in a Carnegie Endowment for International Peace monograph published in 1942, "the benefit of doubt belongs to the old, not to the new laws."[44]

For the above reasons, the High Court does not provide an adequate opportunity to enforce international legal standards in response to controls classified as security measures. Many of the controls which are the subject of this study have been deemed security measures. These include: collective punishments such as tree uprootings, bans on marketing, curfews, and area closures during the harvest; land confiscations for alleged security purposes; certain controls on transportation within the West Bank and from the West Bank to Israel, Jordan, and other destinations; and restrictions on the emergence of local centers of control which could safeguard the interests of farmers, such as municipal governments and farmers' organizations.[45] In such instances the High Court has almost always been unwilling to stand in the way of the military commander. As we have discussed, few if any of the controls studied qualify as military necessities under international law.

High Court review has also been closely circumscribed over controls justified as being for the benefit of the population of the territory. As discussed earlier, certain actions which would otherwise be prohibited by international law, such as amendments to pre-existing law, are permissible if executed for the benefit of the inhabitants of the occupied territory.

As mentioned in the section on settlements (above), since 1972 the High Court has considered Jewish settlers as part of the local communities whose interests the military authorities may take into account.[46] In Eyal Benvenisti's words, "When [the court] considered whether the administrative act in question benefitted the indigenous population, it was satisfied if the act had been intended to benefit *also* the local community. The fact that the act served primarily Israeli interests was not seen as relevant."[47] For example, in *Tabib v. Minister of Defense*, the High Court allowed a confiscation of Palestinian land for a road which connected West Bank settlements but purposely bypassed Arab town centers. The High Court held that although the confiscation served primarily Israeli interests it incidentally benefited the Palestinians who might use the road.[48]

Many of the controls studied above would pass such a low threshold, including land confiscations for roads and other projects intended primarily to benefit Jewish settlers; water regulations designed primarily to ensure ample water supplies to these settlers but which may also serve to control overuse of acquifers for the benefit of all users; and restrictions on crop planting by Palestinian farmers designed primarily to prevent competition with West Bank settlers but which may also avoid gluts in a market shared by Palestinians, settlers, and Israelis.

Article 43 of the Hague Regulations, which forbids amendment of preexisting law except for reasons of military necessity or

for the benefit of the territory's population, clearly did not intend
to allow deviation for the benefit of the occupier's population which
has settled in the territory. In fact, settlement is expressly prohibited by international law. However, the High Court's interpretation allows Jewish settlement in the West Bank, then allows the
government to alter the legal framework of the territory for the
benefit of the settlers. Such interpretations defeat the purpose of
the legal norm, which was intended to minimize the occupier's
involvement in the territory.

Even without factoring in the settlers, Israeli determinations
of what is in the interests of the local population are suspect. In
the *Abu-Aita* case, the High Court adopted a test devised by Professor Yoram Dinstein to analyze claims that a given action is for
the benefit of the inhabitants of the occupied territory.[49] Pointing
out that there is no objective criterion to distinguish between sincere and insincere concern for the inhabitants, Dinstein suggested
that a good test would be "whether or not the occupant is equally
concerned about his own population . . . whether there is a similar
. . . law, in his own country." If there is such a law, then Dinstein
would conclude that the enactment satisfies the requirements of
Hague Article 43; if not, he would conclude that the enactment
would violate the Hague regulation.[50]

While Dinstein's inquiry would be valuable in determining
whether Israeli involvement in the occupied territories truly
sought to promote the interests of the inhabitants, it would not be
conclusive. Even if similar laws or regulations were implemented
in both the occupied territories and in Israel, there could be substantial differences in the application of those laws. The well-
known United States Supreme Court case of *Yick Wo v. Hopkins*
displays how a facially neutral law can be applied in discriminatory
fashion.[51] In *Yick Wo* a California statute simply required all laundries to be in stone buildings; however, the statute was applied
only to laundries owned by Asians. The research outlined above
shows how very similar controls often operate inside Israel to the
advantage of farmers, but operate in the West Bank to subordinate
the territory's economy to that of Israel.

The *Abu-Aita* case displays the peculiar outcomes which may
result from the Dinstein test. The case was brought by Palestinians
who charged that the new value added tax (VAT) of 15 percent,

which was to be applied to almost all sales, violated Articles 48 and 49 of the Hague Regulations.[52] Articles 48 and 49 state that if the occupier collects taxes, these must be "as far as possible" in accordance with the preexisting tax law of the territory and that any additional taxes may only be levied to defray costs of administering the territory.[53]

The High Court adopted the Dinstein test and noted that the same tax was applied inside Israel. The court sided with the government authorities who argued that if the tax were applied only inside Israel then economic borders would have to be erected along the green line to restrict the flow of commerce in order to compensate for the economic advantage created in the West Bank. This, the court held, would be to the detriment of the West Bank population, basing its decision in part on the proposition that the West Bank has already benefited greatly from the economic relationship with Israel. The result is that any taxes levied in Israel can now be applied equally in the West Bank, all allegedly for the benefit of the inhabitants of that territory. Eyal Benvenisti points out that this decision creates a situation in which Israeli voters and legislators make policy for the West Bank, while the Palestinians have no say in deciding what is in their own best interest.[54] The odd result is that the 15 percent tax on Palestinians is held not only to be permissible, but to be in the interests of those who must pay it. Despite the absence of official statistics, it seems clear that taxes collected from West Bank Palestinians far exceed governmental expenditures for the benefit of that population.[55]

Many of the agricultural controls we studied also have analogues within Israel. With the aim of avoiding production surpluses and shortfalls, the government controls Israeli production with legislation similar to that used in the West Bank, such as quotas and restrictions on crop planting. Since the legal form of the controls over the two societies is often quite similar, the Dinstein test permits the same unsatisfactory results as in the VAT case. Israeli farmers' lobbies and interest groups play a role in setting production quotas and controlling competition in the entire region and so can protect their own interests, while in the West Bank the government has impeded or prohibited the development of similar local bases of authority, such as municipal governments and farmers' organizations. Consequently, only Israeli groups are effectively able to influence decisions regarding agricultural controls. As discussed above, the outcome is skewed in favor of these more influential players.

Even when Palestinian parties are able to bring claims before the High Court alleging that agricultural controls imposed by the military government have violated international law, there is little possibility of success. Esther Cohen points out that of ninety-one petitions filed by residents of the occupied territories with the High Court in 1979 and 1980, only five were successful.[56] Eli Nathan, a judge of the District Court of Jerusalem and former senior assistant state attorney and head of the Department of International Affairs in the State Attorney's Office, noted that

> in accordance with the test proposed by the Court, any legislation enacted ostensibly for the declared object of improving existing private law could be considered to be within the authority conferred upon military government under Article 43 [of the Hague Regulations, requiring respect for preexisting law]. One doubts whether such a test would be in conformity with the intentions of the Article. The general principle expressed in the Article is rather that existing law should remain in force unless changed circumstances, in particular changes in economic and social conditions, or the security requirements of the military authorities *necessarily* demand changes and to the extent only that it is so necessary.[57]

Those controls studied which have been justified as being for the benefit of the inhabitants of the West Bank do not appear to have been enacted in response to a necessity which rose to the level of that required by Article 43, yet under the relaxed standard of review established by the High Court such measures would most likely satisfy judicial review.

High Court Enforcement of Procedural Due Process

Due to self-imposed limits on the High Court's review, the primary role it has played in supervising military government action in the territories has been in enforcing procedural requirements, especially with respect to the proceedings of military tribunals.[58] The High Court has strictly required that government officials abide by procedural guidelines established in the laws governing the West Bank. The court has imported Israeli administrative law in enforcing these procedural guidelines. Unfortunately, the High Court's vigilance with respect to procedural matters has not translated into adequate enforcement of substantive international legal norms. The *Kawasme* cases provide an illuminating example.

Kawasme I was brought on behalf of three elected West Bank mayors who had been summarily deported to Lebanon by the military commander for alleged security reasons.[59] In 1980 the High Court invalidated two of the three deportations because a British emergency regulation required that the deportee have a right to raise objections before an advisory board, but the mayors had been deported before having an opportunity to make their cases in a hearing before the board. The court held this procedural omission sufficient to nullify the deportations of two of the mayors. The High Court did not reverse the deportation of the third mayor because he had allegedly given speeches calling for the extermination of the State of Israel.

After the decision in *Kawasme I*, the two mayors were admitted back into the West Bank and allowed to argue before the advisory board that they should not be deported. The board rejected the mayors' arguments and upheld the order for deportation. The mayors again petitioned the High Court for relief, arguing that Article 49 of the Fourth Geneva Convention plainly prohibited deportations of the inhabitants of occupied territories. The first paragraph of that Article states, "Individual or mass forcible transfers, as well as deportations of protected persons from occupied territory to the territory of the Occupying Power or to that of any other country, occupied or not, are prohibited, regardless of their motive."[60] In *Kawasme II* the Court refused to reverse the deportations, since the procedural requirements had now been satisfied. The High Court expressly refrained from testing the validity of the deportation orders against Article 49 on the grounds that the Geneva Conventions do not apply to the West Bank:

All of Article 49, as the Fourth Geneva Convention in general, does not form part of *customary* international

law, and therefore the deportation orders do not contra-
vene the domestic law of the State of Israel, or of the
Judea and Samaria Region. . . . The decision of the Israeli Government to apply *de facto* the humanitarian provisions of the Fourth Geneva Convention is a political
one, not pertaining to the legal plane with which this
Court is concerned.[61]

Clearly, the High Court's strict enforcement of procedural requirements does not necessarily result in adequate enforcement of international legal norms, nor does the government's *"de facto"* adherence to the Fourth Geneva Convention.

Even the High Court's role in enforcing procedural norms has
been limited by the military government. When procedures enforced by the High Court have become too cumbersome, the laws
have simply been amended to remove the impediment.[62] An example is the expropriation of land for public purposes. Jordanian
law required a lengthy procedure before such expropriations could
be executed, including publication of notice of the seizure. According to Eyal Benvenisti, in the *Tabib v. Minister of Defense*
case, "when it was discovered that notices had not been served
according to the law, the authorities changed the law retroactively
to legitimize the confiscation, and to prevent the court from declaring the confiscation illegal."[63] Other procedural requirements
of the Jordanian law have also been eliminated by the military government.[64]

In short, the High Court's review of the actions of the military
government has been insufficient to enforce international legal
norms adequately. Most of the agricultural controls have ostensibly
been justified either as necessary for security reasons or as being
for the benefit of the population of the West Bank. In either case,
the High Court's scope of review is quite narrow. While the court
can be relied upon to require the military commander to abide by
procedural guidelines established in the law of the territories, once
these requirements have been satisfied the court has not been willing to enforce the underlying substantive international law adequately.

Military Tribunals

Since 1967 the military government has created a number of quasi-judicial military tribunals called "objections committees," with jurisdiction over a wide variety of civil matters in the West Bank.[65] The objections committees now hear claims against government authorities regarding some of the most critical of the controls over agriculture, including: decisions to expropriate land for "public purposes"; decisions to declare land to be state property (allegedly unregistered and uncultivated land); decisions concerning the use of and the regulations regarding natural resources, including permits required for dams, wells, and irrigation projects; decisions concerning the registration and licensing of companies; and decisions regarding permits required for the planting of fruit trees, decorative flowers, and other crop varieties pursuant to Military Orders No. 818 and 1015.[66]

By placing these matters within the jurisdiction of the objections committees, the High Court is "effectively divested of supervisory power in this respect."[67] The *Elon Moreh* case, involving a proposed Jewish settlement in the West Bank, provides a clear example. The High Court held that the *Elon Moreh* land requisition and settlement were neither a security concern nor temporary in nature. However, rather than slowing the settlement drive, in the following year the military government began the process of large-scale declarations of West Bank land to be state property, as described above. The High Court was effectively circumvented because jurisdiction for such declarations of state property were within the realm of the military objections committees rather than that of the High Court.[68] This meant that West Bank residents who lost their land to settlements would now most likely have as their only recourse a complaint before a military objections committee rather than the High Court.

Review by an objections committee is inferior to review by the High Court. The decisions of these committees are merely recommendations which the military commander may accept or reject.[69] The committees are staffed entirely by military officers, who sit in panels of three, only one of whom need have legal training.[70] The natural bias of a military officer in favor of her or his own government is exacerbated by the fact that the military commander has the power to both appoint and dismiss committee members.[71] As a general rule, military tribunals do not have the authority to question the validity of military orders, but only to determine if the procedures established by the existing orders were followed.[72] While the High Court will enforce the principles of due process in the proceedings before the objections committees, it is highly unlikely that the court will even hear a petition challenging the decision of such a committee, since the military commander has the power to reject a committee's recommendation.[73] A recent mission sent to the West Bank by the International Commission of Jurists went so far as to say that "no further appeal [is] possible following the decision of the Objection Committee."[74] In *Al-Nazer v. Commander of Judea and Samaria*, while the High Court required the objections committee to follow its own procedures, the court approved the new technique of declarations of state property developed after the *Elon Moreh* decision, effectively divesting itself of supervisory jurisdiction.[75]

The ICJ mission also pointed out that the very existence of the objections committees is of questionable legality. Several of the subjects within the jurisdiction of these Committees were formerly heard by local West Bank courts, including disputes over unregistered land and disputes over tax assessments.[76] The ICJ mission commented that Article 43 of the Hague Regulations, which requires respect for the existing laws of the territory, also presumably requires respect for the "legal institutions of the country."[77] Article 49 of the Fourth Geneva Convention suggests the same conclusion, stating that "the tribunals of the occupied territory shall continue to function in respect of all offenses covered by the said laws," subject "to the necessity for ensuring the effective administration of justice."[78] These provisions would at the very least make it legally problematic for a military government to strip local courts of jurisdiction in order to place certain cases within the scope of military tribunals. As discussed earlier, in the *Ville d'Anvers v. Germany* case, the Belgo-German Mixed Arbitral Tribunal held just such a practice to violate Hague Article 43.

In the critical areas over which the military objections committees have jurisdiction, supervision of the military commander's actions is even less adequate than in those areas, described earlier, over which the High Court exercises complete jurisdiction. In neither area is international law adequately enforced in accordance with internationally accepted standards. The critical factor is that both are Israeli governmental bodies, neither of which can serve as a neutral arbiter over the actions of its own military in a situation of belligerent occupation when the indigenous population has been denied any effective voice in the matters at issue. Eyal Benvenisti states that a system wherein the occupant is in charge of striking the balance between the interests of the occupant and the needs of the indigenous population "is inherently biased in favour of the occupant."[79] This points out the need for a truly neutral body, such as a protecting power as required by the Fourth Geneva Convention, to resolve disputes as to the applicable international law.

CONCLUSION

The Obligation of
the International Community

The concept of human rights represents a consensus of the international community as to those minimum standards of respect and dignity with which individuals and communities should be treated. Useful and necessary criticism is often directed at regimes that fail to abide by human rights standards. Yet the concept of human rights becomes an effective tool for change only when standards can be enforced and victims protected.

In the context of the human rights—and their violation—covered in this particular study, it is important to note that international law places an obligation upon third party governments to ensure compliance with applicable norms. Common Article 1 of the Four Geneva Conventions states, "The High Contracting Parties undertake to respect and to *ensure respect* for the present Convention in all circumstances [authors' emphasis]."[1] Jean Pictet's authoritative commentary on the Geneva Conventions states with regard to Article 1:

> [I]n the event of a power failing to fulfil its obligations the other Contracting Parties (neutral, allied or enemy) may,

and should, endeavour to bring it back to an attitude of respect for the Convention. The proper working of the system of protection provided by the Convention demands in fact that the Contracting Parties should not be content merely to apply its provisions themselves, but should do everything in their power to ensure that the humanitarian principles underlying the Conventions are applied universally.[2]

In the absence of a protecting power to enforce international legal standards, certain political channels may provide effective means for foreign governments to protect the rights of Palestinians in the West Bank and to fulfill their obligation under international law. Foreign governments, especially those having extensive interaction with Israel, can exert, and have exerted, pressure upon the Israeli government with the goal of encouraging conformity with international law. As discussed earlier, the United States government has repeatedly urged Israel to abide by the Fourth Geneva Convention in its occupation of the West Bank, as have almost all of the governments of the world. Unfortunately, mere moral suasion has proven inadequate. A combination of economic and diplomatic pressure from third party governments may be more effective at encouraging compliance with international law.

For instance, third party governments could condition aid to Israel or preferential trade status for Israel upon its conformity with international law in the West Bank. The United States government has consistently opposed Jewish settlement in the West Bank and in the summer of 1990 threatened to withhold $400 million worth of housing aid if Soviet Jews were settled in the West Bank.[3] Although this plan was eventually scuttled in Congress, it could potentially have helped to stem the tide of West Bank settlement. Aid could similarly be withheld if it is to be used all or in part to finance tree uprootings, land expropriations, and other violations of international law.

Examples from another region of the world are the sanctions which the United States and several other governments have imposed against South Africa. These sanctions have been credited as a key factor in helping to force the South African government to repeal several of the main legal pillars of apartheid. In an act known as the Anti-Apartheid Program,[4] the United States Congress imposed a ban on certain economically important exports from South Africa, such as gold, coal, and uranium, and also upon certain strategically important imports to South Africa, such as nuclear technology and computers. At the same time, South Africa was isolated from the international community through various formal and informal bans on South African participation in international sporting events and a ban on foreign entertainers performing in the country. All of these forms of economic and social pressure were contingent upon the elimination or relaxation of apartheid laws.

A model which might be more feasible in the case of Israel would be the withholding of "most favored nation" trading status (MFN). MFN is a preferential trading status which allows a foreign nation to have access to the United States market with substantially reduced tariffs. MFN status has been withheld from numerous governments in order to pressure those regimes to respect the human rights of their populations. For example, MFN was withheld from the minority white government of Rhodesia, and preferential trade status was extended when power was handed over to the black majority in Zimbabwe (post-emancipation Rhodesia).[5]

While the United States government has been reluctant to employ economic measures to encourage Israeli observance of international law, European governments have been far more willing to move in this direction. Recent negotiations between representatives of the European Economic Community (EEC), the Israeli government, and Palestinian businesspeople provide a model for using diplomatic and economic leverage as a means of enforcing international law. Prior to the EEC negotiations, all agricultural exports from Israel *and* the occupied territories were required to go through either Agrexco or the Citrus Marketing Board, both Israeli-run monopolies. Unlike Israeli farmers, Palestinian growers have no voice in the operation of these monopolies. Further, products exported through these avenues bear Israeli labels and give no indication of their origin in the occupied territories. These issues were raised in a series of negotiations involving the ratification of a trade agreement between Israel and the EEC. Finalization of the agreement was linked to Israel's facilitation of a free-trade agreement between the EEC and the occupied territories. The

end result was a formal agreement with Israel detailing the procedures for direct export of agricultural produce from the occupied
territories to the EEC.

Negotiations began in October 1986, when the EEC Council
of Ministers directed its commission to work out a system with
Israel that would allow for the direct exports and give growers in
the West Bank and Gaza some degree of autonomy in marketing
their produce abroad. At the time of the negotiations, the European Parliament awaited three trade and financial protocols that
would expand Israel's preferential status by reducing customs taxes
and provide aid to Israeli small industry. The commission delayed
submitting those protocols to the Parliament, using the delay as
leverage to spur the Israelis to produce a timely and satisfactory
agreement regarding direct exports from the occupied territories.

Substantial negotiation and pressure ensued, including a trip
by members of Al-Haq, a Palestinian human rights organization,
to the European Parliament to brief them on Israel's failure to comply with the EEC's directives to facilitate direct agricultural exports. Negotiations culminated in May 1988, with an Israeli memorandum detailing the procedure for direct exports from the
occupied territories. The EEC Parliament approved the three new
trade and financial protocols with Israel in October 1988.

As of the time of our research, Palestinian farmers had attempted only four direct agricultural export shipments; and for a
variety of reasons (including delays in shipment and refrigeration
problems in the shipping vessels) none of them were particularly
successful. Some members of the Palestinian agricultural community suspect sabotage on the part of the Israelis; others say that
regardless of the source of the damage, the growers should have
taken routine precautions to protect themselves, such as insurance
contracts.

Palestinian agricultural experts disagree over whether additional attempts at direct exports would be profitable for the community as a whole in the near future. While direct exports provide
a badly needed outlet for agricultural surpluses in the occupied
territories, some experts say that Palestinian growers presently do
not have the sophistication, technology, and/or low production
costs required to compete on the European market. In addition,
some economists contend that without a government to oversee

and guide the process, direct exports could exacerbate the instability of the agricultural market in the occupied territories.

However, virtually all community agricultural leaders agree that the exports represent a tremendous political victory for Palestinian growers. To have crops sold in an international market as West Bank and Gaza produce instead of as Israeli produce is to take a significant stride in the direction of autonomy. Similarly, the EEC's actions leading to the implementation of direct exports from the occupied territories offer a new and promising avenue toward persuading the Israelis to allow Palestinians to realize their individual and economic rights.

Besides encouraging the Israeli government to comply with international law, the United States, Jordan, and the EEC, among others, have also assisted by aiming direct investment at areas that have suffered under the Israeli occupation. Such foreign investment in projects to develop the West Bank Palestinian agricultural economy helps to counteract the illegal Israeli actions which impede the development of that economy. This approach looks less to forcing the Israeli government to stop violating the law and more toward enabling Palestinians to safeguard their own rights in the face of existing Israeli contraints. In addition, when foreign governments assist Palestinians in their efforts to continue tending the land, it becomes more difficult for the Israeli government to continue the illegal policy of land confiscation and settlement in the territories.

There is no shortage of examples in which direct investment in the occupied territories has been used to alleviate the results of the occupation and violations of international law. Third party governments and international organizations have financed or attempted to finance, in whole or in part, projects such as the Hebron grape-juice factory, the Gaza citrus factory, and the irrigation project in Wadi Fara'a, as well as numerous smaller-scale agricultural projects, ranging from small canning and pickling enterprises to alternative-crop development programs.[6] All of these projects will help to increase the viability of West Bank agriculture and consequently will help the Palestinians to retain control of their land.

Foreign governments channel much of their direct investment funds through several nonprofit, private, voluntary organizations which provide credit, training, and technical assistance to farmers. These organizations often provide the most effective mechanism for development since they offer expertise, experience, and connections to the local population which governmental organizations often lack; these efforts have been especially important because of the attrition in the agricultural extension services of the Department of Agriculture of the Civil Administration.

International organizations active in promoting West Bank agriculture include Save the Children, Catholic Relief Services, the United Nations Development Program, and American Near East Refugee Aid, better known as ANERA. There is also the USAID-funded Cooperative Development Project, which is attempting to revive and enrich the agricultural marketing cooperatives by providing technical assistance and training for their personnel. In addition, there are local groups like the Arab Development Society, which runs an eight-thousand-dunam dairy farm and boarding school, and receives funding from the EEC, USAID, and the Ford Foundation. The United Agricultural Company provides assistance to small farmers and receives much of its funding from the EEC. Other organizations assist in the provision of agricultural credit; these include the Economic Development Group and the Arab Development and Credit Company, both of which receive some funding from the EEC.

Not surprisingly, foreign-sponsored development projects, like indigenous projects, often encounter substantial resistance from the Israeli government. All foreign-sponsored development projects must be approved by the Israeli authorities, and about 40 percent of the proposals submitted are rejected. Administrators at various organizations report that although Israeli officials may be hesitant to directly refuse projects proposed by international organizations, the government tends to thwart implementation in other ways, such as by conditioning approval on a series of elaborate demands or by prolonging the approval process indefinitely. It generally takes six to nine months to receive approval, even for routine projects.

Most frequently the rejected proposals are for projects that deal with agricultural mechanization, land development, marketing, and food processing, which could potentially create competition with Israeli enterprises.[7] Projects which do receive approval usually revolve around service and "quality of life" infrastructures—sewage, road, or domestic water installation, for example—services which the Israeli government would otherwise be responsible for providing. These projects also tend to be consumer-oriented, providing facilities or equipment (often purchased from Israeli sources) which, again, contribute little in the long run to the creation of an economy independent from that of Israel.

The international organizations involved are not without their critics, who point out that such organizations often engage in "safe" projects that are likely to win Israeli approval and do little to further real development in the occupied territories. Although these organizations provide farmers with badly-needed technical and financial assistance, the scope of the assistance is limited. Others point out that since local Palestinian organizations are so few and their operations so tenuous, international organizations often devise and implement projects independent of Palestinian input. This results in piecemeal development without a coherent, long-term strategy and often without sensitivity to the needs of the community. Further, some critics contend that the farmers who receive the most help tend to be those who are wealthy and politically well connected.

However, direct investment in the West Bank does not suffer from the shortcomings of the South Africa policy of the Reagan administration, known as "constructive engagement." Unlike in South Africa, where investment was channelled into white-owned South African businesses with the hope that the benefits would "trickle down" to black South Africans, in the West Bank investment is being made in Palestinian-owned and -operated enterprises and projects. During our stay in the West Bank, leaflets distributed by the pro-PLO underground leadership of the *intifada*, known as the "unified command," called for agricultural and agro-industrial development. At the same time, conservative Palestinians sometimes identified with Jordan, such as those involved with the marketing cooperatives and the Civil Administration itself, were advocating the same course of action. To the extent that development aid contributes to the development of the Palestinian agricultural economy, it meets with support from Palestinians across the political spectrum.

The international law of belligerent occupation points out the extent to which the occupation has fallen short of human rights standards. The impact of the occupation on agriculture and the Palestinian economy has been particularly harsh. In these areas, Israel has bureaucratized and entrenched a status quo of ongoing violations of Palestinian human rights. Recognition and enforcement of the broad range of these rights will serve as a bulwark against this process, defusing the status quo and countering the tenacity of the occupation.

APPENDIX A

Abstracts of Military Orders
Pertaining to Agriculture*

ORDER NO. 2: Order Regarding Quarantine. Effective 7 June 1967. (Cancelled by Order No. 47.)
Prevents transport of any plant or animal from the West Bank.

ORDER NO. 32: Order Regarding Tobacco Law. Effective 27 June 1967.
Imposes taxes on and regulates sale of tobacco.

ORDER NO. 47: Order Regarding the Transport of Agricultural Products. Effective 9 July 1967. (Order No. 47 cancels Order No. 2. It is amended by Orders No. 155, 305, 1010, and cancelled by Order No. 1252.)
Prohibits the transport into or out of the West Bank of any plants or animals or products (except for canned goods) without a permit.

ORDER NO. 92: Order Concerning Authority for the Requirements of Water Decrees. Effective 22 August 1967. (Amended by Order No. 158, 1 October 1967, not included.)
Gives an appointed official plenary power over water and water projects and serves as the basis for Israeli controls over West Bank water resources and allocation.

ORDER NO. 134: Order Prohibiting the Operation of Tractors and Agricultural Machinery From Israel. Effective 20 September 1967 (although dated 29 September 1967).
Prohibits bringing a tractor or other agricultural machine from Israel to the West Bank, and prohibits the operation of such, unless a permit to this effect has been obtained from administration authorities.

*Abstracted by the authors.

ORDER NO. 149:   Order Concerning the Labeling of Merchandise. Effective 5 November 1967.

Allows authorities to order that merchandise be labeled in a specified fashion; any merchandise that is not in compliance may be confiscated.

ORDER NO. 155:   Order Amending the Order Regarding the Transport of Agricultural Products. Effective 24 October 1967. (Amends Order No. 47. Cancelled by Order No. 1252.)

This modifies Order No. 47 to allow the authorities to designate the routes by which goods may be shipped (presumably into or out of the West Bank). It allows the search of transport vehicles and the seizure of products shipped without a permit or in a manner not in compliance with a given permit, i.e., different goods, route, or time of transport than stated on the permit. The authority may order the seized goods to be transported up to fifty kilometers from the point of seizure; if the owner does not comply, the goods can be transported by another means at the owner's expense.

ORDER NO. 305:   Order Concerning the Transport of Agricultural Products (Amendment No. 2). Effective 22 September 1968 (although signed in January of 1969. (Amends Order No. 47. Cancelled by Order No. 1252.)

Expands exemption from canned foods to processed foods in general. Also expands authority to seize any products or goods to include not just those in violation of this order, but any which the competent authority has reason to believe are in violation of any order or regulation.

UNNUMBERED ORDER: dated 1 December 1969. Order Concerning Security Instructions; Instructions Concerning Transport (The Dead Sea).

Prohibits movement by sea or non-sea transport in the Dead Sea area between five in the evening and five in the morning.

ORDER NO. 474:   Order Concerning the Amendment of the Law Maintaining Trees and Plants (Inspectors). Effective 1 August 1972.

Increases the authority of inspectors under Jordanian law No. 85 of 1966* to allow them to ask for identification or certificates, take people to police stations, etc.

ORDER NO. 1002:   The Nursery Law No. 20 for the Year 1958, An Order Concerning the Amendment of the Law of Nurseries (Judea and Samaria) (No. 1002). Effective March 1983. Amended by Order No. 1248.

This order is a very complex, detailed, and extensive regulation of nurseries, i.e., the use of some land is restricted for five years prior to use of such land for a nursery, a five-thousand-meter border free of citrus trees must exist around

---

*Jordanian Law No. 85 for the Year 1966, For the Preservation of Trees and Plants. Effective 21 December 1966. (Amended by Israeli Military Order No. 474. Effective 21 December 1966.

Allows for inspection of intentional damage to fields, and allows for collective punishment of all males in the area if the culpable party cannot be isolated; provides for court procedures, etc. Does not cover arson.

the land used for the nursery. Substantial administrative discretion may be exercised to relax or enforce these requirements, which include regulations covering the health and labelling of plants and exacting requirements for record keeping and methods of plant propagation.

ORDER NO. 1010: Order Concerning the Transport of Agricultural Products (Amendment No. 3). Effective 1 September 1982. (Amends Order No. 47. Cancelled by Order No. 1252.)

Allows the authority to sell seized goods if they are going to go bad; the proceeds are then treated as if they are the goods. Seized goods can also be destroyed. The authority may fine the party up to the amount of the maximum amount allowable by law. Upon payment, the owner can retrieve the goods or the proceeds from the sale of such goods, if all relevant taxes have been paid and if any other laws would not be violated.

ORDER NO. 1015: Order Regarding Monitoring the Planting of Fruitful Trees. Effective 27 August 1982. (Amended by Orders No. 1039 and 1147.)

Requires permission from the relevant authorities to have or to plant fruit trees, prepare seedlings, or to prepare a plant for grafting, other than for personal consumption (less than twenty trees). The permit may specify certain conditions. Residents are to send in reports about their holdings within ninety days of the order being signed. There are severe penalties for noncompliance, such as uprooting of unregistered trees (for which the owner has to pay the expenses), one year in prison, fines, etc. This order covers grapes and plums; later regulations add to the appendix of regulated plants.

ORDER NO. 1039: Order Concerning Planting Fruitful Trees (Amendment). Effective 31 January 1983. (Amends Order No. 1015.)

Expands Order No. 1015 to include vegetables in the Jericho region, which are listed as eggplants and tomatoes. Vegetables for personal consumption do not require permits.

ORDER NO. 1051: Order Concerning the Marketing of Agricultural Products. Effective 28 March 1983. (Order No. 1051 is amended by the "bases for Marketing of Agricultural Products (Taxes) (Amendment) and by Order No. 1147 and amendments, *infra*.)

Establishes a fund for agricultural products, ostensibly to aid agriculture and agricultural marketing and agro-industry. This is financed "by the Civil Administration" and by taxes raised in accordance with this order. The Civil Administration has wide discretion in establishing the taxes under this order. Noncompliance is punishable by imprisonment, as well as fines and confiscations of produce, the proceeds from which then go into the fund.

ORDER NO. 1051 (AMENDMENT): Order Concerning Marketing of Agricultural Products (Judea and Samaria) of 1983: Bases for the Marketing of Agricultural Products (Taxes) (Amendment). Effective 15 July 1983.

Apparently to finance the fund established by Order 1051, this amendment places a tax on peaches and grapes of 700 shekels/ton.

ORDER NO. 1147:   Order Concerning Inspection of Fruit Trees and Vegetables (Amendment No. 2). Effective 1 August 1985. (Amends Order No. 1015.)

Redefines vegetables in Orders 1015 and 1039 such that eggplants and to-matoes, in appendix 2, remain restricted in the Jericho region, and those items in appendix 3, onions and onion seeds are restricted throughout the West Bank. Permission is required for these items.

ORDER NO. 1248:   Order Amending the Law of Nurseries (Arboretum) (Amendment). Effective 11 August 1988. (Amends Order No. 1002.)

Allows the appointment of extra inspectors to implement Order No. 1002, who shall have the same powers as soldiers under Section 80 (A) of Order No. 378. (order no. 378, Sec. 80(A), effective date 12 April 1981, grants all soldiers the authority to seize any merchandise, equipment, papers or objects that have been used or are about to be used to help break any of the rules of this order, or if these items have been given in payment for helping to break any of these rules.)

ORDER NO. 1252:   Order Concerning Merchandise Transport. Effective 1 September 1988. (Terminates Order Nos. 47 and 49.)

Regulates the shipping of any merchandise into or out of the West Bank, including agricultural goods and all organic products (except for hard fruits); real property is exempted. Permission is required to take merchandise in or out of the region, and the authority may specify in the permit any conditions he desires, including date and route of transport. Penalties for noncompliance include fines and a possible five-year prison sentence.

APPENDIX B

Sample Texts of Military Orders Pertaining to Agriculture*

ISRAELI DEFENSE FORCES

ORDER NO. 2†

ORDER REGARDING QUARANTINE

I, *Aluf* Haim Herzog, acting on the authority invested in me as the commander of the Israeli Defense Forces in the West Bank region, order the following:

Imposition of Quarantine

1. This Order imposes a quarantine on the entire West Bank region.

Prohibition

2. It is prohibited to transport any plant or animal, of any kind, from the West Bank region to any location outside this region.

Punishments

3. Any person violating Article 2 of this Order will be punished by three years imprisonment.

Implementation of this Order

4. The implementation of this Order commences on 7 June 1967.

---

*Our translations were made from official Arabic versions of the original Hebrew texts. See Chapter 3, especially note 2.
†Order No. 2 was cancelled by Order No. 47, *infra*.

Title

5. This Order will bear the title "Order Regarding Quarantine (West Bank Region) (No. 2) for the Year 1967."

7 June 1967

Aluf Haim Herzog
Commander of the Israeli Defense Forces
West Bank Region

ISRAELI DEFENSE FORCES

ORDER NO. 32

ORDER REGARDING TOBACCO LAW

As I believe this Order is necessary for the purpose of maintaining public order, I hereby issue the following:

Definitions

1. In this Order:
   "Tobacco Law"—Tobacco Law (No. 32) of 1952 as implemented on 7 June 1967.
   "Law of Unified Fees"—Law Unifying Fees and Additional Taxes Collected on Imported, Exported, and Locally Produced Goods (No. 25) of 1966 as implemented on 7 June 1967.
   "Regulation of Unified Fees"—Unified Additional Fees Regulation (No. 80) of 1966, issued in accordance with the Law of Unified Fees, as implemented on 7 June 1967.

Unless otherwise indicated, these terms will bear the above definitions in the following articles of this Order.

Payment

2. A) This Order imposes additional unified fees on tobacco and tobacco products (except cigarettes) of 20% (twenty percent) of the fees collected in accordance with the Tobacco Law, in addition to the fees imposed by the Tobacco Law.

   B) This Order imposes additional unified fees on cigarettes in the following manner:

(1) 42 (forty-two) fils on each pack of cigarettes consisting of 20 (twenty) cigarettes and costing more than 60 (sixty) fils.

(2) 11 (eleven) fils on each pack of cigarettes consisting of 20 (twenty) cigarettes and costing less that 60 (sixty) fils.

Production and Marketing Licensing

3. It is prohibited to produce and market cigarettes which cost less than 60 (sixty) fils per pack, unless pursuant to a license issued by the responsible official and in accordance with the conditions of this license.

Retention of Validity

4. To prevent any confusion, it is hereby ordered that, with the exception of the matters dealt with in this Order, the Tobacco Law, the Law of Unified Fees, and the Regulation of Unified Fees will remain entirely valid, in accordance with the regulations issued in Order No. 2 by the Israeli Defense Forces Commander of the West Bank region.

Implementation

5. The implementation of this Order commences on 27 June 1967.

Title

6. This Order will bear the title "Order Regarding Tobacco Law (West Bank Region) (No. 32) of 1967."

27 June 1967

Aluf 'Uzi Narkiss
Officer in Charge of the Central Command
Commander of the Israeli Defense Forces
West Bank Region

ISRAELI DEFENSE FORCES

ORDER NO. 47*

ORDER REGARDING THE TRANSPORT
OF AGRICULTURAL PRODUCTS

In accordance with the authority vested in me, and in my capacity as the commander of the Israeli Defense Forces in the West Bank region, I hereby order as follows:

Definitions

1. In this Order:
   "The person"—Includes all bodies [hay'a ma'nawiyya] and any association of persons not organized into a body.
   "The region"—The West Bank region.
   "Competent authority"—The person appointed by me as the competent authority for the purposes of this order.
   "Agricultural product"—Includes plants, any animal (dead or alive), vegetables, fruits, or any agricultural product whose source is a plant or animal, but not canned goods.

Prohibition

2. It is forbidden to remove or bring any agricultural product from or into the region without a permit from the competent authority.

Punishments

3. Any person who violates Article 2 of this Order or any specification regarding the requisite permit will be punished by a period of three years imprisonment, a fine of 3,000 dinars, or both.

Cancellation of Order No. 2

4. The Order Regarding Quarantine (West Bank Region) (No. 2) of 1967 is hereby cancelled.

Implementation of this Order

5. The implementation of this Order commences as of 9 July 1967.

---

*Order No. 47 cancels Order No. 2. It is amended by Orders No. 155, 305, 1010, and cancelled by Order No. 1252, *infra*.

Title

6. This Order will bear the title "Order Regarding the Transport of Agricultural Products (West Bank Region) (No. 47) of 1967."

9 July 1967

Aluf 'Uzi Narkiss
Officer in Charge of the Central Command
Commander of the Israeli Defense Forces
West Bank Region

ISRAELI DEFENSE FORCES

ORDER NO. 92

ORDER CONCERNING AUTHORITY FOR THE REQUIREMENTS OF WATER DECREES

In accordance with the authority vested in me in my capacity as commander of the Israeli Defense Forces in the West Bank region, I hereby issue the following Order:

Definitions

1. In this Order:
   "The day fixed"—(suspended as of this date)- May 5727 (7 June 1967).
   "Water decrees"—All the decrees including laws, rules, orders, pamphlets, and instructions which were effective until the day of halting and which are related to water, transferring it, digging it, exporting it, consuming it, selling it, distributing it, supervising its use, appointing shares of it, establishing water projects, measuring it, stopping its pollution, preparing booklets and studies of all that is related to it, fixing areas for the work of different institutions and organizations for water, issuing licenses which are demanded within the frame of the decrees mentioned earlier, fixing and collecting fees, taxes, and profits related to the decrees mentioned above and any other order which was not mentioned directly or was not dealt with in any way in water subjects.
   "The area"—The West Bank Region.
   "The official"—Whoever I appoint from time to time to carry out the steps of this Order.
   "The Jordanian Government"—The Hashemite Kingdom of Jordan.

The Authority of the Competent Authority

2. From the day this Order is issued the competent authority has all the privileges related to water decrees.

Privilege

3. In accordance with his authority after his appointment the official can appoint other people to help him indefinitely or for a fixed period of time and either with or without conditions, depending on what he deems best.

Appointing

4. The official can appoint anybody to carry out any of the jobs related to the water decrees or whatever arises from them.

Establishing and Operating Water Organizations

5. The official has the authority to order the continuation of the work of any organization or governmental entity or institution working in the field of water decrees. He also can stop the work of any of these organizations and form new ones and appoint a director, including himself.

Cancelling Privileges

6. In accordance with this he can cancel any of the privileges mentioned above and which were effective unless it is renewed by the competent authority according to the privileges granted by this Order.

Effectiveness

7. The implementation of this Order applies also to any change or development which affects the water decrees.

Continuation

8. If any of the operations mentioned above were executed during the period between the halting and the beginning of the effectiveness of the Order, it is considered as if it was carried out in accordance with this rule.

Implementation

9. The implementation of this Order commences as of 16 August 5727 (22 August 1967).

Title

10. This Order will bear the title "Order Concerning Authorities for the Requirements of Water Decrees (West Bank Region) (No. 92) for the Year 5727—1967."

9 August 5727 (15 August 1967)

Aluf 'Uzi Narkiss
Officer in Charge of the Central Command
Commander of the Israeli Forces
West Bank Region

ISRAELI DEFENSE FORCES

ORDER NO. 134

ORDER PROHIBITING
THE OPERATION OF TRACTORS AND
AGRICULTURAL MACHINERY FROM ISRAEL

In accordance with the authority vested in me in my capacity as the commander
of the Israeli Defense Forces in the West Bank region, I hereby order the following:

Definitions

1. In this Order:
   "The region"—The West Bank Region.
   "The person"—Includes a body [*hay'a ma'nawiyya*] or an association of persons not incorporated into a body.
   "The official"—The person appointed by me to be the official for the purposes
   of this order, and also any person authorized in writing by the official for the
   purposes of this order (the subsidiary official).
   "Tractor or agricultural machine from Israel"—A tractor or agricultural machine registered in Israel in accordance with any law, or a tractor or agricultural machine which is or was present in Israel on the eve of the implementation of this order, or a tractor or agricultural machine imported into Israel
   thereafter.

Operating Prohibition

2. It is prohibited for any person to bring a tractor or other agricultural machine
from Israel to the region, and it is prohibited for any person to operate a tractor
or any other agricultural machine brought from Israel, either directly or indirectly, unless a permit to this effect has been obtained from the official.

Punishment

3. Any person who commits one of the following:
   (1) A violation of any article of this Order,
   (2) An action in violation of the permit conditions issued by the official,
will be punished by imprisonment for a period of three months, a fine of 1,000
IL (Israeli lira), or both.

Implementation of this Order

4. The implementation of this Order commences as of 20 September 1967.

Title

5. This Order will bear the title "Order Prohibiting the Operation of Tractors and
Agricultural Machinery from Israel (West Bank Region) (No. 134) of 1967."

29 September 1967

Aluf Mishna Shlomo Lahat
Authorized Officer in Charge of the Central Command
Commander of the Israeli Defense Forces
West Bank Region

ISRAELI DEFENSE FORCES

ORDER NO. 149

ORDER CONCERNING THE
LABELING OF MERCHANDISE

Acting in accordance with the authority vested in me as commander in chief of
the Israeli Defense Forces in the region, I hereby issue the following Order:

Definitions

1. In this Order:
   "The inspector"—Whoever is appointed as an inspector to guarantee the ex-
   ecution of the requirements of this law concerning the laws of taxes (The West
   Bank Region) (No. 31) for the year 5727—1967.

Labeling the Merchandise

2. The official can order the labeling of merchandise by the owner and the latter must comply at the time and in the way the official orders.

Keeping the Orders

3. The orders in this Order are to be read in addition to the orders in any security law and do not in any way decrease their force.

Confiscation

4. The official or the taxation employees have the authority to enter any places which they have reason to think contain merchandise covered by this Order and confiscate any merchandise which does not meet the requirements of this Order.
5. The implementation of this Order will commence as of 5 November 1967.
6. This Order will bear the title "Order Concerning the Labeling of Merchandise (The West Bank Region) (No. 149) for the Year 5728—1967."

22 October 1967

Aluf 'Uzi Narkiss
Officer in Charge of the Central Command
Commander of the Israeli Defense Forces
West Bank Region

ISRAELI DEFENSE FORCES

ORDER NO. 155

ORDER AMENDING THE ORDER
REGARDING THE TRANSPORT
OF AGRICULTURAL PRODUCTS

In accordance with the authority vested in me in my capacity as commander of the Israeli Defense Forces in the West Bank region, I hereby issue the following Order:

Addition to Article 2, Sections A and B

1. In the Order Regarding the Transport of Agricultural Products (West Bank Region) (No. 47) of 1967, add after Art. 2:

Permit Conditions

2) (A) (a) The competent authority may specify in a permit the route by which agricultural products are transported and their destination.

(b) Any person who transports products in a manner not in accordance with the specifications contained in the permit will be considered to have transported the products without a permit.

Authority to Confiscate

2) (B) (a) The competent authority will, in writing, appoint inspectors.

(b) The inspector appointed in accordance with this article is authorized to take any of the following actions so long as he has reasonable grounds for thinking that it is necessary for the execution of this Order:

(1) To stop and search any transport vehicle.

(2) To seize agricultural products, containers, and certificates which may reasonably be believed to be in violation of this Order.

(3) To order every person who transports or possesses agricultural products to submit all certificates related to the agricultural products, and to provide the inspector with any relevant details.

(4) To order every person who transports agricultural products seized in violation of this Order to transport the products to a destination ordered by the inspector, provided that the destination is not more than fifty kilometers away from the site of the seizure.

(5) If the person engaged in transport refuses to transport the agricultural products as provided for in paragraph (4) above, the inspector may contract any person to transport the agricultural products in the vehicle in which they were seized. The contracted person will be considered the executor of the transport and the cost will be borne by the violator.

(c) Products seized in accordance with this Order will be disposed of in the manner ordered by the competent authority.

(d) The competent authority and the inspector may exercise the authority vested in them in accordance with this article whether a person has been legally accused in relation to said agricultural products or not.

(e) This article does not detract from the authority which vests in accordance with any law or security regulation.

Implementation of this Order

2. The implementation of this Order commences on the date it is signed.

Title

3. This Order will bear the title "Order Amending the Order Regarding the Transport of Agricultural Products (West Bank Region) (No. 155) of 1967."

24 October 1967

Aluf 'Uzi Narkiss
Officer in Charge of the Central Command
Commander of Israeli Defense Forces
West Bank Region

ISRAELI DEFENSE FORCES

ORDER NO. 305

ORDER REGARDING THE
TRANSPORT OF AGRICULTURAL PRODUCTS
(AMENDMENT NO. 2)

In accordance with the authority vested in me in my capacity as commander of
the region, I issue the following Order:

Amendment to Article 1

1. In the Order Regarding the Transport of Agricultural Products (West Bank
   Region) (No. 47) of 1967 (hereinafter the Original Order), in Article 1, instead
   of "Agricultural Product", the following will be substituted:
   "Agricultural Product"—Plant or any section thereof, including fruits, except
   dried fruits, and any animal, whether alive or dead, and anything whose source
   is a plant or animal and which does not undergo preparation.
   "Preparation"—Includes drying, pressing, freezing, pasteurization, steriliza-
   tion, melting, smoking, boiling, salting, or canning in any manner whatsoever.

Amendment of Article 2B

2. In Section 2B of the Original Order:
   1) In the beginning of paragraph (b) delete "for the purpose of implementing
   this Order" and substitute the following for Article 2:
      (2) Seizure of
        (a) Agricultural products, containers, and their certificates, if there is a
        basis for believing that they are in violation of any law or any security
        regulation.
        (b) Goods, if there is a basis for believing that they are in violation of
        the Order Concerning Closed Areas (Prohibition on Transport of Goods)

(West Bank) (No. 49) of 1967 or the Order Concerning Tariff Zone (West Bank) (No. 96) of 1967.

2) In paragraph (c), instead of "anything seized," it should state "the seized agricultural product."

Implementation and Continuation

3. (A) The implementation of this Order will commence as of 22 September 1968.

(B) Any permit issued in relation to agricultural products by the official in charge of implementing the Order Concerning Closed Areas (Prohibition on Transport of Goods) (West Bank) (No. 49) of 1967 and issued before the beginning of the implementation of this Order will be considered as if it has been issued in accordance with the Original Order.

Title

4. This Order will bear the title "Order Regarding the Transport of Agricultural Products (West Bank) (Amendment No. 2) (Order No. 305) of 1969."

16 January 1969

Tat-Aluf Raphael Fardi
Commander of the West Bank Region

ISRAELI DEFENSE FORCES

ORDER CONCERNING SECURITY INSTRUCTIONS

INSTRUCTIONS CONCERNING TRANSPORT (THE DEAD SEA)

In accordance with the authority vested in me as the commander of the region and in accordance with Article 68 (1) from the Order concerning transport instructions, I hereby issue the following instructions:

Definitions

1. In these instructions:
    "The Dead Sea"—The area marked in black on the map.
    "The map"—The map with the measurements 100,000:1 carrying the name (Dead Sea) and which is kept with this Order with the officer in the instructions section at the area leadership.

Banning Transportation

2. It is prohibited to move, using either sea transport or using non-sea transport, in the Dead Sea area between 17:00 hrs. and 05:00 hrs. the next morning.

Distribution

3. Edited copies of these instructions and the map will be kept at the police station offices in the strip laying within the borders of the Dead Sea for whomever wishes to have a look at them.

Implementation

4. The implementation of this Order commences as of 1 December 1969.

Title

5. This Order will bear the title "Instructions Concerning the Transport and Transportation [*sic*] (The Dead Sea) (The West Bank), for the Year 5730—1969."

1 December 1969

Tat-Aluf Raphael Fardi
Commander of the West Bank Region

ISRAELI DEFENSE FORCES

ORDER NO. 474*

ORDER CONCERNING THE AMENDMENT OF THE LAW MAINTAINING TREES AND PLANTS (INSPECTORS)

In accordance with the authority vested in me in my capacity as the commander of the region and because I believe this Order is necessary for the residents' welfare, I hereby issue the following Order:

Addition of Articles 3A and 3B

1. In the law Maintaining Trees and Plants No. 85 of 1966, insert the following after Article 3:

*Order No. 474 amends Jordanian Law No. 85 for the Year 1966. The text of Jordanian Law No. 85 is reproduced at the end of this appendix, see *infra*.

Appointment of Inspectors

3A. The military commander has the right to appoint inspectors.

Authority of Inspectors

3B. (a) The inspector will oversee the implementation of this law and any instruction issued in accordance with it, and is permitted to himself order its implementation.

(b) In addition to paragraph (a) above, the inspector will be authorized to:

(1) Demand that any person who the inspector believes has committed a violation of this law submit his identification papers or any other certificate he has on his person which is deemed satisfactory.

(2) Evict from any planted land any person obstructing his work or violating this law.

(3) Take any person to the police station who the inspector thinks has violated this law and refused to identify himself in accordance with paragraph (b)(1) above.

Implementation of this Order

2. The implementation of this Order will commence as of 1 August 1972.

Title

3. This Order will bear the title "Order Concerning the Amendment of the Law Maintaining Trees and Plants (Inspectors) (West Bank) (No. 474) of 1972."

26 July 1972

Tat-Aluf Raphael Fardi
Commander of the West Bank Region

ISRAELI DEFENSE FORCES

THE NURSERY LAW NO. 20 FOR THE YEAR 1958

AN ORDER CONCERNING
THE AMENDMENT OF THE LAW OF NURSERIES
(JUDEA AND SAMARIA) (NO. 1002)*

In accordance with the authority vested in me as competent authority concerning the Nursery Law No. 20 for the Year 1958 and depending on Articles 7, 16, and 18 of the law and Article 3 from the Order Concerning the Modification of the Nurseries (Judea and Samaria) (No. 1002) 5742—1982/1, I issue this operating system:

Definitions

1. In this rule:
   "The agriculture office"—The office of the officer in charge of agricultural affairs in the civil administration.
   "The nursery committee"—A committee appointed by me to improve the quality of productivity for and the marketing of good nursery plants.
   "Section to supervise the seeds and nursery plants"—The section of the agriculture office that has supervision over seeds and plants.
   "Nursery plant"—A joint [cutting] of a productive tree taken from vines or roses and which has been prepared for planting.
   "Nursery"—The place where these plants are planted and developed.
   "Salesman"—A person who receives a permit to sell nursery plants according to this rule.
   "The nursery administrator"—A person who is appointed by me to supervise the nurseries and to issue licenses and permits with my agreement.
   "Licensed nursery"—A nursery which is operated under the regulations of this law.
   "Nursery person"—The person who runs and takes care of a licensed nursery.
2. **Good Nursery Plants**—The nursery plants to which the articles of this rule have been applied are considered good nursery plants.
3. **The production and sale of different nursery plants**—No one is allowed to grow for sale or to sell nursery plants unless these plants meet the quality requirements mentioned in the appendices to this law.
4. **Ways of growing nursery plants**—The nursery committees suggest to the agricultural office a list of orders including those necessary to improve the production of nursery plants.
5. **The nursery license**—A) It is prohibited for anybody to run a nursery or to sell nursery plants unless he has a license in effect, and has followed the specifi-

*Amended by Order No. 1248, *infra*.

cations in the license. B) The license is not valid for more than one year and it expires on 15 June of every year.

6. **A permit to grow nursery plants**—Whoever receives a license to start a nursery is not allowed to grow anything other than whatever has been defined for him, unless he gets a permit from the nursery administrator.

7. **Application for a license**—The administrator of the nurseries has the right to create an application form for a nursery license including several demands and details. When a form is created only whatever is included in the form can be provided.

8. **The time during which an application may be submitted**—The application may be submitted to the competent authority between the 1st and the 15th of June every year.

9. **The provision of the license**—A) The competent authority has the right to issue a license, refuse it, suspend it, or cancel it. B) If the competent authority rejects an application he has to inform the applicant of this rejection in writing.

10. **The fee for a license and its renewal**—A) The fee for a licensed nursery is five Jordanian dinars. B) As for the renewal of a license it is two Jordanian dinars.

11. **The inspection of the nursery**—According to Article 9, the competent authority will issue the license only after an inspection of the place designed for the nursery. Moreover, he will check if the equipment suits the needs of the place and the demands of this law.

12. **The specifications of the nursery plants for sale**—It is forbidden to sell nursery plants whose physical appearance does not resemble their type specifications, or if the condition of their development is not satisfactory, or if they are damaged or diseased.

13. **The requirements for a nursery:**

1) The place designed to grow nursery plants and the surroundings should be vacant of any harmful bushes.

2) There should be a road that allows easy access to every piece of land on which the nursery plants are grown.

3) The piece of land upon which the nursery plants are to be grown should be prepared, in accordance with the opinion of the competent authority, in a way that is fit to grow nursery plants and which allows for their unobstructed development.

14. **The possession of a map**—A) Every nursery owner must own a map showing the whole area of the nursery not smaller than 1/500 and which very clearly points out the pieces of land and briefly describes the type of nursery plant growing on it. B) Every nursery owner must have the map available in the nursery to show the competent authority whenever he is asked to do so.

15. **Storage of nursery plants**—The nursery plants prepared for sale should be kept in a place with a lot of light and away from any disease-causing insects.

16. **Transferring nursery plants**—The nursery plants prepared for sale should be transferred from one place to another in a way that keeps their quality and does not cause any damage to them.

17. **The danger of selling nursery plants that do not meet the required specifi-**

cations—It is forbidden to sell nursery plants unless they meet the specifications
required by this law.

18. **Licensing the sale of nursery plants with lower quality**—A) Notwithstanding
Article 17, the nursery committee, under the conditions that the committee determines, can sell nursery plants that do not meet any of the requirements mentioned in this law. B) The committee is not allowed to use its authority concerning
defective nursery plants, granted under paragraph (A), except to aid in the development of these plants.

19. **Licensing the place of sale**—A) It is prohibited to sell nursery plants except
in a place found suitable to store the nursery plants, and a license must first be
issued by the administrator of the nursery. (Here is a sales license.) B) The competent authority has the right to issue a sales license or refuse it, suspend, or even
cancel it. C) The license to sell is effective for one year only, and it expires on 30
June every year.

20. **The fee for a license to sell**—The fee for such a license is three Jordanian
dinars per year.

21. **Labeling the nursery plants**—The nursery plants may not be sold or bought
unless they are labeled according to the instructions in paragraph (B). (Here is
the label.)

    B) 1) The name of the variety.

        2) The name of the plant.

        3) The name of the nursery or the special label it is given by the compe-
tent authority to show where the plant was produced.

        4) If the plant was prepared through an intermediary, the name and the
label of the intermediary should be mentioned.

        5) The age of the plant.

        6) The date when the plant was labeled.

22. **The marking of the label**—The marking is to be printed very clearly on the
back of a special label so as to be easily readable. (Here is the label.)

23. **Sticking the label**—The label is to be fixed on each plant in a different way
and in a way that it can not be easily removed.

24. **Labeling stickers**—It is not allowed to add any sticker or label related to the
plants on the bundles without the authorization of the competent authority.

25. **Changing a label or any other details**—Nobody except the consumer may
change, destroy, damage, remove, or scratch any typing on the label; or any other
details on the nursery plant, barrel, or bundle.

26. **The exemptions from the labeling requirement**—

    A) The administrators of the nurseries can offer an exemption from the reg-
ulations under Article 23 for the nursery plants if the following conditions are
met:

        1) The nursery plants should be in a securely sealed bundle.

        2) The competent authority must be convinced that the nursery plants
will be sold from the producer to the consumer.

        3) With each bundle there must be a label showing the number of nursery
plants in that bundle.

4) As mentioned in paragraph (3), one label must be inserted into the bundle.

B) The exemption mentioned in Section (A) and which is given by the competent authority is confined to specific nursery plants and for a fixed period of time.

27. **Objection to the decision of the competent authority**—A) To fulfill the demands of this law the agricultural office will appoint a committee of three people to take care of the objections. B) Anybody may object in front of the committee to a decision taken by the competent authority within seven days from the day he receives the decision of the latter. C) The objections committee will issue its decision within ten days from the day it receives the objection.

28. **Documentation**—A) The nursery owner must keep documentation on the dates of planting and anything concerning the plants themselves, and he must show it to the competent authority whenever he is asked to. B) The documentation will be prepared according to the form designed by the competent authority. C) The nursery owner must keep the documents for at least three years after selling the plants concerned.

29. **Information**—The competent authority must inform the nursery owner about things related to his work in writing. For example, the results of any test carried out by the competent authority must be reported to the nursery owner.

30. **Obligatory selling of nursery plants**—Every single plant in the nursery should be sold.

31. **Application**—This law will be in effect from the day it is signed.

32. **Name**—This law will bear the title "Law Concerning the Planting of Nursery Plants and Selling Them [*sic*] (Judea and Samaria) 5743—1983."

[Appendixes concerning further extensive regulation of the raising and selling of various nursery plants, especially vines and olive and citrus trees, have been omitted here due to their length (in translation, thirty manuscript pages).]

March 5743 (March 1983)

Yoreh Artzi
Officer for Agricultural Affairs in the Civil Administration
of Judea and Samaria
Competent Authority

ISRAELI DEFENSE FORCES

ORDER NO. 1010

ORDER CONCERNING THE
TRANSPORT OF AGRICULTURAL PRODUCTS
(AMENDMENT NO. 3)

In accordance with the authority vested in me, and in my capacity as the commander of the Israeli Defense Forces in the West Bank region, I order the following:

Addition of Articles 2D and 2E

1. In the Order Regarding the Transport of Agricultural Products (Judea and Samaria) (No. 47) 5727—1967, after Article 2 comes the following:

Destroying the Product and Merchandise:
2. D) The merchandise or the product may be destroyed in accordance with any relevant legislation or security legislation.

Selling the Agricultural Product and Merchandise:
E) a) The supervisor can sell at the market rate any agricultural products or merchandise seized according to Article 2B which is ready to go bad for any reason.
b) If the product is sold as mentioned above the money it brings can be considered as the product itself.

Addition of Articles 3A–3C

2. After Article 3 of the original Order comes:

Cash Atonement:
3. A) If the suspect commits a violation the authority in charge can order a cash atonement, with the agreement of the owner and his attorney. This atonement may not be more than the maximum fine permitted to be taken because of the same violation. If this measure is taken against a person, he will be released if he has been imprisoned.

Returning the Agricultural Product and the Merchandise:
3. B) If the suspect is fined the official in charge can, according to his judgment, return the merchandise or the money that come from its sale on the condition that obtaining the merchandise does not cause any rule violation.

Taxes:
3. C) Notwithstanding Article (3B) the authority shall not return the merchandise except after all the different taxes falling due are paid.

Implementation of this Order

3. The implementation of this Order commences as of 13 September 5742 (1 September 1982).

Title

This Order will bear the title "Order Concerning the Transport of Agricultural Products (Amendment No. 3) (Judea and Samaria) (No. 1010) 5742—1982."

5 August 5742 (24 July 1982)

Aluf Uri Or
Commander of the Israeli Defense Forces

ISRAELI DEFENSE FORCES

ORDER NO. 1015*

ORDER REGARDING MONITORING
THE PLANTING OF FRUITFUL TREES

Based upon my authority as the commander of the forces of the Israeli Dense Army in the Area, and whereas I believe the matter to be important for the well being of the population and in order to preserve the water resources and the agricultural production of the area for the public good, I hereby order as follows:

Definitions

1. In this Order:
    "Field"—every area of land planted with fruitful trees, with the exception of trees which have been planted for personal consumption or for experimentation purposes, and which do not exceed twenty in number.
    "Fruitful trees"—trees listed in the appendix of this order.

*Amended by Orders No. 1039 and 1147.

"The relevant authority"—whoever is appointed as the relevant authority for the purposes of this Order by the head of the Civil Administration.

"Objections committee"—as is defined by the Order Regarding Objections Committees (the West Bank) (Number 172) for the Year 1967.

Prohibition on Planting

2. No person shall plant, prepare a seedling for, or plant a fruitful tree except after obtaining a written permission from the relevant authority, and only according to the conditions provided by that authority.

Changing Plants

3. No person shall change the type of trees planted in the lands, nor shall he graft them except pursuant to a written permit from the relevant authority and according to the conditions provided by that authority.

Submitting a Report

4. Every person who owns, possesses, or controls a field must give the relevant authority notification of that in the manner that the relevant authority provides, and that within 90 days from the date of signing of this Order.

Authorities

5. a) The relevant authority may appoint inspectors for the purpose of this Order;
   b) The inspectors may enter upon any land planted with trees in order to insure compliance with this Order.

Objections

6. Any person who considers that he has been injured by virtue of any act or decision issued by the relevant authority may object to this before the objections committee within 15 days of the date of notification of that decision or of the action which he considered to have injured him.

Preservation of Laws

7. Nothing stated in a declaration given according to this Order exonerates from the need to obtain a permit or license required by any other legislation or security legislation.

Fees

8. The relevant authority may determine fees to be levied in return for issuing a permit according to the provisions of this Order and these fees shall be according to regulations issued by the relevant authority.

Altering the Appendix

9. The head of the Civil Administration may alter the appendix of this Order and that by means of regulations he issues.

Penalties

10. a) Any person who commits a crime according the provisions of this Order shall be punished by one year or a fine of 15,000 shekels or both penalties, and if his contravention of the provisions of this Order continues, he shall pay an additional fine of 500 shekels for every day that he continues to commit the crime.

   b) If a person was convicted of a crime under the provisions of this Order, the court may, based on the request of the general prosecutor, order the uprooting of the trees planted without a permit by the person so convicted, and may order the levying upon such a person of all the costs of executing the order to uproot.

   c) If a person is convicted but did not carry out the order of the court to uproot trees which had been planted without a permit, the relevant authority may uproot the trees which had been planted without a permit and impose upon the accused person all the expenses of the uprooting (hereinafter "uprooting expenses").

   d) If a person who was ordered by a court to uproot trees refused to carry the uprooting expense, such uprooting expenses shall be considered as levies not paid in time and will be subject to the provisions of the law regarding collecting unpaid levies of 1952.

Delegation of the Authorities of the Head of the Civil Administration

11. In the Order Regarding the Setting Up of the Civil Administration (West Bank) (Order No. 947) of 1981, at the end of the second appendix shall appear: "Order Regarding Monitoring the Planting of Fruitful Trees (West Bank) (Order No. 1015) of 1982."

Commencement

This Order shall be effective as of the date when it is signed.

The Title

This Order shall be called "Order Regarding Monitoring the Planting of Fruitful Trees (West Bank) (Order No. 1015) of the Year 1982."

Appendix

1) Plums.
2) Grapes.

27 August 1982

Uri Or-*Aluf*
Commander of the Forces of the
Israeli Defense Army
West Bank Area

ISRAELI MILITARY FORCES

ORDER NO. 1039

ORDER CONCERNING PLANTING FRUITFUL TREES (AMENDMENT)

In accordance with the authority vested in me, and in my capacity as commander of the Israeli Military Forces in the region and because I believe that this order is necessary for the welfare of the residents, and with the intention of preserving the water sources and the agricultural product in the region for the general benefit, I hereby order the following:

Change of name

1. In the Order Concerning the Planting of Fruitful Trees (Judea and Samaria) (Order No. 1015) for the Year 5742—1982. Wherever the name of the Order appears the phrase "Planting fruitful trees" is replaced by "Fruitful trees and vegetables."

Amendment of Article 1

2. In Article 1 of the Order:
   A) In the definition of "Fruitful trees" the words "The first" should be added after "Appendix."
   B) After the definition "Fruitful trees" comes:
      1) "The vegetables"—agricultural development of the plants shown in appendix 2.
      2) "Jericho region"—The region which carries this name and which is described on the map signed by the commander of the Israeli forces in the region and which is attached to the Order (Judea and Samaria) (No. 675) for the year 5736—1976/3".

Addition to Articles 2A and 2B

3. **Supervising the development of vegetables**—2) A) It is prohibited to develop any vegetables in the Jericho district except after obtaining a written license from the relevant authority according to the conditions the latter demands.

Growing for consumption—2) B) The orders of Article 2 do not apply to people who grow vegetables not for marketing but for personal consumption for himself and the members of his family.

Amendment of Article 5

4. In Article 5 of the Order the words "Land planted with trees" in paragraph (B) should be changed to "Place."

Amendment of Article 9

5. In the title of Article 9 and also in the contents, the word "Appendix" is replaced by the word "Appendices."

Amendment of Article 10

6. In Article 10 of the Order—
1) In paragraph (B) the phrase "The trees which were planted" is replaced by "The fruitful trees which were planted and the vegetables which were grown."
2) Paragraph (C) is omitted and replaced by "If someone is convicted in court of planting and developing fruitful trees or vegetables without a license and does not follow the court's order to uproot these fruitful trees or vegetables, the authorities can uproot them and the convicted person must pay the expenses. (Here are the fees for uprooting.)"
3) In paragraph (D) the word "Trees" is replaced with the phrase "Fruitful trees or vegetables."

Amendment of the Appendix

7. The appendix should be called "First Appendix" and after it comes:

"The second appendix

1) Tomatoes
2) Eggplants"

Implementation of the order

8. The implementation of this Order commences as of 31 January 1983.

Uri Or-*Aluf*
Commander of the Israeli Defense Forces
Area of the West Bank

ISRAELI DEFENSE FORCES

ORDER NO. 1051*

ORDER CONCERNING THE
MARKETING OF AGRICULTURAL PRODUCTS

In accordance with the authority vested in me as commander of the Israeli military forces in the region and because I think that this Order is necessary for the benefit and comfort of the residents I hereby order the following:

Definitions

"Agricultural products"—Fruits and vegetables, according to what is mentioned in the attachment of the order concerning the supervision of fruit trees and vegetables (Judea and Samaria) (No. 1015) for the year 5742—1982/1.

"Objections committee"—The objections committee established in the order concerning the objections committees (Judea and Samaria) (No. 172) for the year 5728—1967/2.

"The person who carries out the marketing"—A person or a cooperative organization which works on marketing the agricultural products and which is given a permit to take the agricultural products out of the region.

"Authority in charge"—Whoever is appointed by the head of the Civil Administration; an authority in charge of the objectives of this Order.

"Marketing"—Wholesale of agricultural products, legally transferring ownership of them, or conveying them.

The Funding of Agricultural Products

2. A) A fund for the agricultural products is established (Following is the fund). Its purpose is to compensate for any excessive agricultural product, and to compensate for the usage of agricultural products in industry, and to fund the expenses used to organize the marketing of agricultural products and several other aims specified in any order.

B) The fund will be financed by the Civil Administration and taxes implemented according to this Order and the rules which come from it.

C) The head of the Civil Administration will issue a system through which this fund shall be created and operated; he will determine the level of its funding and its aims. He will also issue directions on how the money of the fund should be used in the region.

---

*Order No. 1051 is amended by the "Bases for Marketing of Agricultural Products (Taxes) (Amendment)" and by Order No. 1147 and amendments, *infra*.

Taxation

3. By issuing the appropriate rules the specialized authority can:

1) Place taxes upon people engaged in marketing, which can be general or specific to the kinds of agricultural products concerned, taking into consideration the region of production, the season of the product's marketing, its type, weight, and the way in which it is packed.

2) Set the dates for and the ways of paying the taxes.

3) Determine the duties required of those engaged in marketing, which are keeping files and filing reports on the forms specified by the competent authority.

4) If any damage is caused to anybody because of any of the decisions and rules of this Order, he can complain to the appeals committee within 15 days from the day he is informed of the decision or the rule which has caused him the damage.

Punishment

Whoever violates any of the rules of this Order, including any decisions issued in accordance with it, shall be punished by either one year of imprisonment or by a fine according to what is mentioned in article 1 (A) (2) of the Order Concerning the Fines Fixed in the Security Rule (Judea and Samaria) (No. 845) for the Year 5740—1980/3, or by both together. According to what is mentioned in article 1 (A) (3) of the same order, the maximum fine can be four times the value of the thing in question. In addition to the above punishments, the court can confiscate the agricultural product in question and the containers in which it is packed, or when sold, it can confiscate its monetary equivalent, which amount is transferred to the agricultural product fund. The confiscations can either be full or partial.

Supervisors

6. A) The authority in charge can appoint supervisors to make sure that this Order, its rules and conditions, are followed. These supervisors have the same authority granted to any soldier according to article 80(A) of the Order Concerning Security Instructions (Judea and Samaria) (No. 378) for the year 5730—1970/4.*

B) Every payment for marketing agricultural products is used according to what the authority in charge decides.

Progression

7. All payments taken for marketing agricultural products before the implementation of this Order are considered as if they were taken after its implementation.

Preservation of Legislation

8. This Order cannot decrease the effectiveness of the rules of any legislation or security legislation.

*Article 80(A) of Order No. 378 is reproduced *infra*.

Amendment Of The Order Concerning The Establishment Of The Civil Administration

9. In the end of the second appendix of the Order Concerning the Establishment of the Civil Administration (Judea and Samaria) (No. 947) for the Year 5742—1981/5 comes: "Order Concerning the Marketing of Agricultural Products, (Judea and Samaria) (No. 1051) for the Year 5743—1983.

Implementation

10. The implementation of this Order commences from the day it is signed.

Title

11. This Order shall bear the title: "Order Concerning the Marketing of Agricultural Products (Judea and Samaria) (No. 1051) for the year 5743—1983".

April 14th 5743
March 28th 1983

Aluf Uri Or
Commander of the Israeli Defense Forces
Region of Judea and Samaria

[Appendix is in following amendment.]

ISRAELI DEFENSE FORCES

ORDER NO. 1051

ORDER CONCERNING MARKETING OF AGRICULTURAL PRODUCTS (JUDEA AND SAMARIA) OF 1983

BASES FOR THE MARKETING OF AGRICULTURAL PRODUCTS (TAXES) (AMENDMENT)

Acting in accordance with the authority vested in me as the competent authority pursuant to Article 3 of the Order Concerning the Marketing of Agricultural Products (Judea and Samaria) (No. 1051) of 1983, I decide as follows:

1. In the Bases for the Marketing of Agricultural Products (Taxes) (Judea and Samaria) of 1983, the appendix is replaced by the articles following.
2. These bases will be implemented as of 1 August 1983.
3. These bases will bear the title "Bases for the Marketing of Agricultural Products (Taxes) (Judea and Samaria) of 1983."

APPENDIX

Agricultural Product	Taxes (In Shekels) Imposed on Every Ton of Agricultural Product or the Percentage Cost on Part of One Ton
1. Grapes	700 shekels per ton
2. Peaches	700 shekels per ton

15 July 1983

Yoreh Artzi
Officer for Agricultural Affairs
in the Civil Administration of Judea and Samaria
Competent Authority

ISRAELI DEFENSE FORCES

ORDER NO. 1147

ORDER CONCERNING INSPECTION OF FRUIT TREES AND VEGETABLES (AMENDMENT NO. 2)

In accordance with the authority vested in me as the commander of the Israeli Defense Forces in the region, and because I believe this Order is necessary for the interests of the residents, and in order to protect the production of agricultural products in the region for the interests of the residents, I hereby order the following:

Amendment of the Article of the Order

1. In the Order Concerning the Inspection of Fruit Trees and Vegetables (Judea and Samaria) (No. 1015) of 1982 (hereafter the Original Order), in Article 1 the

words "vegetables—agricultural development of plants shown in the Second Appendix" are deleted.

Amendment of Article 2A

2. In Article 2A of the Original Order:
   (1) That which is mentioned in the Article will be known as (a), and after the word "vegetables" will come: "included in the second appendix."
   (2) Addition after Article (a)
      "(b) A person may not raise vegetables included in Article 3 until he receives a permit from the competent authority.
      "(c) The competent authority may issue a general permit for categories of agricultural products and may, at most, specify orders for specific areas."

Addition of Third Appendix

3. After the second appendix in the Original Order it should state:

"Third Appendix:

1. Onions
2. Onion Seeds"

Implementation

4. The implementation of this Order will commence as of 1 August 1985.

Title

5. This Order will bear the title "Order Concerning the Inspection of Fruit Trees and Vegetables (Amendment No. 2) (Judea and Samaria) (No. 1147) of 1985."

30 July 1985

Aluf Amnon Shahak
Commander of the Israeli Defense Forces
Judea and Samaria

ISRAELI DEFENSE FORCES

ORDER NO. 1248

ORDER AMENDING
THE LAW OF NURSERIES (ARBORETUM)
(AMENDMENT)

In accordance with the authority vested in me as commander of the Israeli Defense Forces in the region, and because I believe this Order is required to maintain public order and the comfort of the region's residents, I hereby order the following:

Addition of Article 3A to the Order

1. In the Order Concerning the Law of Nurseries (Judea and Samaria) (No. 1002) of 1982, insert after Article 3:

"Inspectors 3(A)(a): The official has the right to appoint inspectors in order to guarantee the execution of this Order and the related laws, regulations and orders.

"(b) For the purpose of fulfilling this job the inspector has the right to enter any place, and has the same rights as a soldier, as specified in Article 80 (A) of the Order Concerning Security Instructions (Judea and Samaria) (No. 378) of 1970."

Implementation

2. The implementation of this Order commences as of the date on which it is signed.

Title

3. This Order will bear the title "Order Amending the Law of Nurseries (Arboretum) (Amendment) (Judea and Samaria) (No. 1248) of 1988."

11 August 1988

Aluf 'Amram Mitzna
Officer in Charge of the Israeli Defense Forces
Region of Judea and Samaria

ISRAELI MILITARY FORCES

ORDER NO. 1252

ORDER CONCERNING MERCHANDISE TRANSPORT

In accordance with the authority vested in me as commander of the Israeli Military Forces in the region, I order the following:

Definitions

1. In this Order:
   "The authority"—Every person appointed by me to fulfill the requirements of this Order, who shall deal with special kinds of merchandise or special kinds of people.
   "The Merchandise"—All possessions including agricultural products except real property.
   "Agricultural products"—Plants (every section of the plant, including its fruits, excepting hard fruits); animals (alive or dead); anything that comes from plants or animals or is used in any of the stages of planting.

Permission to Bring Merchandise In or Out of a Region

2. A) Transporting merchandise into or out of the region requires a permit issued by the competent authority.
   B) According to this Order this permit can be general, specific or personal.
   C) A permit to enter or leave the area cannot be effective in the case of bringing merchandise into or taking it out of the region.
   D) A permit issued according to this Order does not cancel the instructions in effect on importing or exporting merchandise set by the law.
   E) Whoever claims that he has a permit based on this Order must prove it.

The Requirements for Bringing Merchandise Into or Taking It Out of the Region

3. The competent authority can include some conditions in the permit, including conditions on how to treat the merchandise after it is brought into the region and the way it is transported to its destination.
4. A) If anybody breaks any of the rules of this Order or breaks any of the conditions of the permit, then the competent authority has the right to fine him with an amount that does not exceed the maximum financial penalty fixed for such a case. If such a measure is taken, no judicial measures can be taken, and if an indictment sheet is applied no fine can be collected until the judicial consultant orders the cancelling of the court measures.
   B) The person who pays the fine, as mentioned in paragraph (A), must treat

the merchandise in question in accordance with the dictates of the competent authority.

Disobedience

5. Whoever violates the rules in the articles of this Order or the conditions of the permit issued by the competent authority is sentenced to 5 years imprisonment.

Amendment

6. A) In the Order Concerning the Establishment of the Civil Administration (Judea and Samaria) (No. 946) 5742—1981; in the end of the second amendment comes:
"Order Concerning the Transportation of Merchandise (Judea and Samaria) (No. 1252) 5748—1988".

B) In the Order Concerning the Authorities of the Customs (Judea and Samaria) (No. 309) 5729—1969 in Article 1: In the definition "Merchandise" and in the definition "The customs' fines which are included in the security legislation", instead of "Order Concerning Closed Areas (Prohibition of Merchandise Transport) (Judea and Samaria) (No. 49) 5727—1967" comes "Order Concerning Merchandise Transport (Judea and Samaria) (No. 1252) 5748—1988."

C) In the Order Concerning the Objections Committee (Judea and Samaria) (No. 172) 5728—1967 in the attachment. Instead of detail 6 comes, "Assortment of the Merchandise According to the Order on Merchandise Transport (Judea and Samaria) (No. 1252) 5748—1988."

Instructions

7. The competent authority can issue instructions in order to fulfill the purpose of this Order, including any instructions concerning the orderly transportation of merchandise into or out of the region.

Termination

8. The Order Concerning the Closed Areas (Banning of Merchandise Transport) (Judea and Samaria) (No. 49) 5727—1967, and the Order Regarding the Transport of Agricultural Products (Judea and Samaria) (No. 47) 5727—1967 are hereby terminated.

Implementation

9. The implementation of this Order commences on the day it is signed.

Title

10. This Order shall bear the title: "Order Concerning Transport of Merchandise (Judea and Samaria) (No. 1252) 5748—1988."

19 September 5748
1 September 1988

Aluf Amram Mitzna'
Commander of the Israeli Defense Forces
Region of Judea and Samaria

JORDANIAN LAW

LAW FOR THE PRESERVATION OF TREES AND PLANTS

NO. 85 FOR THE YEAR 1966

Article 1

This law will bear the title: "Law for the Preservation of Trees and Plants for the year 1966," and its implementation begins on the date it is published in the official newspapers.

Article 2

The following terms and words will carry the meanings they are given below unless mentioned otherwise.
"Administrative governor"—The governor or his assistant, the Director of the region, or the director of the district.
"Justice officer"—Any officer or person from the general security people in the region.
"Plants"—Plants such as vegetables, nursery plants, flowers, and what comes from them such as seeds, tubercles, bulbs, joints, grain, or vegetables.
"Animal"- Domestic animals such as cattle, livestock, and camels.

Article 3

A) If the plants are damaged by any person or animal the person concerned should take his grievance to the administrative governor or the justice officer immediately.
B) If the grievance is brought before anyone other than the governor it should be transferred to the governor. And the governor or his assistant should go to the scene of the incident with one or more experts and start an investigation to determine who caused the damage, or the owner of the animal which did it, so as to estimate the amount of damage.

Article 4

If the administrative governor does not look into the complaint personally, his assistant must pass all papers relevant to the investigation to the governor.

Article 5

A) The grievance is to be registered in a file, and a summary of the complaint, with attendance warrantee attached, is to be sent to the accused. Such warrantee must include the date of trial which proceed *in absentia* if the accused does not attend.

B) The administrative governor makes all the announcements and executes the verdicts and orders.

Article 6

On the day appointed for trial the administrative governor will listen to the arguments of the complainant and the accused and the suspects, and he will pose several questions related to the case. After that he will attempt a reconciliation, and if he succeeds he will prepare the reconciliation paper and reads the contents to both sides in very simple language. Then the complainant, the accused and the administrative governor will sign the paper. The administrative governor has the right to punish the accused according to the penalty mentioned in this law.

Article 7

If a reconciliation does not take place and if the administrative governor is convinced that the accused has caused some damage, he will order the accused to pay the amount of the damage caused to the complainant. If there is more than one complainant the administrative governor will decide the percentage of compensation each receives. In addition, the following punishments are inflicted on the accused and their partners:

A) If the damage does not exceed twenty Jordanian dinars, a fine not exceeding five dinars, or one week imprisonment, or both of them together are inflicted on the accused.

B) If the damage exceeds twenty Jordanian dinars, a fine amounting up to approximately fifty percent of the amount of damage caused, from one week to two months imprisonment, or both of them together are to be inflicted on the accused.

C) he verdicts against the accused are to be taken in accordance with the penal code.

Article 8

A) If the administrative governor is convinced that the damage was caused by unknown persons and that they belong to a specific family or live in a specific area, he will take the verdict against all the adult males of that family or of the people living in the area mentioned above, to pay for all the damage and the expenses. The administrative governor can also fine any person he sees directly or indirectly involved in the action by not more than five Jordanian dinars

B) If the accused is a very young person they are to be prosecuted according to what is mentioned in paragraphs (A) and (B) of Article 7 of this law, taking into consideration the jail punishments of the juvenile law. Furthermore, the administrative governor can fine the parents of the youth as mentioned in the previous paragraph and force them to pay the damage and expenses.

C) If the person or persons are hired stockmen or shepherds they are to be punished according to the previous article in this law, and the administrative governor can also include the owners of the livestock as it is mentioned in the previous article. Only the imbecile, the lunatic, the handicapped, and whoever does not live permanently with the family or in the area are excluded from any ruling based on this article.

Article 9

If, during the trial, the administrative governor does not adhere to the penalty established by law, he must give the accused the right to defend himself.

Article 10

The administrative governor will sign the verdict and one copy will be placed in a visible place in the office and in another visible place to make it easy for the defendant to read and understand it.

Article 11

The administrative governor can either decide the imprisonment penalty immediately or release the defendant on bail until the time the appeal decision is taken.

Article 12

If the defendant attended the trial, an appeal can be made against the decision of the administrative governor to the Minister of the Interior ten days from the day the decision was taken. If the defendant did not attend the trial the appeal can be made within ten days from the day the two copies of the verdict are posted in the visible places as mentioned in Article 10.

Article 13

A) The Minister of the Interior will look into the appeal and his decision will be final.

B) The Minister of the Interior can completely or partially nullify the validity of the verdict, amend it, decrease the punishment inflicted, cancel it, completely or partially pardon all those involved or some of them if the appeal is signed by all the defendants or some of them.

C) The administrative governor will take the necessary measures to carry out the decision of the Minister of Interior immediately after it is taken.

Article 14

The complainant must pay all the expenses the administrative governor decides. The complainant will then obtain them from the defendant as if they were part of the amount of compensation.

Article 15

The decisions and orders issued according to this law are considered as if they were issued from a regular court.

Article 16

Any damage caused by fire is excluded from the orders of this law, and in this case the administrative governor will transfer the papers of the case to the prosecutor to take the necessary measures if the person who caused the damage is known.

Article 17

It is not possible to apply Article 100 of the criminal law for the year 1960 unless if the damage inflicted on the plants and trees was done on purpose.

Article 18

Nothing in this law can prevent the administrative governor from using the measures and decisions provided by any other law against whomever he considers responsible for causing damage to trees and plants.

Article 19

The administrative governor has the right to transfer the case to a regular court if he sees that the crime discussed is so serious that the penalty level this law offers is not enough.

Article 20

The Law for the Preservation of Plants No. 20 for the year 1937 is considered cancelled.

Article 21

The Prime Minister and the ministers are accountable for the execution of the orders of this law.

21 December 1966
Hussein Ibn Talal

ADDENDUM

The Law for the Protection of Plants and Nursery Plants No. 30 for the Year 1937 was published in the official newspaper, issue no. 560, on 1 May 1937. And it was published before as a project in issue no. 553 of the newspaper, published 1 March 1937. The privileges granted to the Prime Minister according to this rule were transferred to the Minister of Interior according to the Law Concerning the Jobs of the Ministers No. 21 for the Year 1939, which was published in the official paper, issue no. 643, on 16 July 1939.

This order was amended while it was in effect according to the Law No. 2 for the year 1941, which is published in issue no. 699 of the official paper on 16 February 1941 and the amended Law No. 18 for the year 1942, which was published in issue no. 744 of the official newspaper on 16 July 1942. The Law Concerning the Protection of Plants and Nursery Plants No. 20 for the year 1937 cancelled, upon its issue, the Law for the Protection of Plants and Nursery Plants issued in the year 1935. And the fourth article of the law was amended as mentioned on page 135 of issue no. 520 of the official newspaper issued on 1 April 1942.

Article 2 of the Law for the Protection of Plants and Nursery Plants No. 21 for the year 1952, which was published on page 153 of issue no. 1104 of the official newspaper published on 1 April 1952, provided that the Law for the Protection of Plants and Nursery Plants No. 20 for the year 1937, in effect in the east bank of the Hashemite Kingdom of Jordan, is in effect on its west bank as well.

APPENDIX C

International Legal Provisions Cited

FOURTH GENEVA CONVENTION (EXCERPTS)

Geneva Convention Relative to the Protection of Civilian
Persons in Time of War of August 12, 1949.

ARTICLE 1

The High Contracting Parties undertake to respect and to ensure respect for the
present Convention in all circumstances.

ARTICLE 2

[Para. 1.]* In addition to the provisions which shall be implemented in peace-
time, the present Convention shall apply to all cases of declared war or of any
other armed conflict which may arise between two or more of the High Contracting Parties, even if the state of war is not recognized by one of them.
[Para. 2.] The Convention shall also apply to all cases of partial or total occupation
of the territory of a High Contracting Party, even if the said occupation meets
with no armed resistance.

ARTICLE 6

[Para. 3.] In the case of occupied territory, the application of the present Convention shall cease one year after the general close of military operations; however, the Occupying Power shall be bound, for the duration of the occupation, to

*Paragraph numbers are given where the article is not quoted in its entirety.

the extent that such Power exercises the functions of government in such territory, by the provisions of the following Articles of the present Convention: 1 to
12, 27, 29 to 34, 47, 49, 51, 52, 53, 59, 61 to 77, 143.

ARTICLE 30

Protected persons shall have every facility for making application to the Protecting Powers, the International Committee of the Red Cross, the National Red
Cross (Red Crescent, Red Lion and Sun) Society of any country where they may
be, as well as to any organizations that might assist them.

These several organizations shall be granted all facilities for that purpose by
the authorities, within the bounds set by military or security considerations.

Apart from the visits of the delegates of the Protecting Powers and of the
International Committee of the Red Cross, provided for by Article 143, the Detaining or Occupying Powers shall facilitate as much as possible visits to protected
persons by the representatives of other organizations whose object is to give spir-
itual aid or material relief to such persons.

ARTICLE 33

No protected person shall be punished for any offence he or she has not personally
committed. Collective penalties and likewise all measures of intimidation or of
terrorism are prohibited.

Pillage is prohibited.

Reprisals against protected persons and their property are prohibited.

ARTICLE 46

In so far as they have not been previously withdrawn, restrictive measures taken
regarding protected persons shall be cancelled as soon as possible after the close
of hostilities.

Restrictive measures affecting their property shall be cancelled, in accordance with the law of the Detaining Power, as soon as possible after the close of
hostilities.

ARTICLE 47

Protected persons who are in occupied territory shall not be deprived, in any case
or in any manner whatsoever, of the benefits of the present Convention by any
change introduced, as the result of the occupation of a territory, into the institutions or government of the said territory, nor by any agreement concluded between the authorities of the occupied territories and the Occupying Power, nor
by any annexation by the latter of the whole or part of the occupied territory.

ARTICLE 49

Individual or mass forcible transfers, as well as deportations of protected persons from occupied territory to the territory of the Occupying Power or to that of any other country, occupied or not, are prohibited, regardless of their motive.

Nevertheless, the Occupying Power may undertake total or partial evacuation of a given area if the security of the population or imperative military reasons so demand. Such evacuations may not involve the displacement of protected persons outside the bounds of the occupied territory except when for material reasons it is impossible to avoid such displacement. Persons thus evacuated shall be transferred back to their homes as soon as hostilities in the area in question have ceased.

The Occupying Power undertaking such transfers or evacuations shall ensure, to the greatest practicable extent, that proper accommodation is provided to receive the protected persons, that the removal [is] effected in satisfactory conditions of hygiene, health, safety and nutrition, and that members of the same family are not separated.

The Protecting Power shall be informed of any transfers and evacuations as soon as they have taken place.

The Occupying Power shall not detain protected persons in an area particularly exposed to the dangers of war unless the security of the population or imperative military reasons so demand.

The Occupying Power shall not deport or transfer parts of its own civilian population into the territory it occupies.

ARTICLE 53

Any destruction by the Occupying Power of real or personal property belonging individually or collectively to private persons, or to the State, or to other public authorities, or to social or cooperative organizations, is prohibited, except where such destruction is rendered absolutely necessary by military operations.

ARTICLE 64

The penal laws of the occupied territory shall remain in force, with the exception that they may be repealed or suspended by the Occupying Power in cases where they constitute a threat to its security or an obstacle to the application of the present Convention. Subject to the latter consideration and to the necessity for ensuring the effective administration of justice, the tribunals of the occupied territory shall continue to function in respect of all offenses covered by the said laws.

The Occupying Power may, however, subject the population of the occupied territory to provisions which are essential to enable the Occupying Power to fulfil[l] its obligations under the present Convention, to maintain the orderly government of the territory, and to ensure the security of the Occupying Power, of the members and property of the occupying forces as administration, and likewise of the establishments and lines of communication used by them.

HAGUE REGULATIONS (EXCERPTS)

Convention (No. IV) Respecting the Laws and Customs of War on Land, With Annex of Regulations
Done at The Hague, Oct. 18, 1907.

ARTICLE 43

The authority of the legitimate power having in fact passed into the hands of the occupant, the latter shall take all the measures in his power to restore, and ensure, as far as possible, public order and safety, while respecting, unless absolutely prevented, the laws in force in the country.

ARTICLE 46

Family honour and rights, the lives of persons, and private property, as well as religious convictions and practice, must be respected.

ARTICLE 48

If, in the territory occupied, the occupant collects the taxes, dues, and tolls imposed for the benefit of the State, he shall do it, as far as possible, in accordance with the rules in existence and the assessment in force, and will in consequence be bound to defray the expenses of the administration of the occupied territory on the same scale as that by which the legitimate government was bound.

ARTICLE 49

If, in addition to the taxes mentioned in the above Article the occupant levies other money contributions in the occupied territory, this shall only be for the needs of the army or of the administration of the territory in question.

ARTICLE 50

No general penalty, pecuniary or otherwise, shall be inflicted upon the population on account of the acts of individuals for which they cannot be regarded as jointly and severally responsible.

ARTICLE 52

Requisitions in kind and services shall not be demanded from municipalities or inhabitants except for the needs of the army of occupation. They shall be in proportion to the resources of the country, and of such a nature as not to involve the inhabitants in the obligation of taking part in military operations against their own country.

Such requisitions and services shall only be demanded on the authority of the commander in the locality occupied.

Contributions in kind shall as far as possible be paid for in cash; if not, a receipt shall be given and the payment of the amount due shall be made as soon as possible.

ARTICLE 53

An army of occupation can only take possession of cash, funds and realizable securities which are strictly the property of the State, depots of arms, means of transport, stores and supplies, and, generally, all movable property belonging to the State which may be used for military operations.

All appliances, whether on land, at sea, or in the air, adapted for the transmission of news, or for the transport of persons of persons or things, exclusive of cases governed by naval law, depots of arms, and, generally, all kinds of ammunition of war, may be seized, even if they belong to private individuals, but must be restored and compensation fixed when peace is made.

ARTICLE 55

The occupying states shall be regarded only as administrator and usufructuary of public buildings, real estate, forests, and agricultural estates belonging to the hostile State, and situated in the occupied country. It must safeguard the capital of these properties, and administer them in accordance with the rules of usufruct.

ARTICLE 56

The property of municipalities, that of institutions dedicated to religion, charity and education, the arts and sciences, even when State property, shall be treated as private property.

All seizure of, destruction or wilful damage done to institutions of this character, historic monuments, works of art and science, is forbidden, and should be made the subject of legal proceedings.

CHARTER OF THE UNITED NATIONS (EXCERPTS)

ARTICLE 77

(1) The trusteeship system shall apply to such territories in the following categories as may be places thereunder by means of trusteeship agreements:

(a) territories now held under mandate; . . .

ARTICLE 80

(1) Except as may be agreed upon in individual trusteeship agreements, made under Articles 77, 79, and 81, placing each territory under the trusteeship system, and until such agreements have been concluded, nothing in this Chapter shall be construed in or of itself to alter in any manner the rights whatsoever of any states or any peoples or the terms of existing international instruments to which Members of the United Nations may respectively be parties. . . .

PROTOCOLS ADDITIONAL TO THE GENEVA CONVENTIONS OF 1949 (EXCERPT) GENEVA, 1977

ARTICLE 3

BEGINNING AND END OF APPLICATION

Without prejudice to the provisions which are applicable at all times:
(a) the Conventions and this Protocol shall apply from the beginning of any situation referred to in Article 1 of this Protocol;
(b) the application of the Conventions and of this Protocol shall cease, in the territory of Parties to the conflict, on the general close of military operations and, in the case of occupied territories, on the termination of the occupation, except, in either circumstance, for those persons whose final release, repatriation or re-establishment takes place thereafter. These persons shall continue to benefit from the relevant provisions of the Conventions and of this Protocol until their final release, repatriation or re-establishment.

COVENANT OF THE LEAGUE OF NATIONS (EXCERPTS)

ARTICLE 22

(1) To those colonies and territories which as a consequence of the late war have ceased to be under the sovereignty of the States which formerly governed them and which are inhabited by peoples not yet able to stand by themselves under the strenuous conditions of the modern world, there should be applied the principle that the well-being and development of such peoples form a sacred trust of

civilization and that securities for the performance of this trust should be embodied in this Covenant.

(2) The best method of giving practical effect to this principle is that the tutelage of such peoples should be intrusted to advanced nations who, by reason of their resources, their experience or their geographical position, can best undertake this responsibility, and who are willing to accept it, and that this tutelage should be exercised by them as Mandatories on behalf of the League. . . .

(4) Certain communities formerly belonging to the Turkish Empire have reached a stage of development where their existence as independent nations can be provisionally recognized subject to the rendering of administrative advice and assistance by a Mandatory until such time as they are able to stand alone. The wishes of these communities must be a principal consideration in the selection of the Mandatory. . . .

(6) There are territories, such as Southwest Africa and certain of the South Pacific islands, which, owing to the sparseness of their population or their small size, or their remoteness from the centers of civilization, or their geographical contiguity to the territory of the Mandatory, and other circumstances, can be best administered under the laws of the Mandatory as integral portions of its territory, subject to the safeguards above mentioned in the interest of the indigenous population.

NOTES

Introduction

1. Fawzi Gharaibeh, *The Economies of the West Bank and Gaza Strip* (Boulder, Colo.: Westview Press, 1985), p. 59.

2. Given the confrontational nature of the situation in the West Bank, bias is a concern when weighing information from any source. Palestinians may place blame on the Israeli occupier for problems which have sources within the Palestinian community, or even within third countries, while Israeli authorities may tend to overlook the adverse effects of government interventions and to focus disproportionately on benefits which have accrued to the West Bank population over the course of the occupation. In our work we tried to filter out such tendencies for bias by checking and cross-checking our sources. We have carefully listed all of our sources, provided that we could do so without compromising their security. The reader should be aware that most Department of Agriculture workers interviewed were Palestinians, and were often sympathetic to the concerns of the West Bank population.

3. Antonio Cassese, "Powers and Duties of an Occupant in Relation to Land and Natural Resources," unpublished paper delivered at the Al-Haq/Law in the Service of Man conference in Jerusalem, January 22–25, 1988, on file at Al-Haq, Ramallah, West Bank. (Hereinafter papers from this conference will be referred to as "Al-Haq Conference papers.")

4. See Georg Schwarzenberger, *International Law*, vol. 2 (London: Stevens, 1968), p. 20; Allan Gerson, *Israel, the West Bank and International Law* (Lanham, Md.: Biblio Distribution Center, 1978).

5. See Meron Benvenisti, *The West Bank Handbook: A Political Lexicon* (Jerusalem: Jerusalem Post, 1986), p. 67. The situation arises as much from the very nature of occupation as it does from malevolent intent. "Closer scrutiny of the economic decision-making process . . . shows that the 'consistent' policy is merely a haphazard *post facto* consequence of decisions made without forethought, in

response to pressures, or as compromises or concessions to Israeli pressure groups." Ibid.

6. A recent United Nations Food and Agriculture Organization (UNFAO) resolution reflects a growing sense in the international community that "the policies and practices of the Israeli occupation authorities impede the basic requirements for the development of the economy of the occupied Palestinian territory, including the agricultural sector," and also that these policies are related to "the Israeli confiscation of Palestinian land and expropriation of Palestinian water resources." UNFAO resolution entitled "Provision of Technical Assistance to the Palestinian People," November 1989. (The authors obtained a copy of this resolution directly from the UN FAO office in Washington, D.C.)

1. Israel, Palestine, and the West Bank

1. See Fred J. Khouri, *The Arab-Israeli Dilemma*, 3d ed. (Syracuse, N.Y.: Syracuse University Press, 1985), p. 16.

2. Ibid.

3. See Peter Mansfield, *A History of the Middle East* (New York: Viking, 1991), pp. 118, 205, 235.

4. See James A. Bill and Carl Leiden, *Politics in the Middle East* (Little, Brown, & Co., Texas, 1984), p. 333.

5. See David Kahan, *Agriculture and Water Resources in the West Bank and Gaza (1967–87)* (Jerusalem: Jerusalem Post, 1987), pp. 1–5.

6. Ibid., p. 9.

7. Don Peretz, *The West Bank: History, Politics, Society, and Economy* (Boulder, Colo.: Westview Press, 1986), p. 33.

8. See Khouri, p. 260.

9. Population figures for 1967 from Meron Benvenisti, *The West Bank Data Project: A Survey of Israel's Policies* (Jerusalem: Jerusalem Post, 1984,), p. 2. The current figure includes Arab East Jerusalem. See Meron Benvenisti and Shlomo Khayat, *The West Bank and Gaza Atlas* (Jerusalem: Jerusalem Post, 1988), pp. 27–31, 109.

10. See Sarah Graham-Brown, "The Economic Consequences of the Occupation," in *Occupation: Israel Over Palestine*, Naseer H. Aruri, ed. (Belmont, Mass.: Association of Arab American University Graduates, 1983), p. 171.

11. See, for example, Esther Cohen, *Human Rights in the Israeli-Occupied Territories 1967–1982* (U.K.: Manchester University Press, 1985) pp. 235–50; *Abu-Aita v. Commander of the Judea and Samaria Region*, H.C. 69/81 and 493/81, 37(2) P.D. 197 (1983), English case summary in 13 *Israel Yearbook on Human Rights* 348 (1983); Israeli Ministry of Defense, *A Fourteen Year Survey (1967–1981)*, p. 3, cited in Peretz, *The West Bank*, p. 109. (*Israel Yearbook on Human Rights* hereafter cited as *IYBHR*.)

12. See Cohen, *Human Rights*, p. 236.

13. Ibid.

14. See Gharaibeh, p. 18.

15. See Cohen, *Human Rights*, p. 238.

16. Ibid., p. 237.

17. Ibid., pp. 239, 244; Shmuel Sandler and H. Frisch, *Israel, the Palestinians and the West Bank: A Study of Intercommunal Conflict* (Lexington, Mass.: Lexington Books, 1984), p. 55.

18. See Cohen, *Human Rights*, p. 237.

19. UNRWA administers refugee camps built for Palestinians who fled or were driven from their homes in the 1948 and 1967 wars. The agency has an annual budget of approximately U.S. $230 million. See R. C. Gross, *Washington Times*, Nov. 15, 1990, A-9. See also M. Benvenisti, *West Bank Data Project*, p. 10.

20. See Sandler and Frisch, p. 51; Cohen, *Human Rights*, p. 237.

21. See Gharaibeh, pp. 9, 18.

22. See *Financial Times*, June 10, 1989.

23. See Sandler and Frisch, p. 49.

24. See Cohen, *Human Rights*, p. 243.

25. See Gharaibeh, p. 13.

26. Ibid., p. 22.

27. See Cohen, *Human Rights*, pp. 56, 57.

28. Sandler and Frisch, p. 55.

29. See M. Benvenisti, *West Bank Data Project Survey*, p. 12.

30. See Kahan p. 3.

31. Ibid., p. 27.

32. See Gharaibeh, pp. 64–65.

33. Kahan, p. 15.

34. Some Palestinian agriculturalists we interviewed blamed the shift from subsistence to cash crops, in part, for the West Bank's current dependence on Israeli agricultural products.

35. See M. Benvenisti, *West Bank Handbook*, p. 1; Gharaibeh, pp. 65–77.

36. See Peretz, *The West Bank*, p. 114.

37. Ibid., p. 242.

38. See Mansfield, pp. 294–296.

39. M. Benvenisti, *West Bank Data Project Survey*, pp. 9–10.

40. Ibid.

41. Kahan, pp. 118–19.

42. See Graham-Brown, p. 173.

43. Ibid., p. 204.

44. Mohammed Rabie, "Foreign Aid and the Israeli Economy," 25 *American Arab Affairs* 64 (Summer 1988).

45. See also *Abu Aita v. Commander of the Judea and Samaria Region*; Israeli Ministry of Defense, *A 14 Year Survey (1967–1981)*, p. 3, cited in Don Peretz, *Intifada* (Boulder, Colo.: Westview Press, 1990), p. 9.

46. Kahan, p. 117.

47. See Cohen, *Human Rights*, p. 241.

48. Quoted in Kahan, p. 16.

49. See Gharaibeh, pp. 53, 134.

50. Kahan, p. 16.

51. Graham-Brown, p. 187. "It is to be noted that all this 'technology' is imported either from or through Israel, both increasing Israeli trade and importing Israeli inflation into agricultural costs." Ibid.

52. See Hisham Awartani, "Agriculture," in *A Palestinian Agenda for the West Bank and Gaza,* Emile A. Nakhleh, ed. (Washington, D.C.: American Enterprise Institute, 1980). See also J. Bainerman, "The Uprising and Israel's Economy," *Jerusalem Post,* Dec. 12, 1990.

53. See Al-Haq/Law in the Service of Man, *Punishing a Nation—Human Rights Violations During the Palestinian Uprising—December 1987–1988* (Ramallah, West Bank: 1989), p. 272.

54. R. L. Coles, "Economic Development in the Occupied Territories," 25 *American Arab Affairs* 82 (Summer 1988).

55. Ibid. See also Gharaibeh, p. 137; report of a mission sent by the Netherlands government, entitled "Export of Agricultural Produce from the West Bank and the Gaza Strip: Difficulties and Opportunities," June 1987, p. 11; (hereafter cited as *Netherlands Government Mission*); Palestinian Agricultural Relief Committee, *Agricultural Development and the Uprising* (Jerusalem: May 1988), p. 1; John Quigley, *Palestine and Israel: A Challenge to Justice* (Durham, N.C.: Duke University Press, 1990), pp. 185–87; and Kahan, *generally,* on government subsidies for several specific agricultural products.

56. See Kate Rouhana, "The Other Intifada: The Crucial Economic War Heats Up," *The Nation,* Jan. 1, 1990, p.1.

57. See Gharaibeh, pp. 50–51.

58. See Peretz, *Intifada,* p. 11.

59. See Quigley, p. 25.

60. See Gharaibeh, p. 136.

61. See Cohen, *Human Rights,* p. 238.

62. See Gharaibeh, pp. 51, 136.

63. See Rouhana.

64. See George Abed, "The Economic Viability of a Palestinian State," 19(2) *Journal of Palestine Studies* 8 (Winter 1990). The number of workers does not include the 20,000–50,000 that work illegally within the green line. Ibid., note 23. See also Bainerman, "The Uprising and Israel's Economy," *Jerusalem Post,* Dec. 12, 1990; S. Roy, "The Political Economy of Despair," 20(3) *Journal of Palestine Studies* (Spring 1991), pp. 58, 61.

65. See Peretz, *The West Bank,* p. 114.

66. See Jordanian Department of Statistics, *Population and Employment in Agriculture, 1967* (Amman: 1968), Table 1, as cited in Gharaibeh. See also Kahan, pp. 3, 26–27, citing Israeli Central Bureau of Statistics.

67. See Kahan, pp. 26–27.

68. See *Netherlands Government Mission,* pp. 9–11; Kahan, pp. 71–72.

69. See Kahan, p. 71. See also *Netherlands Government Mission,* p. 9.

2. Economic Developments since the Intifada

1. See J. Diehl, "Boycott Spurs Palestinian Businesses," *Washington Post,* Sept. 8, 1989, p. A-25.

2. See M. Dunsky, "Palestinians Plant Seeds of Struggle," *Chicago Tribune*, June 26, 1988, p. C-3.
3. See J. Hilterman, "The Women's Movement During the Uprising," 20(3) *Journal of Palestine Studies* 48 (Spring 1991).
4. See Peretz, *Intifada*, pp. 76, 90.
5. See Rouhana.
6. See Roy, pp. 61–62.
7. *Financial Times*, citing Awartani, June 10, 1989.
8. See Peretz, *Intifada*, pp. 148–51.
9. See Rouhana.
10. Ibid.
11. Ibid.; Bainerman, "The Uprising and Israel's Economy," *Jerusalem Post* (Dec. 12, 1990); Joel Bainerman, "The Economic Growing Pains for Palestinian Autonomy," 6(5) *Middle East Insight* 49 (Spring 1989).
12. Abed, p. 8.

3. The Institutions of Occupation

1. See Raja Shehadeh and Jonathan Kuttab, *The West Bank and the Rule of Law*, 2d ed. (Geneva: International Commission of Jurists, 1980); Israel National Section of the International Commission of Jurists, *The Rule of Law in the Areas Administered by Israel* (Tel Aviv: Israel National Section of the International Commission of Jurists, 1981).
2. See Eyal Benvenisti, *Legal Dualism: The Absorption of the Occupied Territories into Israel* (Boulder, Colo.: Westview Press, 1990), p. 1. See also Peretz, *Intifada*, p. 5. Al-Haq/Law in the Service of Man, the West Bank affiliate of the International Commission of Jurists, has compiled, through painstaking effort, a nearly complete set of the military orders, which are housed at the Al-Haq office in Ramallah. See Appendix D for sample English texts of several of the most significant military orders directly affecting agriculture. Abstracts of those orders are found in Appendix C. The military orders are written in Hebrew with an Arabic translation. Our translations were made from an Arabic set at the Al-Haq offices in Ramallah, West Bank. Currently, copies of such orders are distributed to lawyers, but the quality of the Arabic can be bad, and often the copies do not include schedules, maps, and sections found in the original Hebrew. Most military orders can be obtained in pamphlets from the publisher in Tel Aviv, but some of the most important orders never appear in these publications, and they are not published by the occupation authorities in an official gazette or in the press. Regulations amending the military orders, if they exist in any formal form at all, are often impossible to get hold of. See Jordan Paust, Gerhard von Glahn, and G. Woratsch, *Inquiry into the Israeli Military Court System in the Occupied West Bank and Gaza* (Geneva: International Commission of Jurists, 1989), p. 13; E. Benvenisti, pp. 1–2.
3. See Quigley, pp. 184–88.
4. In the Camp David meetings, United States President Jimmy Carter brokered an accord between Egyptian President Anwar Sadat and Israeli Prime Minister Menachem Begin, in which Egypt agreed to end its long-standing war with Israel

in exchange for the Sinai peninsula, which Israel had occupied following the 1967 war. The Camp David Accords were rather vague with respect to the West Bank, stating only that Israel was to institute a five-year "autonomy" plan. See Peretz, *The West Bank*, pp. 54–55.

5. See Quigley, pp. 10, 23–24.

6. See Peretz, *The West Bank*, pp. 83–84, 98–99; Quigley, p. 180; M. Benvenisti, *West Bank Handbook*, pp. 217–220.

7. U.S. Department of State, *Country Reports on Human Rights Practices for 1982*, pp. 1165–66, quoted in Quigley, p. 180.

8. See *Kawasme et al. v. Minister of Defense (Kawasme II)* H.C. 698/80, 35(1) P.D. 617, English case summary in 11 *IYBHR* 350 (1981).

9. See Peretz, *The West Bank*, pp. 85, 103.

10. Ibid., pp. 98–100. See also M. Benvenisti, *West Bank Handbook*, pp. 217–20.

11. See Asher Arian, *Politics in Israel, the Second Generation* (Chatham, N.J.: Chatham House, 1985), pp. 188–216; Don Peretz, *The Government and Politics of Israel* (Boulder, Colo.: Westview Press, 1979), pp. 75–119.

12. See Yaval Elizur and Eliahu Salpeter, *Who Rules Israel?* (New York: Harper & Row, 1973), pp. 275–82; Arian, pp. 210–16.

4. The Permit System

1. E. Benvenisti, *Legal Dualism*, p. 48.

2. See also *Netherlands Government Mission*, p. 15; Palestinian Agricultural Relief Committee, "Agricultural Development and the Uprising," p. 1.

3. See Kahan, pp. 36–37; Quigley, p. 186.

4. Interview with high-ranking agricultural officer in the Civil Administration; interview with Samir Hillele, Economic Development Group, in E. Jerusalem (July 1, 1989).

5. See *Netherlands Government Mission*, p. 15; Palestinian Agricultural Relief Committee, *Agricultural Development*, p. 1.

6. Interview with staff member, Arab Thought Forum, in E. Jerusalem (June 28, 1989).

7. Interview with Baoud Istanbuli, former (17-year) Department of Agriculture officer, now employed at Cooperative Development Project, in Jerusalem (July 7, 1989).

8. Interview with Khalid A. Qutob, secretary, Agricultural Cooperative Union, chair of the Jericho Marketing Cooperative, in Beit Hanina, West Bank (July 21, 1989); *Netherlands Government Mission*, pp. 11, 13.

9. Interview with staff members, Palestine Agricultural Relief Committee, in Shufat, West Bank (July 4, 1989); interview with Department of Agriculture official, in Jenin, West Bank (Aug. 20, 1989).

10. See Kahan, p. 36.

11. Interview with Ibrahim Matar, deputy director of ANERA and board member of the Arab Development and Credit Co., in E. Jerusalem (July 10, 1989).

12. Interview with Department of Agriculture officers, Jenin office (Aug. 20, 1989); interview with I. Matar; interview with S. Hillele.

13. See Kahan, p. 35; interview with Department of Agriculture officers in Jenin.

14. See Raja Shehadeh, *Occupier's Law: Israel and the West Bank*, 2d ed. (Washington, D.C.: Institute for Palestine Studies, 1989), p. 89; interview with K. A. Qutob.

15. Interview with S. Hillele; interview with staff members, Arab Development and Credit Co., in E. Jerusalem (July 20, 1989). See also Kahan, p. 38; M. Benvenisti, *West Bank Data Project Survey*, pp. 34–35.

16. See M. Benvenisti, *West Bank Handbook*, p. 120; E. Benvenisti, p. 48.

17. Interview with Charles Shammas, Mattin Ltd; board of directors, Al-Haq, in E. Jerusalem (June 29, 1989); interview with S. Hillele; interview with Department of Agriculture officers in Jenin.

18. Amendments to Order No. 47 allowed authorities to specify the route of transport, and for stop and search, and seizure for noncompliance. Penalties included confiscation and/or cost of transportation to a designated destination.

19. See *Netherlands Government Mission,* pp. 4–11; Kahan, pp. 71–72.

20. See Gharaibeh, pp. 136–37.

21. See Jerusalem Media and Communication Centre, "Bitter Harvest: Israeli Sanctions Against Palestinian Agriculture During the Uprising" (May 1989), on file at Jerusalem Media and Communications Centre, p. 10.

22. Interview with staff members, Palestine Agricultural Relief Committee; interview with staff members, Arab Development and Credit Company.

23. Jerusalem Media Centre, "Bitter Harvest," pp. 10–11.

24. See Kahan, p. 71; Quigley, p. 185–86; Gharaibeh, p. 137.

25. See Kahan, p. 121; interviews with regional officials of the Department of Agriculture of the Civil Administration, West Bank (June, July 1989).

26. E. Benvenisti, pp. 36–37, citing Military Orders No. 1093 and 1252; Kahan, p. 71; Quigley, p. 186; Gharaibeh, p. 137.

27. See E. Benvenisti, p. 37. See also Kahan, p. 71.

28. Interview with official, United States Consulate, Jerusalem (July 1989).

29. Ibid.

30. Interview with Ghrassan El-Khatib, Bir Zeit University professor of economics (July 11, 1989); interview with assistant manager, Jenin Agricultural Marketing Cooperative, in Jenin, West Bank (July 18, 1989); interview with official, United States Consulate, Jerusalem (July 26, 1989); interview with officers of Department of Agriculture of the Civil Administration.

31. See Peretz, *Intifada*, p. 99.

32. See Quigley, p. 187.

33. See *Netherlands Government Mission*, p. 11; Kahan, p. 71.

34. Interview with director, Nablus Marketing Cooperative; interview with Professor Salim Tamari of Bir Zeit University, Ramallah, West Bank (Aug. 4, 1989).

35. See *Netherlands Government Mission*, p. 11; interview with director, Nablus Marketing Cooperative.

36. Interview with Department of Agriculture official in Jenin, West Bank (July 27, 1989).

37. See Kahan, p. 71; interview with director, Nablus Marketing Cooperative.

Prof. H. Awartani of An-Najah Research Center lists the costs of Israeli regulation of produce transport from Israel to Jordan (January 1988) as follows:

	NIS	$ U.S.
Exit permit for owner of merchandise/trip	114	74
Permit for truck driver/mo.	225	154
Inspection fee of truck on return/trip	29	20
Custom Service Fee/trip	21	14

H. Awartani, "Israel's Economic Policies in the Occupied Territories," Al-Haq Conference paper.

38. Interview with director, Nablus Marketing Cooperative.
39. See Kahan, p. 71.
40. Interview with director, Nablus Marketing Cooperative.
41. See *Netherlands Government Mission*, p. 11; H. Awartani, Al-Haq Conference paper; interview with Department of Agriculture official in Jenin.
42. Ibid.; interview with Department of Agriculture official, in West Bank (July 27, 1989).
43. Interview with director, Nablus Marketing Cooperative.
44. Interview with high-ranking Department of Agriculture official, in Jenin, West Bank (July 27, 1989). This figure roughly corresponds to estimates made by relief organizations working with West Bank farmers. In an interview, representatives of the Catholic Relief Services estimated the cost of shipping produce to Amman at 70 Jordanian dinars per ton in 1987.
45. See Awartani, Al-Haq Conference paper.
46. Interview with S. Tamari.
47. Interview with Professor Hisham Awartani, An-Najah Research Center of Nablus, in Ramallah, West Bank (Aug. 7, 1989).
48. See Peretz, *Intifada*, p. 72.

5. Restrictions on Farmers' Organizations

1. See Kahan, p. 121; interview with S. Dijani, Arab Development Society, in Jericho (July 24, 1989); interview with UNDP representative, in E. Jerusalem (July 27, 1989); interview with B. Istanbuli.
2. Interview with B. Istanbuli; *Netherlands Government Mission*, p. 12.
3. Interviews with numerous West Bank farmers; *Netherlands Government Mission*, p. 12.
4. Interview with B. Istanbuli
5. See Palestinian Agricultural Relief Committee, *Annual Report for 1988* (Shufat, West Bank: 1988).
6. Interview with Palestine Agricultural Relief Committee staff members in Shufat, West Bank (Aug. 7, 1989).
7. See M. Benvenisti, *The West Bank Handbook*, pp. 154–55.

8. Interview with staff members, Arab Development and Credit Co., in E. Jerusalem (July 27 1989).

9. See M. Benvenisti, *West Bank Handbook*, 156–57.

10. Ibid., p. 167.

11. See Awartani, Al-Haq Conference paper.

12. See M. Benvenisti, *West Bank Handbook*, p. 167; interview with H. Awartani.

13. Meron Benvenisti, *West Bank Data Project 1986 Report*, p. 33; see also Baheh, *West Bank Data Project Report* (1989). Benvenisti also writes, "To all intents and purposes [the HPC's] efforts were limited to preventing Arab construction in sensitive military areas slated for Jewish settlement by the Allon Plan . . . [After 1977] physical planning became a central instrument in carrying out settlement policy . . . [and] severe restrictions were placed on physical planning for the Palestinian population." He states further that "the Israeli authorities attempt to block projects for the development of economic infrastructure," especially when those projects would compete with Israeli ventures. M. Benvenisti, *West Bank Handbook*, p. 94. See also ibid., p. 67; Quigley, pp. 184–86.

14. Interview with staff members, Arab Development and Credit Co.

15. Interview with staff member, Arab Development and Credit Co.; interview with staff members, Palestine Agricultural Relief Committee.

16. Interview with staff member, Arab Development and Credit Co.; interview with staff members, PARC, *supra*.

17. See Netherlands Government Mission, p. 15.

18. See M. Benvenisti, *West Bank Handbook*, pp. 112–13.

19. Ibid., p. 113.

20. Quigley, p. 186.

21. S. Bahiri, *Jerusalem Post*, January 4, 1991.

22. As quoted in *Jerusalem Post*, Feb. 15, 1985.

23. Interview with UNDP representative, E. Jerusalem (July 27, 1989); interview with H. Awartani.

24. See P. Ford and G. Moffett, "Israel Eases Restrictions to Encourage Palestinian Business," *Christian Science Monitor*, Jan. 9, 1991; Bainerman, *Jerusalem Post*, Jan. 4, 1991.

25. See *Netherlands Government Mission*, pp. 8, 10.

26. Ibid., p. 15.

27. Interview with UNDP representative.

28. Interview with H. Awartani.

29. Interview with UNDP representative; Quigley, p. 186; Bainerman, *Jerusalem Post*, Jan. 4, 1991.

30. See *Netherlands Government Mission*, p. 7.

31. Interview with H. Awartani.

32. American Near East Refugee Aid is one of the three largest organizations funded by USAID. ANERA is involved with development of the economic infrastructure, agriculture, industry, and water works.

33. Interview with UNDP representative.

34. Interview with staff members, Arab Development and Credit Co.

35. Interview with H. Awartani.

36. Interview with UNDP representative; interview with S. Dijani.

37. See Kahan, p. 40.

38. See Awartani, Al-Haq Conference paper.

39. Interview with staff members, Arab Development and Credit Co.; interview with UNDP representative.

40. Interview with C. Shammas.

41. Interview with S. Dijani.

42. Interview with Ramallah Poultry Cooperative representative, in Ramallah, West Bank (Aug. 17, 1989).

43. Interview with Ramallah Poultry Cooperative representative; interview with staff members, Arab Development and Credit Co.

44. Interview with staff members, Arab Development and Credit Co.; interview with UNDP representative.

45. Interview with Ramallah Poultry Cooperative Representative.

46. UNDP representative, *supra*, citing a high-ranking Israeli government official.

47. See Bainerman, *Jerusalem Post*, Jan. 4, 1991.

48. Interview with S. Hillele.

49. See Kahan, pp. 39–40; interview with S. Dijani.

50. See Kahan, pp. 40–41.

51. Interview with official, U.S. Consulate, in Jerusalem (July 12, 1989).

52. Interview with S. Dijani.

53. Interview with staff member, Arab Development and Credit Co.

54. Interview with staff members, Palestine Agricultural Relief Committee.

55. Interview with Save the Children relief workers (July 15, 1989).

56. Interview with organizers of the Beit Sahour Dairy Cooperative, in Bethlehem, (July 27, 1989).

57. Interview with S. Hillele, Economic Development Group.

58. Interview with staff members, Palestine Agricultural Relief Committee.

59. Ibid.

6. Collective Punishment

1. See Palestinian Agricultural Relief Committee, *Agricultural Development*, pp. 3–5; D. Williams, "Rural Economy Hit: Israelis Using Olives, Figs to Subdue Arabs," *Los Angeles Times*, Oct. 13, 1988, p. 1.

2. Interviews with numerous West Bank farmers and development workers; Palestinian Agricultural Relief Committee, *Agricultural Development*, pp. 3–5.

3. Jerusalem Media Centre, "Bitter Harvest," p. 14, citing *Ha'aretz*, March 29, 1989; Palestine Human Rights Information Center, *Uprising in Palestine* (Jerusalem: 1988).

4. Al-Haq, *Punishing a Nation*, p. 400.

5. See Jerusalem Media Centre, "Bitter Harvest"; Palestine Human Rights Information Center, *Uprising in Palestine*; files of the Arab Studies Center in E. Jerusalem; files of Al-Haq in Ramallah.

6. Interview with religious group relief worker in Jerusalem, June 25, 1988.

7. See A. Ashkar, *Middle East International* 18 (Sept. 8, 1989).

8. Jerusalem Media Centre, "Bitter Harvest," p. 15.

9. Interview with H. Awartani; *Christian Science Monitor*, Sept. 27, 1988; Al-Haq, *Punishing a Nation*, p. 402.

10. *Jerusalem Post*, Sept. 9, 1988, p. 24.

11. Al-Haq, *Punishing a Nation*, p. 401.

12. See Palestinian Agricultural Relief Committee, *Agricultural Development*, p. 5.

13. See Peretz, *Intifada*, p. 72.

14. Ibid., p. 67.

15. Interview with Omar Daoudi, Agricultural Engineers' Union and Cooperative Development Project (July 12, 1989), citing Jericho curfew which disrupted watermelon harvest; Palestinian Agricultural Relief Committee, *Agricultural Development*, p. 5.

16. See Peretz, *Intifada*, p. 68.

17. *Jerusalem Post*, Sept. 22, 1988, p. 1.

18. Quoted in *Christian Science Monitor*, Sept. 27, 1988, p. 1.

19. See Al-Haq, *Punishing a Nation*, pp. 402–06.

20. See Palestinian Agricultural Relief Committee, *Agricultural Development*, p. 4.

21. Interview with Palestinian relief workers in Gaza City (July 1989).

7. Land and Water

1. M. Benvenisti, *West Bank Handbook*, p. 115. Meron Benvenisti of the West Bank Data Project states: "Israeli authorities, in their quest to take possession of land in the territories, have been using every legal and quasi-legal means in the book and are inventing new ones to attain their objectives. . . . The declared plan objective is 'to disperse maximally large Jewish population in a relatively short period by using the settlement potential of the West Bank and to achieve the incorporation [of the West Bank] into the [Israeli] national system.'" He cites from the World Zionist Organization 1983–86 plan, which was based on the work of numerous Israeli government representatives, and, in his words, "cannot be viewed as other than the official land use plan for the West Bank." M. Benvenisti, *West Bank Data Project Survey*, pp. 27–30.

2. See M. Benvenisti, *West Bank Handbook*, pp. 120–21.

3. See M. Benvenisti, *West Bank Data Project Survey*, p. 30.

4. See Shehadeh, p. 36.

5. See M. Benvenisti, *West Bank Handbook*, p. 114.

6. Ibid., p. 116.

7. Ibid., pp. 116–17.

8. *Beit-El* case, *Ayoub v. Minister of Defense*, H.C. 606/78, 33(2) P.D. 113 (1979), English transl. in Meir Shamgar, ed., *Military Government in the Territories Administered by Israel 1967–1980* (Jerusalem: Hebrew University, 1982), p. 371, English case summary in 9 *IYBHR* 337, 377 (1979).

9. See M. Benvenisti, *West Bank Handbook*, p. 115.

10. See J. Brinkley, *New York Times*, May 24, 1991, p. A-3.

11. According to Meron Benvenisti, this method arose to satisfy a need to find more land for Jewish settlements after the late 1970s when other methods proved insufficient. M. Benvenisti, *West Bank Data Project Survey*, p. 32. Under the new approach, "Israeli officials . . . view 'all land as national patrimony, except what the [Arab] villages can prove is theirs under the narrowest interpretation of the law' . . . The assumption was that all uncultivated land in the West Bank would be seized if it was not registered." Ibid., quoting Ian Lustick, *Arabs in the Jewish State* (Austin: University of Texas Press, 1980), p. 171.

12. See M. Benvenisti, *West Bank Handbook*, pp. 114–15; M. Benvenisti, *West Bank Data Project Survey*, p. 3. By some accounts, Israel has seized land which has lain fallow for as little as one year. J. Brinkley, *New York Times*, May 24, 1991, A-3.

13. See M. Benvenisti, *West Bank Data Project Survey*, p. 32.

14. See M. Benvenisti, *West Bank Handbook*, p. 115.

15. This method of state land acquisition was approved by the Israel High Court of Justice in *Al-Nazer v. Commander of Judea and Samaria*, 36(1) P.D. 701 (1982), cited in E. Benvenisti, p. 75, n. 290. See also M. Benvenisti, *West Bank Data Project Survey*, p. 33.

16. See Shehadeh, *Occupier's Law*, pp. 23–24.

17. Ibid., p. 23; M. Benvenisti, *West Bank Data Project Survey*, p. 32.

18. See Shehadeh, *Occupier's Law*, pp. 22–23.

19. See M. Benvenisti, *West Bank Data Project Survey*, p. 34.

20. Of the total area under Israeli control, it has been calculated that at the very least one million dunams are either cultivable or are grazing land (Jerusalem Media Centre, "Bitter Harvest," p. 3). A mission sent by the Netherlands Government to the West Bank concluded that as a result of Israeli land acquisition in the West Bank, the area devoted to rainfed cultivation has fallen to one third of the 1964 level. (*Netherlands Government Mission*, p. 6). A West Bank Data Project researcher estimates that the area of cultivated land in the West Bank declined by 20 percent between 1967 and 1985 (See Kahan, pp. 18–19). According to Kate Rouhana, by the mid-1980s, work in Israel had attracted so many agricultural laborers that the area of land under cultivation in the territories diminished by 21 percent from the 1967 levels (Rouhana, p. 1). In contrast, Benvenisti asserts that there has been no significant decline in the extent of either irrigated or non-irrigated cultivation since 1967 (M. Benvenisti, *West Bank Handbook*, p. 3).

21. See *Netherlands Government Mission*, p. 7; M. Benvenisti, *West Bank Data Project Survey*, p. 19; Gharaibeh, p. 69; numerous interviews with West Bank Palestinians.

22. See *Netherlands Government Mission*, p. 7; see also Kahan, pp. 37–39.

23. See J. Broder, "Olive Trees Grow to Mystical Proportions," *Chicago Tribune*, Dec. 25, 1986, p. 5 (discussing political symbolism of olive trees in the West Bank).

24. Interviews with Bir Zeit University students and professors, in Ramallah (July-August 1989); interview with S. Hillele.

25. Interview with a West Bank Palestinian, near Ramallah (July 1989).

26. The committee was created pursuant to Military Order No. 172 of 1967.

27. See Shehadeh, *Occupier's Law*, pp. 29–33; M. Benvenisti, *West Bank Data Project Survey*, p. 34.

28. Interview with the *muhktar* (village leader) of Dura-Hebron and other village members, including owners of the disputed property in Dura-Hebron (July 1989).

29. Planting has become more difficult during the *intifada* because so many young Palestinian males in the village of Dura have been arrested and detained without charge for up to six months since the start of the uprising.

30. Interview with lawyer working with Al-Haq, Ramallah (July 1989).

31. See J. Dillman, "Water Rights in the Occupied Territories," 19(1) *Journal of Palestine Studies* 46, 47 (Autumn 1989), p. 47; Gharaibeh, p. 134.

32. Shehadeh, *Occupier's Law*, p. 153.

33. See Dillman, p. 53. Military Order No. 158 states that "it shall not be permissible for any person to set up or to assemble or to possess or to operate a water installation unless he has obtained a license from the area commander."

34. See Ze'ev Schiff and Ehud Ya'ari, *Intifada: The Palestinian Uprising—Israel's Third Front* (New York: Simon & Schuster, 1989), p. 97.

35. Interview with Yoreh Artzi, head of Department of Agriculture of the Civil Administration, at the Vulcani Institute near Bet Agon (Aug. 23, 1989); see also Kahan, pp. 25–26.

36. See Dillman, pp. 46–47.

37. See M. Benvenisti, *West Bank Handbook*, p. 223; Kahan, p. 20.

38. See "Hard Facts Defeat Israeli Researcher," *New York Times*, Oct. 21, 1989, p. A-18, citing M. Benvenisti; Jerusalem Media and Centre, "Bitter Harvest," p. 3.

39. See Dillman, p. 57.

40. Interview with Professor Kamaal Abdulfatah, Bir Zeit University, in Ramallah (July 31, 1989).

41. See Shehadeh, *Occupier's Law*, p. 154; M. Benvenisti, *West Bank Data Project Survey*, p. 114; see also Dillman, p. 56, discussing Israeli government claims.

42. See Quigley, p. 187; Dillman, p. 57; Gharaibeh, pp. 134–35; interview with K. Abdulfatah.

43. See Dillman, p. 55.

44. See M. Benvenisti, *West Bank Data Project Survey*, p. 14; Quigley, p. 187; Gharaibeh, p. 63.

45. See Shehadeh, *Occupier's Law*, p. 153; Dillman, p. 53; interview with G. El-Khatib.

46. See M. Benvenisti, *West Bank Handbook*, p. 224; Kahan, p. 114.

47. See M. Benvenisti, *West Bank Data Project Survey*, p. 14.

48. British Consulate, *West Bank: Water Resources and their Exploitation*, p. 12 (1978), as cited in Gharaibeh, p. 63.

49. See Dillman, p. 58.

50. Interview with Save the Children Relief workers (July 1989).

51. See Kahan, p. 114; M. Benvenisti, *West Bank Handbook*, p. 3; interview with K. A. Qutob; interview with S. Dijani. This finding is disputed by the *Netherlands Government Mission* (p. 6), which claims irrigated land area has doubled since 1967.

52. See Kahan, p. 114.

53. Ibid.; interview with S. Dijani.

54. See *Netherlands Government Mission*, p. 6.

55. See Shehadeh, *Occupier's Law*, p. 154; Dillman, p. 57; Gharaibeh, pp. 134–35.

56. See M. Benvenisti, *West Bank Handbook*, p. 224; Dillman, p. 58; M. Benvenisti, *West Bank Data Project Survey*, p. 14; Quigley, p. 187.

57. See M. Benvenisti, *West Bank Handbook*, p. 22.

58. Ibid.

59. See Dillman, p. 55; M. Benvenisti, *West Bank Handbook*, p. 224.

60. See Dillman, pp. 46–48.

61. See Shehadeh, *Occupier's Law*, p. 154, Dillman, pp. 56–58; *Netherlands Government Mission*, p. 11; interview with S. Dijani; interview with K. A. Qutob.

62. Interview with S. Dijani.

63. Interview with Ayn-Sultan farmer, in Ayn-Sultan (July, 1989); Dillman, pp. 56–58; Gharaibeh, pp. 63–64.

64. Interview with Ein El-Bida farmers (July 27, 1989).

65. Interview with H. Awartani; See also Dillman, p. 55.

66. Interview with K. A. Qutob (July 23, 1989); Kahan, p. 35.

67. For further information on land issues, see Shehadeh, *Occupier's Law*, pp. 17–50, 153–54; M. Benvenisti, *West Bank Handbook*, pp. 113–21, 223–25; M. Benvenisti and S. Khayat, *The West Bank and Gaza Atlas*; M. Benvenisti, *West Bank Data Project Survey*, pp. 19–37; Gharaibeh, *The Economies of the West Bank and Gaza Strip*, pp. 59–62. Addressing water issues, see Dillman, "Water Rights in the Occupied Territories"; M. Benvenisti, *West Bank Handbook*, p. 223; Gharaibeh, *The Economies of the West Bank and Gaza Strip*, pp. 62–64; Joyce Starr and Daniel Stoll, *U.S. Foreign Policy and Water Resources in the Middle East: Instrument for Peace and Development* (Washington, D.C.: Center for Strategic and International Studies, 1987).

Introduction

1. See Appendixes A and B for abstracts of military orders pertaining to agriculture and sample texts of those orders

2. E. Benvenisti, pp. 1–2.

3. See Schwarzenberger, vol. 2, pp. 163–64. See Appendix C for complete texts of international legal provisions cited in this paper.

4. Ibid., p. 178.

5. Lassa Oppenheim, *International Law*, H. Lauterpacht, ed., 7th ed., vol. 2 (London, New York: Longmans, Green, 1952).

8. The Hague Regulations and the Fourth Geneva Convention

1. See Shehadeh, *Occupier's Law*, p. xiii. For the text of major provisions of the Hague Convention, see Burns Weston, Richard Falk, Anthony D'Amato, *Basic Documents in International Law and World Order* (St. Paul, Minn.: West Publishing, 1980), pp. 88–95.

2. *Beit-El* case, *Ayoub v. Minister of Defense*, H.C. 606/78, 610/78, 33(2) P.D. 113 (1979) (international customary law is part of municipal law of Israel); *Dwikat v. Government of Israel*, (*Elon Moreh* case) H.C. 390/79, 34(1) P.D. 1 (1979) ("the Hague Rules, which bind the military administration in Judea and Samaria, being part of customary international law . . .").

3. See Ted Meron, "West Bank and Gaza: Human Rights and Humanitarian Law in the Period of Transition," 9 *IYBHR* 106 (1979).

4. See Ted Meron, "The Geneva Conventions as Customary Law," 81 *American Journal of International Law* 348 (1987); (hereinafter cited as *AJIL*); Ted Meron, *Human Rights and Humanitarian Norms as Customary Law* (New York: Oxford University Press, 1989), pp. 41–62.

5. Fourth Geneva Convention, Art. 2(2). See Meron, "West Bank and Gaza," pp. 106, 107. Both Israel and Jordan acceded to the Fourth Geneva Convention in 1951. See G. Willemin & R. Heacock, *The International Committee of the Red Cross* (Norwell, Mass.: Kluwer Academic Publications, 1984), pp. 175–76.

6. *International Review of the Red Cross*, 113 (Aug. 1970), pp. 426–28.

7. See Shehadeh, *Occupier's Law*, p. xi.

8. Meir Shamgar (then attorney general of Israel, later justice of the Israeli High Court of Justice), 1 *IYBHR* 262, 266.

9. See H. Cohn in Israel National Section of the International Commission of Jurists, *The Rule of Law in the Areas Administered by Israel* (Tel Aviv: Israel National Section of the International Commission of Jurists, 1981), pp. vii–viii; M. Benvenisti, *The West Bank Data Project Survey*, p. 37.

10. See Yoram Dinstein, "The International Law of Belligerent Occupation and Human Rights," 8 *IYBHR* 104 (1978), citing *Christian Ass'n for Holy Places v. Minister of Defence*, 26(1) P.D. 574, 580; *Sheikh Suleiman Abu-Hilu v. State of Israel*, H.C. 302/72, 27(2) P.D. 169, 177, English case summary in 5 *IYBHR* 384 (1975).

11. See Schwarzenberger, vol. 2, pp. 163–64.

12. See Shehadeh, *Occupier's Law*, p. 154.

13. See Fourth Geneva Convention, Art. 9.

14. Jean Pictet, ed., *Commentary: Fourth Geneva Convention Relative to the Protection of Civilian Persons in Time of War* (Geneva: International Committee of the Red Cross, 1958), p. 88.

15. See Fourth Geneva Convention, Art. 12; Oppenheim, p. 375.

16. See International Committee of the Red Cross, *ICRC Annual Report, 1972*, pp. 69–70. Egypt, Jordan, Lebanon, and Syria failed to respond to a similar request from the ICRC. *id.*

17. Professor Blum later became Israel's ambassador to the United Nations. See Shehadeh, *Occupier's Law*, p. xi.

18. Published in 3 *Israel Law Review* 279 (1968).

19. Whiteman, 2 *Digest of International Law*, 1163, quoting Arab League statement of Dec. 14, 1948, to King Abdullah of Jordan, cited in Cohen, *Human Rights*, p. 48.

20. See Cohen, *Human Rights*, p. 48.

21. Ibid., p. 53.

22. Fourth Geneva Convention, Art. 47, cited in Cohen, *Human Rights*, p. 53.

23. See Cohen, *Human Rights*, pp. 53–54, citing Pictet, pp. 273–75; Rideau, "Le probleme du respect des droits de l'homme dans les territoires occupes par Israel," 16 *Annuaire Francais de Droit International* (1970), pp. 204–32.

24. See Gerhard von Glahn, "Taxation Under Occupation," Al-Haq Conference paper, p. 13, citing Boyd, 1 *IYBHR* 370 (1971).

25. See von Glahn, *Occupation of Enemy Territory*, (Minneapolis: University of Minnesota Press, 1957), p. 43; von Glahn, Al-Haq Conference paper, pp. 13–4, citing Alan Gerson, 14 *Harvard International Law Journal*. 1, 13 (1973).

26. Concerning the theory of a sovereignty vacuum in the West Bank after 1948, E. Lauterpacht wrote, "Slight though the force of the partition Resolution might be, it is difficult to conceive of it as having opened up Palestine to the law of the jungle, to be carved up on the basis of first come first served." E. Lauterpacht, "Jerusalem and the Holy Places" (London: Anglo-Israel Association, pamphlet no. 19, Oct. 1968), p. 16, quoted in Cohen, *Human Rights*, p. 49.

27. See Eugene Rostow, "'Palestinian Self-Determination': Possible Futures for the Unallocated Territories of the Palestine Mandate," 5 *Yale Studies in World Public Order* 147, 160 (1979).

28. Nathaniel Lorch, 1 *IYBHR* 366 (1971).

29. See Cohen, *Human Rights*, p. 48.

30. See Adam Roberts, "Prolonged Military Occupation: The Israeli-Occupied Territories Since 1967," 84 *AJIL* 44, 52–70 (1990); Paust, von Glahn, and Woratsch, pp. 9–12.

31. See Cohen, *Human Rights*, pp. 52–53; Roberts, "Prolonged Military Occupation, pp. 44, 64–66; Paust, and von Glahn, and Woratsch, pp. 9–12.

32. Pictet, *Commentary*, as quoted in Cohen, *Human Rights*, p. 52.

33. See Shehadeh, *Occupier's Law*, p. xii.

34. Ibid.

35. Brigadier Shlomo Gazit, "The Administered Areas: Aspects of Israel's Policy," information briefing (Jerusalem: Ministry of Foreign Affairs, Information Division, 1972), pp. 19–20, quoted in Cohen, *Human Rights*, pp. 54–55.

36. *International Review of the Red Cross* 113, pp. 426–28, 429–30.

37. ICRC, *Annual Report, 1985*, p. 72.

38. The United Nations has been criticized by certain Israeli commentators for its alleged anti-Israeli bias. See, for example, D. Shefi, "Reports of the U.N. Special Committees," in Shamgar, *Military Government*, pp. 285–334. Certain Arab governments have criticized the United Nations for not taking sufficiently strong actions to ensure Israel's respect for international law. See Republic of

Syria, Palestine Arab Refugees Institution, *Resolutions Adopted by Different Organs of the United Nations on the Palestine Question 1947–53*, 2d ed. (Damascus: Republic of Syria, 1953), p. 4.

39. UN Security Council Resolution 607 (5 Jan. 1988), quoted in Shehadeh, *Occupier's Law*, p. xvi. See also UN Security Council Resolution 446 (22 March 1979); UN Security Council Resolution 465 (1 March 1980); UN General Assembly Resolution 32/91A (13 Dec. 1977); UN General Assembly Resolution 37/123A (16 Dec. 1982).

40. Quoted in Shehadeh, *Occupier's Law*, p. xvi.

41. See Cohen, *Human Rights*, p. 51.

42. See Meron, "West Bank and Gaza," pp. 106, 111.

43. Adam Roberts, "The Israeli-Occupied Territories, 1967–1988: The International Legal Framework of a Prolonged Occupation," Al-Haq Conference paper; Roberts, "Prolonged Military Occupation," p. 55.

44. Roberts, "Prolonged Military Occupation," p. 56.

45. Ibid., p. 55.

46. Meron, "West Bank and Gaza," pp. 106, 117.

47. See Francis Boyle, "Create the State of Palestine!" 25 *American-Arab Affairs* 85–105 (Summer 1988). For an argument which also draws upon the Namibia precedent, but which arrives at radically different conclusions, see Rostow, p. 147; and Eugene Rostow, interview published in *New York Times* and in *Ha'aretz*, Aug. 4, 1978, quoted at length in Shefi, "Reports of U.N. Special Committees," in Shamgar *Military Government*, pp. 285, 315–317.

48. *Namibia* case, 1971, International Court of Justice 16 (Advisory Opinion of June 21, 1971).

49. League of Nations Covenant, Art. 22.

50. League of Nations Covenant, Art. 22, para. 4.

51. League of Nations Covenant, Art. 22, para. 6.

52. See Boyle, p. 88.

53. See Mahnoush Arsanjani, 31 *International and Comparative Law Quarterly* 426 (1982).

54. See Boyle, p. 89, citing UN Charter, Art. 80(1). For text of the UN Charter, see Weston, Falk, and D'Amato, *Basic Documents*, p. 6.

55. 1950 International Court of Justice 128, 136–143 (Advisory Opinion of July 11, 1950). (Internatinal Court of Justice hereafter cited as I.C.J.)

56. 1955 I.C.J. 67, 77–78 (Advisory Opinion of June 7, 1955).

57. See Boyle, p. 91, citing UN General Assembly Resolution 2145, 21 U.N. GAOR Supp. (No. 16), p. 2, U.N. Doc. A\6416 (1966).

58. Ibid., p. 91, citing UN General Assembly Resolution 2403, 23 U.N. GAOR Supp. (No. 18) p. 3, U.N. Doc. A/7218 (1968). For a detailed listing of UN resolutions on the occupation of Namibia, see Roberts, "Prolonged Military Occupation," pp. 44, 49, n.9.

59. 1971 I.C.J. 16 (Advisory Opinion of June 21, 1971).

60. See Boyle, p. 92.

61. 1971 I.C.J. 55 (Advisory Opinion of June 21, 1971).

62. See Roberts, "Prolonged Military Occupation," p. 50, citing UN General Assembly Resoluton 2871 (XXVI)(Dec. 20, 1971).

63. See Boyle, p. 94. See also Quigley, pp. 48–52; "Prolonged Military Occupatin," pp. 44, 50.

64. See Roberts, "Prolonged Military Occupation," p. 69.

9. Agricultural Controls in the West Bank

1. See E. Benvenisti, p. 1.

2. See Cohen, *Human Rights*, p. 17, citing Pictet, *Commentary*, p. 275; Georg Schwarzenberger and E.D. Brown, *The Law of Armed Conflict*, (Stevens & Sons, Ltd., 1968), pp. 166–69; von Glahn, *Occupation of Enemy Territory*, pp. 31–32; Hans Kelson, *Principles of International Law* (New York: Holt, Rinehart and Wilson, 1952), p. 73.

3. Cohen, *Human Rights*, pp. 17–18.

4. See Schwarzenberger, vol. 2, p. 201; Gerson, *Israel, the West Bank and International Law*, p. 4; von Glahn, "Taxation Under Occupation."

5. Gerhard von Glahn, *Law Among Nations: An Introduction to Public International Law* (New York: Macmillan, 1981), pp. 672–73. See also Ernst Feilchenfeld, *The International Economic Law of Belligerent Occupation*, Carnegie Endowment for International Peace Monograph Series, No. 6 (New York: Columbia University Press, 1942, reprinted in 1971), p. 89, para. 324–25.

6. Schwarzenberger, vol. 2, p. 201.

7. Feilchenfeld, p. 86, para. 314.

8. Cohen, *Human Rights*, p. 248, citing von Glahn, *Occupation of Enemy Territory*, pp. 207–08; von Glahn, *Law Among Nations*, pp. 685–86.

9. Oppenheim cites all five provisions; von Glahn cites only the first three.

10. von Glahn, *Law Among Nations*, (3d ed., 1976), p. 685; Oppenheim, pp. 400–01.

11. Oppenheim, p. 401; von Glahn, *Law Among Nations*, p. 685. See also U.S. Department of State, "Memorandum of Law concerning alleged rights of Israel to develop new oil fields in Sinai and the Gulf of Suez," 16 *International Legal Materials* 733, 743–44, n. 14 (1977).

12. *Cooperative Society v. Commander of the I.D.F.*, H.C. 393/82, 37(4) P.D. 785, excerpted in 14 *IYBHR* 301, 304 (1984). See also *Dwikat v. Government of Israel*.

13. U.S. State Department of State, "Memorandum of Law."

14. See Ernst Fraenkel, *Military Occupation and the Rule of Law: Occupation Government in the Rhineland* (Oxford, Toronto: Institute of World Affiars, 1944), p. 17.

15. Ibid., pp. 17–20, 97, 104–05.

16. See Oppenheim, pp. 434, 436–37; Georg Schwarzenberger and E. D. Brown, *Manual of International Law*, 6th ed. (Milton, U.K.: Professional Books, 1976), p. 160.

17. See von Glahn, *Law Among Nations*, p. 685; Cohen, *Human Rights*, pp. 17–18; Gerson, *Israel*, pp. 7–11.

18. Dinstein, citing Hague Regulations, Art. 43.

19. Von Glahn, *Law Among Nations*, pp. 687–88.

20. Gerson, *Israel*, pp. 7–8.

21. See Dinstein, pp. 104, 112.

22. Belgo-German Mixed Arbitral Tribunal (1925), cited in Schwarzenberger, vol. 2, p. 192.

23. Schwarzenberger, vol. 2, pp. 192–93, citing 5 M.A.T. 712, 716.

24. See Schwarzenberger, vol. 2, pp. 192–93.

25. Ibid., pp. 180–83, 192–93.

26. Von Glahn, *Law Among Nations*, p. 688.

27. U.S. Department of the Army Pamphlet No. 27–161–2, *International Law, Volume II* (1962), p. 248.

28. Esther Cohen, "The Fourth Geneva Convention and Human Rights in the Israeli Occupied Territories, 1967–1977," doctoral thesis, Hebrew University (Sept. 27, 1981).

29. Ibid., p. 33.

30. See von Glahn, *Law Among Nations*, p. 685; Cohen, "Fourth Geneva Convention," pp. 17–18; Gerson, *Israel*, pp. 7–11; Dinstein, pp. 104, 112, citing Hague Regulations, Art. 43. Von Glahn writes that the occupant may pass new laws "for the benefit of the population" which "are not dictated by his own military necessity and requirements." Von Glahn, *Occupation of Enemy Territory*, p. 43, n. 14.

31. U.S. Department of the Army Pamphlet No. 27–161–2, p. 169.

32. Feilchenfeld, p. 87, para. 316, and p. 92, para. 340.

33. See Gerson, *Israel*, p. 8; Cohen, *Human Rights*, p. 189.

34. Cohen, *Human Rights*, p. 189.

35. See Gerson, *Israel*, p. 8, citing Myres McDougal and Florentino Feliciano, *Law and Minimum World Public Order* (New Haven: Yale University Press, 1961), p. 746.

36. Pictet, cited in Cohen, *Human Rights*, p. 190.

37. Gerson, *Israel*, p. 10. Yoram Dinstein remarks, "The concern of the occupant for the needs of the civilian population in an occupied territory is not always genuine, and at times it is imperative to guard the inhabitants from the bear's hug of the occupant." Dinstein, p. 112. As a solution, Gerson suggests that the common law jurisprudence regarding trustees be applied to the occupant. Gerson would apply the trusteeship standard starting from the presumption that the occupant was acting illegally: "An occupant undertaking institutional and legal reform will be acting under the rebuttable presumption of illegality, pending a showing that such reform was either minor in character, necessitated by public order and security needs, or, if fundamental in scope, based on genuine humanitarian considerations." Gerson, p. 11. Adam Roberts argues that the idea of trusteeship is inherent in the law of belligerent occupation, and that Israel is not meeting its responsibilities as trustee. See Roberts, "Prolonged Military Occupation," pp. 44, 68; Roberts, Al-Haq Conference paper.

38. *Christian Association for the Holy Places v. Minister of Defense*, 26(1) P.D. 574, 582; *Cooperative Society v. Commander of the I.D.F.*

39. Cassese, p. 15.

40. *Cooperative Society v. Commander of the I.D.F.*, p. 304; see also H.C.J. 390/79 in 9 *IYBHR* 345 (1979).

41. But see *Tabib v. Minister of Defense*, H.C. 202/81, 36(2) P.D. 622, English case summary in 13 *IYBHR* 364 (1983). This case allows the interests of the Jewish settlers to be factored into the analysis as part of the "local population."

42. *Cooperative Society v. Commander of the I.D.V.*, p. 302.

43. Von Glahn, *Law Among Nations*, p. 686.

44. *Cooperative Society v. Commander of the I.D.F.*, p. 304.

10. West Bank Land and Water Resource Control

1. See Dillman, p. 46.

2. Ibid., p. 53.

3. Ibid., p. 52.

4. Hague Regulations, Art. 46.

5. See Dillman, pp. 56, 61.

6. Fourth Geneva Convention, Art. 46.

7. Hague Regulations, Art. 46.

8. Dillman, p. 60.

9. Ibid., p. 53.

10. Julius Stone, *Legal Controls of International Conflict: A Treatise on the Dynamics of Disputes and War Law* (New York: Rinehart, 1959), p. 697. The resolution of the London International Law Conference of 1943 stated, "The rights of the occupant do not include any right to dispose of property, rights or interests for purposes other than the maintenance of public order and safety in the occupied territory . . . this applies whether such property, rights or interests are those of the State or of private persons or bodies." Quoted in U.S. Department of State, "Memorandum of Law," p. 743, n. 14.

11. *Singapore Oil Stocks* case, Wyatt, C. J., 51 *AJIL* p. 808 (1957).

12. See Dillman, p. 60.

13. U.S. State Department, "Memorandum of Law," pp. 745–46.

14. M. Benvenisti, *The West Bank Data Project Survey*, p. 31

15. See von Glahn, *Law Among Nations*, p. 683.

16. *Beit-El* case, *Ayoub v. Minister of Defense*, cited in Shamgar, *Military Government*, pp. 371–98.

17. Cited in Quigley, p. 175, quoting *Ayoub v. Minister of Defense*.

18. *Elon Moreh* case, *Dwikat v. Government of Israel*, cited in Shamgar, *Military Government*, p. 404.

19. Gush Emunim (Bloc of the Faithful) is a religiously motivated movement which favors the construction of Jewish settlements in the West Bank and Gaza as a means of preventing Israeli withdrawal from the territories. M. Benvenisti, *West Bank Handbook*, p. 126.

20. Shehadeh, *Occupier's Law*, p. 20.

21. *Dwikat v. Government of Israel*, in Shamgar, *Military Government*, pp. 404, 428. See also M. Benvenisti, *West Bank Data Project Survey*, p. 31; Quigley, pp. 176, 178.

22. See M. Benvenisti, *West Bank Data Project Survey*, p. 31; Shehadeh, *Occupier's Law*, p. 37.

23. See Shehadeh, *Occupier's Law*, p. 37.

24. See M. Benvenisti, *West Bank Data Project Survey*, p. 31.

25. See M. Benvenisti, *West Bank Handbook*, pp. 16–17.

26. See Schwarzenberger, vol. 2, p. 246.

27. See M. Benvenisti, *West Bank Handbook*, p. 116.

28. Jordanian Law No. 2 of 1953, "Expropriation of Land for Public Purposes," in Shehadeh, *Occupier's Law*, p. 37, citing *Official Gazette of Jordan* 1130 (1 Jan. 1953).

29. Military Orders No. 131, 321, 949.

30. M. Benvenisti, *West Bank Data Project Survey*, p. 31.

31. See Shehadeh, *Occupier's Law*, pp. 37–38.

32. *Tabib v. Minister of Defense.*

33. See M. Benvenisti, *West Bank Data Project Survey*, p. 32; Shehadeh, *Occupier's Law*, p. 38.

34. See *Tabib v. Minister of Defense*. Land confiscation for a road that bypassed Palestinian population centers but connected Jewish settlements was found to benefit incidentally the Palestinian population.

35. E. Benvenisti, p. 54, citing *Electricity Co. for the District of Jerusalem v. Minister of Defense*, H.C. 351/80 27(1) P.D. 124, 138 (1972), English case summary in 11 *IYBHR* 364 (1981), and *Jama'iat Iscan v. Commander of IDF in Judea and Samaria*, 37 (4) P.D. 785 (1983); *Abu-Aita v. Commander of the Judea and Samaria Region.*

36. Oppenheim, p. 397.

37. Schwarzenberger, vol. 2, p. 680.

38. Use of state land for permanent settlements would violate the law of usufruct since that law allows use only for the duration of the occupation. (This issue is discussed in Chapter 11.)

39. See M. Benvenisti, *West Bank Data Project Survey*, p. 31; Shehadeh, *Occupier's Law*, pp. 17–22; Quigley, p. 178.

40. See Roberts, "Prolonged Military Occupation," pp. 44, 91 (1990); Shehadeh, *Occupier's Law*, p. 22.

41. See Quigley, p. 178; M. Benvenisti, *West Bank Data Project Survey*, p. 31.

42. Shehadeh, *Occupier's Law*, p. 21.

43. Ibid., p. 22.

44. Ibid.

45. See M. Benvenisti, *West Bank Data Project Survey*, p. 33; relevant materials reprinted in Richard Clifford Tute, *The Ottoman Land Laws* (Jerusalem: Greek Convent Press, 1927).

46. Ottoman Land Code of 1858, Art. 103, quoted in M. Benvenisti, *West Bank Data Project Survey*, p. 33.

47. See Shehadeh, *Occupier's Law*, p. 24, citing *Jordanian Official Gazette* 1135 (1 March 1953); M. Benvenisti, *West Bank Data Project Survey*, p. 33.

48. M. Benvenisti, *West Bank Data Project Survey*, p. 33.

49. D. Shefi, "Reports of U.N. Special Committees," in Shamgar, *Military Government*, pp. 285, 318.

50. See Shehadeh, *Occupier's Law*, p. 23.

51. See Jesse Dukeminier and James E. Krier, *Property*, 2d ed. (Boston: Little, Brown, & Co., 1988), pp. 86–103.

52. M. Benvenisti, *West Bank Data Project Survey*, p. 33.

53. See Shehadeh, *Occupier's Law*, p. 26.

54. Schwarzenberger, vol. 2, p. 245.

55. Ottoman Land Code of 1858, Art. 103, quoted in M. Benvenisti, *West Bank Data Project Survey*, p. 33.

56. See M. Benvenisti, *West Bank Data Project Survey*, p. 34.

11. Settlements

1. Roberts, "Prolonged Military Occupation"; M. Benvenisti, *The West Bank Handbook*, p. 64.

2. See J. Brinkley, *New York Times*, May 24, 1991, A-3; "Amid Arab Protests, Israel Keeps Building," *Newsday*, July 5, 1991, p. 4.

3. See M. Benvenisti, *The West Bank Data Project Survey*, p. 35. See also Shehadeh, *Occupier's Law*, pp. 22–41.

4. See Roberts, "Prolonged Military Occupation," citing UN resolutions.

5. Shefi, "Reports of U.N. Special Committees," in Shamgar, *Military Government*, pp. 285, 314–15.

6. U.S. Department of State, File No. P780065–0030, in 72 *AJIL* 908–11, 910 (1978).

7. See R. Owen, *New York Times*, "Shamir's Hardline Stance Perplexes Washington," May 3, 1990.

8. See J. Miller, "Nowhere to go," *New York Times Magazine*, July 21, 1991, p. 32.

9. See Dinstein.

10. Roberts, "Prolonged Military Occupation," p. 85. See also Quigley, p. 177.

11. See Peretz, *Intifada*, p. 27, citing *Jerusalem Post International*, Feb. 14, 1987.

12. *Ayoub v. Minister of Defense* (Landau concurring), in Shamgar, *Military Government*, pp. 371, 392.

13. Roberts, "Prolonged Military Occupation," p. 85.

14. See Shehadeh, *Occupier's Law*, p. 45.

15. U.S. Department of State, "Memorandum of Law."

16. *Ayoub v. Minister of Defense*, in Shamgar, *Military Government*, pp. 371, 392; see also *Dwikat v. Government of Israel*, in Shamgar, *Military Government*, p. 404.

17. Quigley, p. 177, quoting "Israeli Settlements in Occupied Territories," 19 *Review of the International Commission of Jurists*, 27, 30–32 (1977).

18. See M. Benvenisti, *West Bank Handbook*, pp. 225–26.

19. Ibid., p. 63.

20. Moishe Dayan in interview with Goldstein for the Israeli newspaper *'Ma'ariv*, 3 Oct. 1980, quoted in Cohen, *Human Rights*, p. 148.

12. Enforcement of International Law

1. For a thorough discussion of the protecting power institution as it applies to the West Bank, see Al-Haq/Law in the Service of Man, *Annual Report, 1989* (Ramallah, West Bank: Al-Haq, 1989). chap. 19.

2. While a well-developed court system existed in the West Bank at the time of occupation, Military Order No. 104 divested these courts of all power to review actions of military government authorities. See Cohen, *Human Rights*, p. 79.

3. See F. Siordet, *The Geneva Conventions of 1949: The Question of Scrutiny* (Geneva: International Commission of the Red Cross, 1953), pp. 26, 44–45; Pictet, p. 88; U.S. Army Pamphlet 27–161–2, p. 352, citing the Fourth Geneva Convention, Art. 9.

4. Fourth Geneva Convention, Arts. 9, 12; Oppenheim, p. 375.

5. See Schwarzenberger, vol. 2, p. 351; Oppenheim, pp. 374–75. Pictet states that "the whole Convention shows that it was intended to exclude any possibility of the protected persons not having the benefit of a Protecting Power or a substitute for such a Power." Pictet, p. 9; see also ibid., p. 92.

6. For a historical background of the protecting power, see Siordet, pp. 3–24. Protecting powers since the Franco-Prussian War have been as follows: Franco-Prussian War (1870–1871)—England for France; United States, Switzerland, and Russia for Germany. Sino-Japanese War (1894–1895)—United States for both belligerents. Boer War (1899–1902)—United States to a limited extent for both belligerents. Spanish-American War (1898)—England for the United States; France and Austria-Hungary for Spain. Greco-Turkish War (1897)—Germany for Turkey; England, France, and Russia for Greece. Russo-Japanese War (1904–1905)—United States for Japan; France for Russia. Italo-Turkish War (1911–1912)—Germany for both belligerents. Balkan Wars (1912–1913)—France and Russia for Montenegro. World War I (1914–1918)—Switzerland for Germany. Sino-Soviet War (1929)—Germany for both belligerents. World War II (1939–1945)—Spain for Japan in the United States; Sweden for Japan in Hawaii; Switzerland for Japan in American Samoa. At one time Switzerland was the protecting power for thirty-five belligerent countries. Toward the end of World War II, Switzerland and Sweden between them were acting as protecting powers for practically all the belligerent states. (Source: U.S. Army Pamphlet 27-161-2.)

7. Pictet on the Fourth Geneva Convention, Art. 11.

8. Fourth Geneva Convention, Art. 11. See also Pictet, p. 106; U.S. Army Pamphlet 27-161-2, pp. 352–53.

9. Oppenheim, p. 375.

10. U.S. Army Pamphlet 27-161-2, p. 77, citing Fourth Geneva Convention, Art. 12. See also Oppenheim, p. 375.

11. See U.S. Army Pamphlet 27-161-2, p. 77.

12. Ibid., p. 354.

13. See D. Betz, *The Intifada, the United Nations and the Non-Governmental Organizations* (Geneva: The International Coordinating Committee for NGOs on the Question of Palestine, 1989), p. 87; Al-Haq/Law in the Service of Man, *Annual Report, 1989*, chapter 19. Several Israeli commentators contend that UNSCOP and other United Nations bodies are strongly biased against Israel. See

Shefi, "Reports of the U.N. Special Committees," in Shamgar, *Military Government*, pp. 285–334. Conversely, certain Arab governments have criticized the United Nations for "encouraging Jewish defiance" of international law (Republic of Syria, *Resolutions Adopted*, p. 4).

14. See International Committee of the Red Cross, *ICRC Annual Report, 1972*, pp. 69–70. Egypt, Jordan, Lebanon and Syria refused to respond to similar requests from the ICRC. See Al-Haq/Law in the Service of Man, *Annual Report, 1989*, chap. 19.

15. See Al-Haq, *Punishing a Nation*, pp. 97–122; *ICRC Annual Report, 1970*; *International Review of the Red Cross* 113, pp. 429–30; Cohen, *Human Rights*, p. 54.

16. See Boyle, pp. 85–105.

17. Ibid.; Al-Haq/Law in the Service of Man, *Annual Report, 1989*, chap. 19.

18. See *New York Times*, Nov. 2, 1990, p. A-1.

19. See Cohen, *Human Rights*, pp. 80–81. For a detailed discussion of the basis of High Court jurisdiction and its legality, see E. Nathan, "Power of Supervision of the High Court of Justice Over Military Government," in Shamgar, *Military Government*, pp. 109–69.

20. *Ayoub v. Minister of Defense*, in Shamgar, *Military Government*, p. 371.

21. *Dwikat v. Government of Israel*, in Shamgar, *Military Government*, p. 404.

22. As a contracting party, Israel is still bound to abide by the Fourth Geneva Convention regardless of whether it has passed incorporating legislation. Article 26 of the Vienna Convention on the Law of Treaties states, "Every treaty in force is binding upon the parties to it and must be performed by them in good faith." (text in Weston, Falk, and D'Amato, *Basic Documents*, pp. 59, 63, 65).

23. See Dinstein, pp. 104, 108.

24. *Mustafa v. Military Commander of the Judea and Samaria Region*, H.C. 629/82, 37(1) P.D. 158, excerpted in 14 *IYBHR* 313, 315 (1984); *Cooperative Society v. Commander of the I.D.F.*

25. Nathan, in Shamgar, *Military Government*, p. 111.

26. Shehadeh, *Occupier's Law*, p. 97.

27. Ibid.

28. *Ayoub v. Minister of Defense*.

29. *Dwikat v. Government of Israel*; *Ha'etzni v. State of Israel*, 34(3) P.D. 595 (1980).

30. See E. Benvenisti, p. 52.

31. Ibid., p. 53, citing *Abu-Gosh v. Military Commander of the Corridor to Jerusalem*, 7 P.D. 941, 943 (1953), and *Ayoub v. Minister of Defense*. See also Cohen, *Human Rights*, p. 88 (the extent of the High Court's review over actions justified on grounds of security is to determine whether the security claim is *bona fide*). The court has also stated that it would invalidate governmental acts which are "unreasonable or an abuse of power." *Al-Sayad v. Commander of Judea and Samaria*, H.C. 771/80, 35(3) P.D. 219, English case summary in 11 *IYBHR* 364, 365 (1981).

32. Shamgar, *Military Government*, p. 150.

33. *Hilu v. Government of Israel*, 27(2) P.D. 177 (1973), quoted in Shamgar, *Military Government*, p. 150.

34. *Korematsu v. United States*, 323 U.S. 214 (1944).

35. Shamgar, *Military Government*, p. 155, quoting *Hilu v. Government of Israel*.

36. *Ayoub v. Minister of Defense*, p. 332.

37. *Falah Hassin Ibrahim Amirah v. Minister of Defense*, H.C. 258/79, 34(1) P.D. 90 (1980), English transl. in Shamgar, *Military Government*, p. 398.

38. See Shamgar, *Military Government*, pp. 400–01.

39. Nathan, in Shamgar, *Military Government*, p. 153.

40. *Taha v. Minister of the Interior*, H.C. 658, 660–62/80, 35 (1) P.D. 249, English case summary in 11 *IYBHR* 361 (1981).

41. *Al-Sayad v. Commander of Judea and Samaria*.

42. E. Benvenisti, pp. 53–54. Benvenisti does not mention *Samara and Ne'imat v. Commander of Judea and Samaria Region* (H.C. 802/79, 34[4] P.D. 1, English case summary in 11 *IYBHR* 362 [1981]), in which the High Court ordered the military commander to issue a permit of permanent residence to a Palestinian man who was living in Germany but wished to be reunited with his wife who lived in the West Bank. The commander had refused the permit for security reasons.

43. See E. Benvenisti, p. 54.

44. Feilchenfeld, p. 89. para. 325. See also Dinstein.

45. See *Kawasme v. Minister of Defense*, H.C. 698/80, 35(1) P.D. 617, English case summary in 11 *IYBHR* 349 (1981) (allowing the military government to deport popularly elected West Bank mayors).

46. See E. Benvenisti, p. 52, citing *Jerusalem Electric* case.

47. E. Benvenisti, p. 54, citing *Jerusalem Electric*; *Jama'iat Iscan v. Commander of IDF in Judea and Samaria*,37(4) P.D. 785, 810 (1983); *Abu-Aita v. Commander of Judea and Samaria*.

48. *Tabib v. Minister of Defense*. See also E. Benvenisti, p. 56; *Cooperative Society v. Commander of the I.D.F.*

49. *Abu-Aita v. Commander of the Judea and Samaria*. Dinstein's test is described in 2 *Tel Aviv University Law Review* 505 (1972, Hebrew), and 8 *IYBHR* 104 (1978, English).

50. Dinstein, p. 113.

51. *Yick Wo v. Hopkins* 118 U.S. 356 (1886).

52. See Roberts, "Prolonged Military Occupation."

53. Hague Regulations, Arts. 48, 49.

54. See E. Benvenisti, pp. 34, 35.

55. See Marc Stephens, *Taxation in the Occupied West Bank 1967–1989* (Ramallah, West Bank: Al-Haq/Law in the Service of Man, 1990), pp. 49–56.

56. See Cohen, *Human Rights*, p. 86.

57. Eli Nathan, "Supervision by the High Court of Justice," in Shamgar, *Military Government*, pp. 165–66.

58. See Paust, von Glahn, and Woratsch, p. 49; E. Benvenisti, p. 54.

59. *Kawasme et al. v. Minister of Defense*, H.C. 320/80, 35(3) P.D. 113, English case summary in 11 *IYBHR* 344 (1981):

60. Fourth Geneva Convention, Art. 49.

61. *Kawasme II*, (*Kawasme et al. v. Ministry of Defense*, H.C. 698/80, 35(1) P.D. 617) as translated in 11 *IYBHR* 350–51 (1981).

62. See E. Benvenisti, p. 56.

63. Ibid.

64. See Shehadeh, *Occupier's Law*, pp. 37–39.

65. See Paust, von Glahn, and Woratsch, p. 58.

66. See Shehadeh, *Occupier's Law*, pp. 88–89; E. Benvenisti, pp. 48–49.

67. E. Benvenisti, p. 56.

68. Ibid.

69. See Paust, von Glahn, and Woratsch, p. 58; E. Benvenisti, p. 49; Shehadeh, *Occupier's Law*, p. 88.

70. See Paust, von Glahn, and Woratsch, p. 58.

71. See E. Benvenisti, p. 49.

72. See Cohen, *Human Rights*, p. 80 (citing A. Pach, 7 *IYBHR* 222 [1977]).

73. See E. Benvenisti, p. 49 (citing, *Shmalawi v. Objection Committee*, 39[4] P.D. 598 [1985] and *Al-Nazer v. Commander of Judea and Samaria*, 36[1] P.D. 701, 707 [1982].

74. Quoted in Paust, von Glahn, and Woratsch, p. 58.

75. *Al-Nazer v. Commander of Judea and Samaria*. See also E. Benvenisti, p. 75, n. 290 and p. 49, n. 261.

76. See Paust, von Glahn, and Woratsch, pp. 58–59; Shehadeh, *Occupier's Law*, pp. 87–88.

77. Paust, von Glahn, and Woratsch, p. 59.

78. Ibid.

79. E. Benvenisti, p. 57.

Conclusion

1. Fourth Geneva Convention, Art. 1. For a detailed discussion of third-party government enforcement of international law, see M. Stephens, Al-Haq/Law in the Service of Man, "Enforcement of International Law in the Israeli-Occupied Territories" (Ramallah, West Bank, Al-Haq, 1989).

2. Pictet, p. 15.

3. R. Owen, *New York Times*, "Shamir's Hardline Stance Perplexes Washington," May 3, 1990.

4. 22 U.S.C. § 5001 et seq.

5. Executive Order No. 12204 (Mar. 27, 1980), 19 U.S.C. § 2462.

6. Interview with UNDP representative; interview with K. Abdulfatah.

7. See Kahan, p. 57.

BIBLIOGRAPHY

BOOKS

Al-Haq/Law in the Service of Man. *Punishing a Nation: Human Rights Violations During the Palestinian Uprising, December 1987–1988.* Ramallah, West Bank: Al-Haq, 1988.

Arian, Asher. *Politics in Israel, the Second Generation.* Chatham, N.J.: Chatham House, 1985.

Aruri, Naseer, ed. *Occupation: Israel Over Palestine.* Belmont, Mass.: Association of Arab-American University Graduates, 1983.

Awartani, Hisham. "Agriculture." In *A Palestinian Agenda for the West Bank and Gaza,* ed. Emile Nakhleh. Washington, D.C.: American Enterprise Institute, 1980.

Baheh, Simha. *West Bank Data Project Report.* Jerusalem: Jerusalem Post, 1989.

Benvenisti, Eyal. *Legal Dualism: The Absorption of the Occupied Territories into Israel.* Boulder, Colo.: Westview Press, 1990.

Benvenisti, Meron. *The West Bank Data Project: A Survey of Israel's Policies.* Washington, D.C.: American Enterprise Institute, 1984.

———. *West Bank Data Project 1986 Report.* Jerusalem: Jerusalem Post, 1986.

———. *The West Bank Handbook: A Political Lexicon.* Jerusalem: Jerusalem Post, 1986.

Benvenisti, Meron, and Shlomo Khayat. *The West Bank and Gaza Atlas.* Jerusalem: Jerusalem Post, 1988.

Betz, D. *The Intifada, the United Nations and the Non-Governmental Organizations.* Geneva: The International Coordinating Committee for Non-Governmental Organizations on the Question of Palestine, 1989.

Bill, James A., and Carl Leiden. *Politics in the Middle East*. Texas: Little, Brown & Co., 1984.

Cohen, Esther. *Human Rights in the Israeli-Occupied Territories: 1967–82*. U.K.: Manchester University Press, 1985.

Dukeminier, Jesse, and James E. Krier. *Property*. 2d ed. Boston: Little, Brown, & Co., 1988.

Elizur, Yaval, and Eliahu Salpeter. *Who Rules Israel?* New York: Harper & Row, 1973.

Feilchenfeld, Ernst. *The International Economic Law of Belligerent Occupation*. Carnegie Endowment for International Peace Monograph Series, no. 6. New York: Columbia University Press, 1942, reprinted in 1972.

Fraenkel, Ernst. *Military Occupation and the Rule of Law: Occupation Government in the Rhineland*. Oxford and Toronto: Institute of World Affairs, 1944.

Gerson, Allan. *Israel, the West Bank, and International Law*. Lanham, Md.: Biblio Distribution Center, 1978.

Gharaibeh, Fawzi. *The Economies of the West Bank and Gaza Strip*. Boulder, Colo.: Westview Press, 1985.

Graham-Brown, Sarah. "The Economic Consequences of the Occupation." In *Occupation: Israel Over Palestine*, ed. Naseer H. Aruri. Belmont, Mass.: Association of Arab-American University Graduates, 1983.

Israel National Section of the International Commission of Jurists. *The Rule of Law in the Areas Administered by Israel*. Tel Aviv: Israel National Section of the International Commission of Jurists, 1981.

Kahan, David. *Agriculture and Water Resources in the West Bank and Gaza (1967–1987)*. Jerusalem: Jerusalem Post, 1987.

Kelson, Hans. *Principles of International Law*. New York: Holt, Rinehart & Wilson, 1952.

Khouri, Fred J. *The Arab-Israeli Dilemma*. 3d ed. Syracuse, N.Y.: Syracuse University Press, 1985.

Lustick, Ian. *Arabs in the Jewish State*. Austin: University of Texas Press, 1980.

Mansfield, Peter. *A History of the Middle East*. New York: Viking, 1991.

McDougal, Myres, and Florentino Feliciano. *Law and Minimum World Public Order*. New Haven: Yale University Press, 1961.

Meron, Ted. *Human Rights and Humanitarian Norms as Customary Law*. New York: Oxford University Press, 1989.

Oppenheim, Lassa. *International Law*, ed. H. Lauterpacht. 7th ed. London and New York: Longmans, Green, 1952.

Palestine Human Rights Information Center. *Uprising in Palestine*. Jerusalem: 1988.

Paust, Jordan, Gerhard von Glahn, and G. Woratsch. *Inquiry into the Israeli-Military Court System in the Occupied West Bank and Gaza*. Geneva: International Commission of Jurists, 1989.

Peretz, Don. *Intifada*. Boulder, Colo.: Westview Press, 1990.

———. *The Government and Politics of Israel*. Boulder, Colo.: Westview Press, 1979.

———. *The West Bank: History, Politics, Society, and Economy*. Boulder, Colo.: Westview Press, 1986.

Pictet, Jean, ed. *Commentary: Fourth Geneva Convention Relative to the Protection of Civilian Persons in Time of War*. Geneva: International Committee of the Red Cross. 1958.

Quigley, John. *Palestine and Israel: A Challenge to Justice*. Durham, N.C.: Duke University Press, 1990.

Sandler, Shmuel, and Hillel Frisch. *Israel, the Palestinians, and the West Bank: A Study of Intercommunal Conflict*. Lexington, Mass.: Lexington Books, 1984.

Schiff, Ze'ev, and Ehud Ya'ari. *Intifada: The Palestinian Uprising—Israel's Third Front*. New York: Simon & Schuster, 1989.

Schwarzenberger, Georg. *International Law*. London: Stevens & Sons, Ltd., 1968.

Schwarzenberger, Georg, and E. D. Brown. *Manual of International Law*. 6th ed. Milton, U.K.: Professional Books, 1976.

———. *The Law of Armed Conflict*. London: Stevens & Sons, Ltd., 1968.

Shamgar, Meir, ed. *Military Government in the Territories Administered by Israel 1967–1980*. Jerusalem: Hebrew University Jerusalem, Faculty of Law, Harry Sacher Institute for Legislature Research and Comparative Law, 1982.

Shehadeh, Raja. *Occupier's Law: Israel and the West Bank*. 2d ed. Washington, D.C.: Institute for Palestine Studies, 1989.

Shehadeh, Raja, and Jonathan Kuttab. *The West Bank and the Rule of Law*. Geneva: International Commission of Jurists, 1980.

Siordet, F. *The Geneva Convention of 1949: The Question of Scrutiny*. Geneva: International Committee of the Red Cross, 1953.

Starr, Joyce, and Daniel Stoll. *U.S. Foreign Policy and Water Resources in the Middle East: Instrument for Peace and Development*. Washington, D.C.: Center for Strategic and International Studies, 1987.

Stephens, Marc. *Taxation in the Occupied West Bank, 1967–1989*. Ramallah, West Bank: Al-Haq/Law in the Service of Man, 1990.

Stone, Julius. *Legal Controls of International Conflict: A Treatise on the Dynamics of Disputes and War Law*. New York: Rinehart, 1959.

Syria, Republic of, Palestine Arab Refugees Institution. *Resolutions Adopted by Different Organs of the United Nations on the Palestine Question 1947–53*. 2d ed. Damascus: Republic of Syria, 1953.

Tute, Richard Clifford. *The Ottoman Land Laws*. Jerusalem: Greek Convent Press, 1927.

U.S. Department of State. *Country Reports on Human Rights Practices for 1982*. Washington, D.C.: U.S. Government Printing Office, 1983.

Von Glahn, Gerhard. *Occupation of Enemy Territory*. Minneapolis: University of Minnesota Press, 1957.

————. *Law Among Nations: An Introduction to Public International Law*. New York: Macmillan, 1981.

Weston, Burns, Richard Falk, and Anthony D'Amato. *Basic Documents in International Law and World Order*. St. Paul, Minn.: West Publishing, 1980.

Willemin, G., and R. Heacock. *The International Committee of the Red Cross*. Norwell, Mass.: Kluwer Academic Publications, 1984.

JOURNAL ARTICLES, PAPERS, AND DOCUMENTS
Abed, George. "The Economic Viability of a Palestinian State," 19(2) *Journal of Palestine Studies* 8 (Winter 1990).

Al-Haq/Law in the Service of Man. *Annual Report, 1989*. Ramallah, West Bank: Al-Haq, 1989.

Arsanjani, Mahnoush. 31 *International and Comparative Law Quarterly* 426 (1982).

Awartani, Hisham. "Israel's Economic Policies in the Occupied Territories." Unpublished manuscript of paper delivered at Al-Haq/Law in the Service of Man conference in Jerusalem, January 22–25, 1988. On file at Al-Haq, Ramallah, West Bank.

Bainerman, Joel. "The Economic Growing Pains for Palestinian Autonomy." 6(5) *Middle East Insight* 49 (Spring 1989).

Blum, Yehuda. "The Missing Reversioner: Reflection on the Status of Judea and Samaria." 3 *Israel Law Review* 279 (1968).

Boyle, Francis. "Create the State of Palestine!" 25 *American-Arab Affairs* 85 (Summer 1988).

Cassese, Antonio. "Powers and Duties of an Occupant in Relation to Land and Natural Resources." Unpublished manuscript of paper delivered at Al-Haq/ Law in the Service of Man conference in Jerusalem, January 22–25, 1988. On file at Al-Haq, Ramallah, West Bank.

Cohen, Esther. "The Fourth Geneva Convention and Human Rights in the Israeli-Occupied Territories, 1967–1977." Ph.D. dissertation, Hebrew University, September 27, 1981.

Coles, R. L. "Economic Development in the Occupied Territories." 25 *American Arab Affairs* 82 (Summer 1988).

Dillman, Jeffrey. "Water Rights in the Occupied Territories." 19(1) *Journal of Palestine Studies* 46 (Autumn 1989).

Dinstein, Yoram. "The International Law of Belligerent Occupation and Human Rights." 8 *Israel Yearbook on Human Rights* 104 (1978).

Gerson, Allan. 14 *Harvard International Law Journal* 1 (1973).

Hilterman, J. "The Women's Movement During the Uprising." 20(3) *Journal of Palestine Studies* 48 (Spring 1991).

International Committee of the Red Cross. *Annual Report, 1970.*

———. *Annual Report, 1972.*

———. *Annual Report, 1980.*

International Review of the Red Cross. 113 (August 1970).

Jerusalem Media and Communication Centre. "Bitter Harvest: Israeli Sanctions Against Palestinian Agriculture During the Uprising." May 1989. On file at Jerusalem Media and Communication Centre, Jerusalem.

Jordanian Department of Statistics. *Population and Employment in Agriculture, 1967.* Amman: 1968.

Lorch, Nathaniel. 1 *Israel Yearbook on Human Rights* 366 (1971).

Meron, Ted. "The Geneva Conventions as Customary Law." 81 *American Journal of International Law* 348 (1987).

———. "West Bank and Gaza: Human Rights and Humanitarian Law in the Period of Transition." 9 *Israel Yearbook on Human Rights* 106 (1979).

Netherlands Government Mission. "Export of Agricultural Produce from the West Bank and the Gaza Strip: Difficulties and Opportunities," June 1987. Report of a mission sent by the Netherlands government, on file at Al-Haq, Ramallah, West Bank.

Palestinian Agricultural Relief Committee. *Annual Report, 1988.* Shufat, West Bank: 1988.

———. *Agricultural Development and the Uprising.* Jerusalem: May 1988.

Rabie, Mohammed. "Foreign Aid and the Israeli Economy." 25 *American Arab Affairs* 64 (Summer 1988).

Rideau. "Le probleme du respect des droits des hommes dans les territoires occupes par Israel." 16 *Annuaire Francais de Droit International* (970).

Roberts, Adam. "Prolonged Military Occupation: The Israeli-Occupied Territories Since 1967." 84 *American Journal of International Law* 44 (1990).

————. "The Israeli-Occupied Territories, 1967–1988: The International Legal Framework of a Prolonged Occupation." Manuscript of paper delivered at Al-Haq/Law in the Service of Man conference in Jerusalem, January 22–25, 1988. On file at Al-Haq, Ramallah, West Bank.

Rostow, Eugene. "'Palestinian Self-Determination': Possible Futures for the Unallocated Territories of the Palestine Mandate." 5 *Yale Studies in World Public Order* 147 (1979).

Rouhana, Kate. "The Other Intifada: The Crucial Economic War Heats Up," 250(1) *The Nation* 1 (January 1, 1990).

Roy, S. "The Political Economy of Despair." 20(30) *Journal of Palestine Studies* (Spring 1981).

Shamgar, Meir. 1 *Israel Yearbook on Human Rights* 262 (1971).

Shehadeh, Raja. "The Land Laws of Palestine." 11(2) *Journal of Palestine Studies* 79 (1982).

Sullivan, A. "What Outlook for Peace: Conversations with Prominent Palestinians and Israelis Discourage Optimism that Any Political Settlement of the Israeli-Palestinian Conflict is Likely Soon." 11(3) *Americans for Justice in the Middle East News* 1 (December/January 1986).

United Nations Food and Agriculture Organization. Resolution regarding "Provision of Technical Assistance to the Palestinian People." November 1989. Office of the UN Food and Agriculture Organization, Washington, D.C.

United States Department of the Army. Pamphlet No. 27–161–2, *International Law, Volume II*. 1962.

United States Department of State. File No. P780065–0030, 72 *American Journal of International Law* 908 (1978).

United States Department of State. "Memorandum of Law concerning alleged rights of Israel to develop new oil fields in Sinai and the Gulf of Suez." 16 *International Legal Materials* 733 (1977).

Von Glahn, Gerhard. "Taxation Under Occupation." Unpublished manuscript of paper delivered at Al-Haq/Law in the Service of Man conference in Jerusalem, January 22–25, 1988. On file at Al-Haq, Ramallah, West Bank.

LEGAL CASES

Abu-Aita v. Commander of the Judea and Samaria Region [*VAT* (Value Added Tax) case]. H.C. 69/81 and 493/81, 37(2) P.D. 197 (1981). English translation in 7 *Selected Judgements of the Supreme Court of Israel* 6, 98–99 (1988). English case summary in 13 *Israel Yearbook on Human Rights* 348 (1983).

Falah Fassin Ibrahim Amirah v. Minster of Defense. H.C. 258/79, 34(1) P.D. 90 (1980), English translation in M. Shamgar, ed., *Military Government in the Territories Administered by Israel 1967–1980* (1982): 398.

Ayoub v. Minister of Defense, [*Beit-El* case]. H.C. 606/78, 610/78, 33(2) P.D. 113 (1979). English translation in M. Shamgar, ed., *Military Government in the Territories Administered by Israel 1967–1980* (1982): 371. English case summary in 9 *Israel Yearbook on Human Rights* 337, 377 (1979). See H.C. 258/79, English case summary in 10 *Israel Yearbook on Human Rights* 332 (1980).

Cooperative Society v. Commander of the I.D.F. H.C. 393/82, 37(4) P.D. 785. English case summary in 14 *Israel Yearbook on Human Rights* 301(1984).

Dwikat v. Government of Israel [*Elon Moreh* case]. H.C. 390/79, 34(1) P.D. 1, English translation in 1 *Palestine Yearbook of International Law* 124 (1984), and in M. Shamgar, ed., *Military Government in the Territories Administered by Israel 1967–1980,* (1982): 404. English case summary in 9 *Israel Yearbook on Human Rights* 345 (1979).

Electricity Co. for the District of Jerusalem v. Minister of Defense. H.C. 351/80, 35(2) P.D. 673, and 27(1) P.D. 124, 138 (1972). English case summary in 11 *Israel Yearbook on Human Rights* 354 (1981).

Hilu v. Government of Israel. 27 P.D. 177 (1973), quoted in M. Shamgar, ed., *Military Government in the Territories Administered by Israel 1967–1980* 150 (1982).

Kawasme, et al. v. Minister of Defense [*Kawasme I*]. H.C. 320/80, 35(3) P.D. 113. English case summary in 11 *Israel Yearbook on Human Rights* 344 (1981).

Kawasme, et al. v. Minister of Defense [*Kawasme II*]. H.C. 698/80, 35(1) P.D. 617. English case summary in 11 *Israel Yearbook on Human Rights* 350 (1981).

Korematsu v. United States, 323 U.S. 214 (1944).

Mustafa v. Military Commander of the Judea and Samaria Region. H.C. 629/82, 37(1) P.D. 158. English case summary in 14 *Israel Yearbook on Human Rights* 313 (1984).

Namibia case. 1950 International Court of Justice 128 (Advisory Opinion of July 11, 1950).

Namibia case. 1955 International Court of Justice 67 (Advisory Opinion of June 7, 1955).

Namibia case. 1971 International Court of Justice 16 (Advisory Opinion of June 21, 1971).

Samara and Ne'imat v. Commander of Judea and Samaria Region. H.C. 802/79, 34(4) P.D. 1. English case summary in 11 *Israel Yearbook on Human Rights* 362 (1981).

Al-Sayad v. Commander of Judea and Samaria. H.C. 771/80, 35(3) P.D. 219. English case summary in 11 *Israel Yearbook on Human Rights* 364 (1981).

Sheikh Suleiman Abu-Hilu v. State of Israel. H.C. 302/72, 27(2) P.D. 169, 177. English Case summary in 5 *Israel Yearbook on Human Rights* 384 (1975).

Singapore Oil Stocks case. 51 *American Journal of International Law* 808 (1957).

Tabib v. Minister of Defense. H.C. 202/81, 36(2) P.D. 622 (1981). English case summary in 13 *Israel Yearbook on Human Rights* 364 (1983).

Taha v. Minster of the Interior. H.C. 658, 660–62/80, 35(1) P.D. 249. English case summary in 11 *Israel Yearbook on Human Rights* 361 (1981).

Yick Wo v. Hopkins, 118 U.S. 356 (1886).

INDEX

217

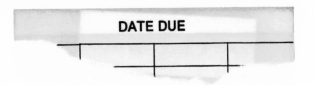

DATE DUE